Challenging Codependency

Feminist Critiques

Edited by

Marguerite Babcock

and Christine McKay

CHALLENGING CODEPENDENCY: FEMINIST CRITIQUES

In the field of addiction research and counselling there has been an increasing investment in the theory of codependency – a theory that holds women partly responsible for perpetuating the alcoholism and addiction of their male partners. This is the first anthology of feminist essays that presents a cogent critique of this theory.

The unifying feature of the eighteen essays collected here is the revelation that solid evidence contradicts, rather than supports, the theory of codependency. Its assumptions are found to be unsubstantiated in theory and practice. The contributors to the volume explore the history of codependency theory and look at reasons for its growing popularity in medical-model politics. A central theme emerges: that codependency theory is essentially misogynist in nature – the result of a male backlash against feminism. The collection leaves no doubt that this backlash is effective. These essays reveal the many ways that codependency therapy promotes advice and counselling that is damaging and ultimately fails women seeking help for their distress.

This anthology, aimed at professionals as well as readers at large reveals a remarkable body of literature questioning the validity of popular addictions philosophy about women and the quality of the scholarship that supports those theories.

MARGUERITE BABCOCK is Unit Director at the Center for Substance Abuse in McKeesport, Pennsylvania.

CHRISTINE McKAY is a counsellor at the Centretown Community Health Centre, Ottawa.

Challenging Codependency: Feminist Critiques

Edited by Marguerite Babcock and
Christine McKay

UNIVERSITY OF TORONTO PRESS
Toronto Buffalo London

59

© University of Toronto Press Incorporated 1995
Toronto Buffalo London
Printed in Canada

ISBN 0-8020-0440-7 (cloth)
ISBN 0-8020-7230-5 (paper)

Printed on acid-free paper

Canadian Cataloguing in Publication Data

Main entry under title:

Challenging codependency

Includes index.
ISBN 0-8020-0440-7 (bound) ISBN 0-8020-7230-5 (pbk.)

1. Feminist theory.   2. Co-dependence (Psychology).
I. Babcock, Marguerite.   II. McKay, Christine (M. Christine).

HQ1190.C53 1995   362.29   C95-930173-9

University of Toronto Press acknowledges the financial assistance to its
publishing program of the Canada Council and the Ontario Arts Council.

Contents

Part III
The Therapeutic Implications of Codependency

Part IV
The Political Implications of Codependency

Foreword

The theme of this multi-authored work is that the rampant pop/psych ideology of addiction/recovery serves to obscure the ongoing political reality of women's oppression as played out on the field of individual personal relationships. The intensive marketing to women of the language of pathology effectively obliterates feminist voices calling for change. It upends 'the personal is political' so it reads 'the personal is [no more than] the personal.'

Of all the labels with which mental health professionals have tried to ensnare and diminish women (in the name of treatment), codependency is th e most downright insidious. While the definition does not hold still for a minute, oozing and slithering and ever-expanding, codependency refers always to a disease-by-association. In the main, it requires only that you have become intimate with someone, usually a man, who is irresponsible or abusive. The havoc he wreaks in your life is transformed into the 'symptoms' of codependency.

I have heard folks opine that the reason this 'disorder' seems to strike only women is that when a man becomes involved with a difficult or troublesome female, he does not hang around. This observation, however, seems churlish. Some men do hang around. They are not then identified as codepedent; rather, they are beatified as saints. Like *masochism, codependency* is no more than macho attitude – medicalized.

A further reason why the concept of codependency is so destructive is that it is so clearly designed to keep women hooked, rather than to free them. It coerces women into looking inward for answers that patently cannot be found there. It sells the idea that the women herself is the pathogen, causing the abusive and irresponsible behaviour that inherently belongs to someone else. She is the provocateur. Behind every no-good man, this dictum goes, is a culpable woman.

Not only does the construct of *codependency* keep women individualized, separated, inward focused – diverting them from analysis and understanding and action for social change – but it does so under the rubric, 'You are not alone.' Orwellian, that. And thus, not only does it keep women hooked into patriarchial oppression, but it keeps them hooked in the pattern of abusive relationships as well; telling them that their task in their next go 'round at this relationship, or in their next relationship (next life?) is to repeat their attempt, but this time to *fix* themselves and, in doing so, make *someone else* better. Rather like administering insulin to the diabetic's wife: you're changing chemistry all right, but your chances of fixing the problem aren't great.

By now, this virulent pathologizing of female partners has spread to attack virtually all women who have suffered abuse or violence at the hands of men, including the mothers who try to protect their children from abuse, and to adult survivors of incest.

Just four of the steps in a Twelve-Step program prescribed for incest survivors (the same kind of 'recovery' group most often recommended for 'codependents') speak volumes:

• Admit to God, yourself and another human being the exact nature of your wrongs [yes, yours].

• Be entirely ready to have God remove these defects of character [yes, *yours*].

• Humbly ask Her/Him to remove your shortcomings.

• Make a list of all persons you have harmed and become willing to make amends to them all.

I ask you. A Twelve-Step program designed by rapists could not have improved on this program of sin and redemption (sin yours, redemption task yours)?

Codependency, then, can be defined as a logical impossibility – on which an entire industry has come to rest (Armstrong, just now). It can best be conceptualized as part of a larger campaign to offer men absolution by providing women with a bogus explanation: the fault is in themselves. This campaign of exoneration of men and implication of women has the virtue of tradition on its side, guaranteeing establishment support. Where *masochism* says, 'She asked for it,' *codependency* says, 'She made me do it.' That it has received such wide media support tells us that it is indeed a triumph – not of human relations insight, but of marketing.

Voices like those included in this volume have largely been denied public exposure throughout the 1980s to now. And that is because,

beneath its medical mantle, the construct of codependency is both politically driven and capitalism compatible. It masks a reactionary agenda
with a veneer of therapeutic credo, whose language is liberal.

These voices are critical and urgently needed. Too many of us have
been too silent too long about the escalating woman blame that inheres
in the medical model – one that is teasing women into the mental
health maw with the promise of 'help' for their very real distress and
then, in the name of empowerment, reducing their experiential reality
to no more than a collection of their own purported shortcomings.

It is only if voices like these are listened to and heard; only if women
are encouraged to look outward, to identify once again the political
realities that play out in their individual personal lives – that women
will be able to find their collective voice and take collective action
for the social change that might actually *enhance* their personal lives.
Then, maybe, we can respond to slogans like 'Codependent no more!'
with the liberating cry of 'What a crock. Never was!'

LOUISE ARMSTRONG
Author of *Kiss Daddy Goodnight* and *Rocking the Cradle of Sexual Politics*

Acknowledgments

I am grateful to Marguerite Babcock for her assistance and support. While 'Max' and I have never met, it has been a comfort to correspond and, more recently, to talk and laugh on the telephone. It is a tribute to feminist networking that this book exists. Thanks Max for all your help.

Sue Pearson also read each draft of my paper with enthusiasm, and her insightful comments and suggestions were helpful.

Colleen Lundy, my research adviser at Carleton University's School of Social Work, supported my initial intuition that the construct of 'codependency' pathologized female experience. Without her encouragement and assistance it is doubtful that I would have settled on this focus of enquiry.

Virgil Duff, executive editor at the University of Toronto Press, was quick to support this project and was instrumental in bringing this book to press.

My thanks as well to numerous friends who have expressed an interest in this project and supported me throughout. They are: Jill Abson, Martha Cockshutt, Evan Frank, Paul Lee, Robert Stanley, and Isobel Salole. My eternal gratitude to Louis Cabri, who provided me with both intellectual and emotional support.

Thanks are also due to my co-workers in the LESA Program, April, Diane, Jane, and Michelle, who have listened to me complain ad nauseum about nights spent at the computer.

Finally, I'd like to acknowledge my parents and my grandmothers. All in their own ways have contributed to my understanding of 'codependency.'

CHRISTINE McKAY

My many thanks to my co-conspirator in this project, Christine McKay. Christine was the one who made the initial effort to reach out and make contact for our professional relationship. Although we have yet to meet face to face, the telephone and letters have also made us friends. Without Christie this book would have been absolsutely impossible. She additionally can take credit for coming up with 'Max.'

I want to thank the following friends for their intellectual and emotional support as I worked on this project: David Krajack of U.S. Steel EAP, and Betty McBride and Gerald Taylor of the Center for Substance Abuse in McKeesport, Pennsylvania, whose sharing with me their ideas and encouraging my own helped my creativity to flower. Freelance journalist Andrew Meacham, my 'little brother,' who has been my partner in hours of fascinating discussions, and who helped me in being published. Michael Taleff, of Pennsylvania State University, who has been another co-conspirator on several pleasantly subversive projects. Sonia Paleos, of Community College of Allegheny County, Pennsylvania, who has greatly encouraged me to teach what is right rather than just what sells.

I am also most thankful for the guidance and patience of Virgil Duff and Agnes Ambrus of the University of Toronto Press, as they helped us in the completion of this book.

MARGUERITE BABCOCK

MARGUERITE BABCOCK, M Ed and
CHRISTINE McKAY, MSW

Introduction

The history of scientific paradigms and knowledge construction involves conflict, with forces taking sides as the struggle evolves over which group will take dominance in the 'objective' expression of reality (Kuhn 1962). Science is constructed within historical, social, and cultural contexts; politics, economics, and prejudice play as much a part in the struggle as any rational assessment of the facts does (Badash 1989). Questioning of the dominant group's view on any given subject has always been in evidence in human thought. More recently this kind of analysis has been given the label 'deconstruction,' which Sands and Nuccio (1992) define as 'a way of analyzing texts that is sensitive to contextual dimensions and marginalized voices' (491).

In addictions work, the dominant trend has been to engage in oversimplified versions of reality. This pattern has developed from the presence of several elements in our culture. One stems from the observation that Gomberg (1989) makes about the greater commercial appeal of simple over complex concepts. Wilsnack and Wilsnack (1992) elaborate: 'Many great scientific achievements have resulted from trying to find simpler ways to explain things. However, in trying to understand human behavior, we often want to believe that life is simpler than it really is ... As behavioral science matures, it should move away from wishful oversimplification toward a more complex, subtle, and difficult understanding of human behavior' (172).

Yet another element is the exhortative, spiritualistic mystique that is embedded in much of addictions work, owing to the role of many recovering addicts and alcoholics as therapists who have moved through spiritually oriented self-help programs such as Alcoholics Anonymous (AA) to gain sobriety. A survey conducted by Sobel and

Sobel (1987) found that 72 per cent of the workers in the more than 10,000 addictions treatment programs in the United States were in recovery from substance abuse. Brown (1991) describes how this factor affects the addictions field: 'Similar to religious converts' salvation through a profoundly redemptive religious experience, professional ex-s' deep career commitment derives from a transforming therapeutic resocialization ... The substance abuse treatment center transforms from a mere "clinic" occupied by secularly credentialed professionals into a moral community of single believers' (222). Unfortunately, the intellectually limiting aspect of a 'single belief' has become present in the thinking of many addictions workers.

This simplistic thinking has culminated in an avoidance in the addictions field of 'rigorous scientific procedures that reduce the risk of reaching a false conclusion' (National Institute on Alcohol Abuse and Alcoholism, 1991, 2). The erroneous ideas that have thus been promoted in the field, however, have been noticed by a vocal although often censored minority. For example, there was a comment at the 1991 conference of Substance Abuse Librarians and Information Specialists to the effect that certain ideas in the addictions field that have some basis, such as the concept of 'responsible' drug or alcohol use, are suppressed by representatives of governmental and private institutional interests (*Alcoholism and Drug Abuse Weekly* 1991).

Add to these limitations the fact that North America is a patriarchal (as well as racist, classist, and heterosexist) society (hooks 1988). The resulting male-oriented, sexist point of view, accepted as the cultural norm, has been explored by several feminist writers (e.g., Miller and Mothner 1971). Women have suffered in several ways from sexism in addictions work as a result of this unadmitted male norm: women's treatment needs are not given adequate attention (Reed 1987); the incidence of addictions in women compared with that in men has been minimized, owing to poor research approaches for women (Babcock 1993; Vannicelli and Nash 1984); and women have erroneously received sole blame for babies born affected by parental drug/alcohol use (see Harrison 1992). The latest expression of sexism in the addictions field is the construct of 'codependency,' a notion that labels the partners of addicts/alcoholics as either 'sick' or 'dysfunctional.'

This last issue is the focus of attention in this anthology of feminist critiques of codependency. Here, feminism is broadly defined as 'a movement to end sexism and sexist oppression' (hooks 1988, 23). While not all of the articles are informed by an explicitly feminist point of view, all of the authors agree that the notion of codependency is harmful to women.

Many overlapping themes emerge in this collection of articles. Many feminist critics, for example, note that the proponents of codependency ignore the literature on alcoholism-complicated relationships, a body of research that disputes the notion that the partners of substance abusers exhibit pathology (Jackson 1954; Edwards, Harvey and Whitehead 1973; Orford 1975). Other feminist critics note the parallels between codependency and the disturbed personality hypothesis, a theory popular in the 1950s that proposed that women in relationships with substance abusers stay in these situations to fulfil their own pathological needs. Other critics argue that codependency theory pathologizes behaviour associated with traditional female sex-role socialization.

Very few proponents or critics of codependency address the issues of race, class, age, or sexual orientation. McKay, in her article, contends that the construct ignores gender, race, and class issues; while Tallen argues that the notion of codependency appeals primarily to white, middle-class women. This anthology only begins to address the lack of feminist critiques from a race, class, or lesbian perspective; further research must be done in these areas.

The first section of this volume provides an overview of the feminist critiques of codependency. What are the historical roots of codependency? Who benefits from the creation and promotion of codependency? The articles in this section situate the construct of codependency in historical, cultural, and economic contexts.

The theme of part II is victim blaming and codependency. The authors of these articles argue that the construct of codependency is harmful to women, especially women who have been abused or are in abusive relationships. These critics believe that the notion of codependency blames women and absolves men of responsibility for their abusive behaviour.

Part III examines the therapeutic implications of codependency. These authors review and critique the dominant models of codependency theory and treatment. Alternative theoretical and therapeutic models are proposed.

In part IV the political implications of codependency are addressed. These authors link the concept of codependency with female oppression. Some critics argue that codependency describes the psychological impact of female oppression; others contend that codependency is the latest psychological concept to oppress women. The first view attempts to determine why the concept of codependency appeals to women, especially white, middle-class women. According to these authors, the 'symptoms' attributed to codependency are the same conflicts and dissatisfactions that many women in contemporary North American society experience. Proponents of codependency, however, fail to situate these so-called 'symptoms' within social, economic, and political contexts, contexts that are oppressive to women.

Feminist critics also suggest that the construct of codependency is part of a 'backlash' against feminism. Many of these authors compare codependency to other psychological and medical constructs that have pathologized female behaviour, for example, hysteria and the masochistic personality disorder. These critics contend that codependency depoliticizes feminism.

Such critiques have been marginalized in the addictions field by the repeated omission of feminist themes concerning the questioning of 'codependency' and other misogynistic constructs in conference presentations and major publications in the field, as well as in treatment and prevention formats (see also Hare-Mustin 1987).

We believe that there are a significant number of professionals in the addictions and mental health fields, as well as consumers, who are ready to 'deconstruct' many of the popularly enforced notions in addictions work, but who have been isolated from each other, owing to the silencing of their ideas in much of the public arena. This anthology lessens that isolation by bringing together some of the feminist critiques that challenge the simplistic and sexist norms embodied in the construct 'codependency.'

REFERENCES

Alcoholism and Drug Abuse Weekly (1991) Info. specialists decry knowledge control efforts (23 October), 6.

Babcock, M. (1993) Does feminism drive women to drink? Manuscript submitted for publication.

Badash, L. (1989) The age-of-the-earth debate. *Scientific American* (August), 90–6.

Brown, J.D. (1991) The professional ex-: an alternative for exiting the deviant career. *Sociological Quarterly, 32*, 219–30.

Edwards, P., C. Harvey, and P. Whitehead, (1973) Wives of alcoholics: a critical review and analysis. *Quarterly Journal of Studies on Alcohol, 34*, 112–32.

Gomberg, E.S.L. (1989) On terms used and abused: the concept of 'codependency.' *Drugs and Society, 3*, 113–32.

Hare-Mustin, R.T. (1987) The problem of gender in family therapy theory. *Family Process, 26*, 15–27.

Harrison, M. (1991) Drug addiction in pregnancy: the interface of science, emotion, and social policy. *Journal of Substance Abuse Treatment, 8*, 261–8.

hooks, b. (1988) *Talking Back: Thinking Feminist – Thinking Black.* Toronto: Between the Lines.

Jackson, J. (1954) The adjustment of the family to the crisis of alcoholism. *Quarterly Journal of Studies on Alcohol, 15*, 562–86.

Kuhn, T.S. (1962) *The Structure of Scientific Revolutions.* Chicago: University of Chicago Press.

Miller, J.B., and I. Mothner (1971) Psychological consequences of sexual inequality. *American Journal of Orthopsychiatry, 41*, 767–75.

National Institute on Alcohol Abuse and Alcoholism (1991) Advances in alcoholism treatment research. *Alcohol Alert Supplement* (July), 1–2.

Orford, J. (1976) Alcoholism and marriage: the argument against specialism. *Journal of Studies on Alcohol, 36*, 1537–63.

Reed, B.G. (1987) Developing women-sensitive drug dependence treatment services: why so difficult? *Journal of Psychoactive Drugs, 19*, 151–64.

Sands, R.B., and K. Nuccio (1992) Postmodern feminist theory and social work. *Social Work, 37*, 489–94.

Sobell, M., and L. Sobell (1987) Conceptual issues regarding goals in the treatment of alcohol problems. *Drugs and Alcohol, 2/3*, 1–3.

Vanicelli, M., and L. Nash (1984) Effects of sex bias on women's studies of alcoholism. *Alcoholism: Clinical and Experimental Research, 8*, 334–6.

Wilsnack, R.W., and S.C. Wilsnack (1992) Women, work, and alcohol: failure of simple theories. *Alcoholism: Clinical and Experimental Research, 16*, 172–9.

PART I

Critiques of Codependency

MARGUERITE BABCOCK, M Ed

Critiques of Codependency: History and Background Issues

A major goal of this paper is to help the reader past the marginalizing of dissident voices in addiction (McKay 1992). Another is to provide a perspective on how 'codependency' is a congruent part of sexism in psychology, psychiatry, and general counselling. This paper is additionally an attempt to express a growing concern about the paucity of scholarly analysis in practical addictions work, which causes harm in a number of ways. Chiauzzi and Liljegren (1993) warn that clinging to assumptions that are without empirical basis causes damage to progress in addictions treatment. They include 'codependency' among such assumptions.

It is difficult to engage in debate about the term *codependency* when its adherents keep shifting what they mean by the word (Asher and Brissett 1988; Harper and Capdevila 1990; Martin 1988). However, this difficulty does not remove the need to examine the negative consequences of its use. Krestan and Bepko (1990), giving a list of several versions by well-known commercial writers, state 'These definitions are irresponsible and so vague as to be meaningless' (p. 220). This author's repeated impression has been that the term is most frequently used, by addictions workers and the public, to mean a disordered syndrome (often called a 'disease') of excessive focus on the other, which typifies most addicts' significant others (especially female), is chronic, and is invested in the continuation of the addiction (as indicated by the prefix *co*) (see also Martin 1988). No features of this description have been verified in research.

One especially alarming aspect of the freely shifting definitions of codependency is that its adherents can claim that 'it' includes any variety of groups. This in turn feeds into the rambling, grandiose assertions made about codependency, such as that it is a syndrome typically passed down in families, that it affects almost anyone from any 'dysfunctional' family, that it is the necessary ingredient for someone to develop a drug/alcohol addiction (see Carson and Baker 1994 or Fischer et al. 1992 for a review of several such claims).

As the bibliography of this paper shows, critiques of the idea of codependency date from at least the mid-1980s. Censorship in the addictions field has prevented their receiving the widespread exposure that has been accorded the profitably popular term *codependency*. This author has seen this censorship in the form of refusal to publish or allow to present, refusal to hire, and the suggestion that the critics themselves are pathological (Whitfield 1991).

The notion of codependency has a decades-long history, both in precursor concepts and in the victim-blaming of women in western psychology and psychiatry. Despite many years of repeated research rebuttals of the ideas that codependency embraces, these ideas have continued to re-emerge. McKay (1992) traces the earliest use of terms linguistically similar to codependency to the 1970s. In the 1980s there was an embracing of the idea of codependency by the addictions field and the general public. Feminist scholars have questioned its focus-on-others core as a pathologizing of the feminine role. Theorists of various schools of behavioural sciences are concerned about the effect of its use on quality of social services. The following section is a historical review of the concepts that finally culminated in the idea of codependency.

HISTORY: THE PATHOLOGY OF COMPASSION

Sexism in western psychotherapy has been reviewed in feminist literature (see Brown and Ballou 1992). Hare-Mustin (1983) gives us a good account. She reports from her historical overview that women have often been labelled as 'pathological,' when in fact their symptoms have been caused by the social stressors and powerlessness of the feminine role (a core element to be seen in 'codependency'). Irvine (1992) discusses the late-nineteenth-century term *neurasthenia*, which pathologized the role assigned to women by framing women's reaction to oppression in medical terms rather than in social reality. A century ago Freud developed the diagnostic idea of the 'masochistic woman.' This notion (lingering still today) holds that women are inherently seekers of pain, by virtue of their anatomy, life experiences, and interactions with others. Karen Horney, MD, began her work in the Freudian psychoanalytic school but broke ranks by intensively questioning many Freudian assumptions about women (Horney 1967). Her question, 'Where are the data?' addresses the fact that there are no empirical data to support the idea of inherent masochism in women. (Notably, both Carson and Baker 1994 and Lyon and Greenberg 1991 trace the origins of the codependency concept to Horney. Horney would be appalled.) Enforced sex roles cause pain for women (Waites 1977–8), but in constructs such as 'masochistic woman' the patriarchal culture then calls them 'sick' for succumbing to these roles. This thinking is victim blaming.

More recently, Deighton and McPeek (1985) write about Bowen's theory on 'differentiation,' explaining that the 'more poorly differentiated' person suffers from emotional problems, owing to greater 'emotional reactivity,' while the 'differentiated' person 'has more control over thinking and feeling functions' (405). Of course, in traditional socialization women are taught to be emotionally reactive, but 'differentiation' labels them 'sick' for conforming to this pattern (see also Lerner 1985). The Gestalt notion of 'confluence' as a disordered response (Gilliland, James, and Bowman 1989) says essentially the same thing. This core concept of closeness as pathological clearly is pursued in the codependency theme.

Recently, there have been attempts to include 'masochistic personality' and then 'self-defeating personality' in the diagnoses described in the *Diagnostic and Statistical Manual of Mental Disorders* (Franklin 1987; Tavris 1992). In the United States the *DSM* is considered to be the official medical manual of psychiatric disorders. Though the proponents of both labels deny it, these labels would be used primarily to diagnose women, since the feminine role creates such 'symptoms.' If either diagnosis were ever accepted as official, the focus again would be on women's alleged pathology rather than on the dynamics of sexism.

The classic Broverman et al. (1970) study, in which mental health clinicians of both genders viewed 'healthy' adult females and males very differently, illustrates the informal process of misogyny in counselling and psychotherapy. This research showed that these clinicians equated the male role more closely with 'healthy' adult, sex unspecified. That is, women are pressured to be 'feminine' but are seen as less healthy for being so (indeed, exactly the formula of the labels 'masochistic,' 'self-defeating,' and 'codependent'). There have been mixed results in attempts to replicate the Broverman findings in later studies (see Phillips and Gilroy 1985). Attempts to test its well-known premises may have been confoundingly transparent to many mental health staffers used as subjects in subsequent research. Also, Bargh (1992) reports the recent findings that subjects may avoid sex-role stereotyping when they are aware that it is at issue but engage in it when unaware that sex roles are at the core of their discussion. Thus, current subjects more versed in gender stereotyping may be less willing to express overtly sexist analyses, although their reluctance says nothing of their actual attitudes.

Women in Relationships with Addicts

Consistent with the sexist view of women, woman-as-other is how females have predominantly been considered in research and theorizing on addictions. In this century, the addict who for decades was most studied was the white, heterosexual, male alcoholic, and the wife of such a man was studied as his ancillary (Reed 1987). Later, young addicts to other drugs were also studied; they too were mostly males, and their mothers were considered their most important family relation (Kaufman 1985). During all this time, women's own addictions were largely ignored (Babcock 1992a). And up to the 1950s all of the literature on those female significant others to addicts and alcoholics consisted of anecdotal, biased speculations or, in a few instances, highly selective interpretations of research results. The consistent theme for wives of alcoholics was to portray them as pathological women who were seeking to fulfil their own disordered needs by marrying the alcoholic partner (Futterman 1953; Lewis 1954; Price 1945; Whalen 1953). Similarly condemning interpretations have been made about the supposedly pathologically 'enmeshed' mothers of young drug addicts (Attardo 1965; Fort 1954; Kaufman 1981).

This view of the wives of alcoholics gave rise to what was called the 'disturbed personality hypothesis.' This was a formalization of the notion that these women were emotionally disturbed themselves, so that they not only selected impaired partners but also were invested in the continuation of the partners' addiction. Accompanying this belief was the 'decompensation hypothesis,' which proposed that these women would emotionally deteriorate further if their spouses became sober – a supposed confirmation of their pathological investment in keeping the addiction active. (See Nace 1982, for a fuller description and a critique of these concepts.) These ideas, of course, begin to sound very much like the current label of 'codependency.' Harper and Capdevila (1990) also write about the appearance of pathologizing descriptions of spouses of alcoholics in the literature of Al-Anon, the Twelve-Step support organization for family members of alcoholics (see also Collet 1990).

In 1954, however, Joan Jackson presented a detailed, factual study (rather than a prejudicial interpretation) of what her sample of wives of alcoholics had actually gone through in adapting their coping with their addicted partners. Jackson found a sequence of stages through which the wives' coping evolved. She followed this article with related pieces in 1956 and 1962. Her work gave credence to the 'stress hypothesis,' in which the significant others to addicts/alcoholics were seen not as pathological but as coping with stress in an exploratory manner. Later, the 'psychosocial hypothesis' combined the stress concept with the acknowledgment that (as in any population) there could be individual pathologies in the significant others, which must also be figured in to the profile of their behaviours. This idea still did not (in contrast to the 'disturbed personality hypothesis' or the current idea of codependency) label the class of significant others of addicts as pathological, but rather took into account a fuller array of factors (Edwards, Harvey, and Whitehead 1973).

RESEARCH REBUTTALS

Following Jackson's contributions, a large body of research showed the disturbed personality and decompensation hypotheses to be without substance. These studies supported instead the stress and psychosocial analyses (and, by extension, refuted the later idea of codependency). For example, the research by Corder, Hendricks, and Corder (1964) on wives of alcoholics showed a profile of these women that is quite similar to what we now call post-traumatic stress disorder. This is similar to Hubbard's (1989) PTSD profile of female spouses of incest perpetrators. Pitman and Taylor (1992) report from their research: 'There is no evidence to indicate that there are characterological problems with either the partners of sexual abusers or the partners of alcoholics'(58). From the viewpoint of the alcoholic woman, two-thirds of the alcoholic females in Macdonald's (1987) study denied the presence of significant others who imperilled their sobriety (i.e., who were invested in the continuation of their addiction). A study by Sisson and Azrin (1986) on the results of teaching the families of problem drinkers new ways of coping describes the more typical wife of such a drinker: 'Out of her concern for him, the wife may indeed inadvertently reinforce his drinking behavior but desires to do otherwise and succeeds when shown how to do so' (20). Love et al. (1993) have developed operational measures of family members' responses to another member's alcoholic drinking. They explored 'punishing sobriety' and 'withdrawing when the patient is abstinent' (1269) as items to be included among such responses, but they had to drop them from their list: 'Neither behavior type was reported with sufficient frequency to warrant their inclusion' (1269). Haberman (1964) summarizes from his own research that 'the results do not support the early [sic] theories about the alcoholic marriage, which usually emphasized the wife's neurotic need for her spouse to continue drinking' (232). It should be noted that such theories, pathologizing these wives' behaviours, appeared in later as well as earlier thinking.

Contrary to the decompensation hypothesis, there is no evidence that partners of addicts typically decompensate when the addict gets sober. Indeed, several researchers report an improvement in the functioning of the spouse and other family members once the addict reaches sobriety (Billings and Moos 1983; Haberman 1964; Moos, Finney, and Gamble 1982; Moos and Moos 1984; Nace 1982; Preli, Protinsky, and Cross 1990; Roberts et al. 1985; van Wormer 1989). Despite the corollary that the emotional status of wives of alcoholics is dependent on the alcoholics' drinking status, Kogan and Jackson (1965) found in their research that the self-perception of wives of alcoholics did not depend on whether their husbands were intoxicated or abstinent.

See earlier summaries of the research on significant others in Edwards et al. (1973); Jacob et al. (1978); Nace (1982); Paolino et al. (1976); Thomas and Santa (1982). For pioneer psychological testing of wives of alcoholics (which clearly refutes the disturbed personality hypothesis) see Corder et al. (1964); Kogan, Fordyce, and Jackson (1963); Kogan and Jackson (1965).

To support the notion that significant others to addicts/alcoholics are pathological, this author has often heard the claim that many women, once romantically involved with addicted males, tend to repeat this pattern. Nici's (1979) study, however, found that daughters of alcoholics were more likely than the general population of women to marry alcoholics, but that women once married to alcoholics were unlikely to repeat that mistake in future unions. A plausible explanation of this is that while daughters of alcoholics may tend naïvely to marry someone 'just like Dad,' if women get out of such a marriage they typically do not have a pathological investment in continuing this pattern. And since the choice about making the union is obviously not unilateral, blaming only the female partners for the choice edits out the logical question of whom the male alcoholics/addicts choose and why. See also Pitman and Taylor (1992), whose research suggests that women from an abused background do not tend to pick abusive partners.

An example of research on significant others that avoids victim blaming or unsubstantiated claims of pathology is the 1992 article by Roman, Blum, and Martin on 'enabling' of problem drinkers on the job. Rather than assuming the presence of a pathological syndrome in co-workers, these researchers explore various functional reasons why such a coping tactic might be adopted by those having to deal with problem drinkers. It is also of interest that they discovered that only 57 per cent of their large sample of problem drinkers experienced 'enabling' by others: 'Thus work-place enabling may be common, but it is far from being a universal phenomenon' (282). Ames and Delaney (1992) found, from their study of how one manufacturing plant handled alcohol problems among employees, that politics and work pressures interfered with effectiveness of resolution. They did not find it necessary to propose pathology on the part of the company or co-workers as an explanation of the difficulties encountered.

Menicucci and Wermuth (1989) critique the tendency of the addictions field to depict families-with-addicts as having an unchanging and consistent profile, at least before 'treatment' (this is argued even now by 'codependency' proponents, with the alleged 'addicted family'). Echoing Jackson (1954), they write: 'Even with drug abuse, adult change and development occurs. It proceeds regardless of the postulated covert desires of the family to hold on to children and to maintain a 'homeostatic balance' (135). This notion of such families as static and uniform persists in spite of over three decades of research that reveals spontaneous changes and multiple variables feeding into how these families' dynamics develop over time (Glynn and Haenlein 1988). Moos and Moos (1984) explain that overall stress on alcoholics' families (from multiple and changing sources) as well as individual variations in the personalities of spouses of alcoholics, affect the functioning of the family. Jacob (1986) and Jacob, Dunn, and Leonard (1983) report that alcoholics who engage in binge rather than steady drinking exert more of a negative effect on family stability.

Kaufman (1980) cautions about the sample bias of theorizing only from data on families that are in treatment for help with an addicted member, noting that other families may present very different dynamics. Orford (1992), who has been involved in years of intensive family research, criticizes the pathologizing of significant others in addictions literature: 'Wives of excessive drinkers, like parents of excessive drug users, appear principally as ogres, or indecisive weaklings' (1513). Orford has been convinced by his research that significant others are struggling to cope with the addiction rather than investing in continuation of it. Writing in a compelling way about the painful conflicts and confusion faced by these families, he comments:

> To ask why a wife does not leave her drinking husband, or why a parent is not tougher with a drug-taking youngster, and to assume that these 'coping failures' imply some kind of pathology is, in my view, to misunderstand the profound dilemmas that excessive behaviour in others poses for those of us who witness it or are affected by it (1516) ... We criticise or pathologize [significant others] when they get emotional, rejecting, over-controlling, over-protective or inconsistent. (1521)

Corrective research on significant others to addicted persons has been primarily focused on adult female partners of male alcoholics. To a lesser extent, it has also been applied to various significant others of addicts to multiple types of substances. For example, Alexander and Dibb (1975) report that only a minority of opiate addicts have families-of-origin engaged in dysfunctional involvement (see also Binion 1982). Orford (1992) emphasizes the need to explore accurately the difficulties faced by these significant others, not only for their own welfare in coping with addiction, but also so that they may learn optimal ways of reducing the overall impact of addiction.

FAMILY THERAPY

Despite the research cited above, the insistence that the significant others to addicted persons are themselves invested in continuation of the addiction has shown popular staying power. Kane-Caviola and Rullo-Cooney (1991), alleging that codependency in the family undermines the addict's sobriety, declare that 'This phenomenon is well known to addiction professionals as the addicted family system' (115). Contributing to such stereotyping has been the growth since the 1940s in the United States of 'systems theory' and related schools of thought in family therapy. This model proposes that all family members are invested on an egalitarian basis in the dynamic dance of the family (again, ignoring social dynamics such as gender power differences), and that each member's behaviour has the primary purpose of maintaining family homeostasis and distracting attention from other problems that are even more severe than members' overt 'symptoms' (such as addiction) (Libow, Raskin, and Caust 1982). Thus it could be argued that significant others to addicts/alcoholics are invested in keeping up the 'front' of the addiction (see, e.g., Steinglass 1976; Steinglass et al. 1987). Several authors have questioned the accuracy of this classic systems view (see, e.g., Bernal and Ysern 1986; Sorensen 1989; van Wormer 1989). Van Wormer writes: 'The systems approach is very compatible with the shift in focus from the alcoholic to the "co-dependent" person or the "co-dependent" family ... The claim is that an individual's problem drinking is an adaptive function for the family. However, evidence indicates that family functioning and cohesion are enhanced, not exacerbated, through the alcoholic's recovery' (58–9).

'CODEPENDENCY' EMERGES

Despite the repeated research rebuttals of victim blaming and pathologizing of significant others of addicts, these elements have emerged once more in the popular term *codependency*, which gained momentum in the 1980s. For example, in a 1989 article, Miller and Millman make the completely baseless statement that 'A common cause of alcoholism is the nonalcoholic ... Without the enabler, alcoholism would dwindle' (41) (a core tenet of the 'codependency' concept). The authors ascribe the significant others' 'enabling' to personal inadequacy, while ignoring the social and sex-role pressures that shape their coping tactics. Velleman et al. (1993) comment on the lack of genuinely in-depth interest in families in addictions work:

Professionals' (and lay) theories have often not only neglected relatives' experiences, they have also often held the families responsible for the drug-taking problems of one member. Examples include the blame for the development of drug problems in the young often being placed quite firmly upon the qualities of parenting and the characteristics of the families from which the young people come; and the current emphasis on 'co-dependency' and 'women who love too much,' implying yet again that the co-dependent woman is also suffering from a 'personality disorder' which led her unconsciously to select a partner who would then develop an addictive problem. (1281-2)

In the absence of any well-thought-out, validated, and professionally accepted definition of codependency, self-appointed experts on this alleged syndrome have felt free to come up with many variants of the profile given at the beginning of this paper (and sometimes descriptions that have little to do with anyone else's definition). The proponents of the term provide virtually endless lists of 'symptoms of codependency' (Tavris 1992). This appears to be debate by evasion, a defensive response to the mounting critiques of 'codependency.' Rather than provoking questions on the part of its adherents, such vagueness seems to have only encouraged a more sweeping use of the word. Whitfield (1992) has even argued that codependency's 'multiple definitions enrich its usefulness.' Hagan (Martin 1988, 1989) and Martin (1988) critique the broadness of the current claim that codependency applies to 'anyone coming from a dysfunctional family' (389; see also Gorski 1992). In fact, the effects of dysfunctional families constitute the complex focus of decades of psychological inquiry, rather than a unitary syndrome that could be given one label. The popular, simplistic, and grandiose claims about codependency are unaccompanied by critical thought (see Gomberg 1989, Harper and Capdevila 1990, and Kaminer 1990 for comments to this point).

None the less, the popularity of the idea of codependency cannot be denied. Addiction treatment facilities and trainers often promote the concept, usually with the blessing of licensing and training organizations. Books on codependency sell quite well. In addition to the sexism implicit in victim blaming of women (discussed below), the financial profits made from pushing 'codependency' are an incentive to maintain the term (Babcock 1991; Martin 1988; McKay 1992; van Wormer 1989). The elements of simplistic thinking (Babcock 1992b) and the illusion of community accord also fuel the wide appeal of this idea (Collet 1990; Haaken 1990; Kaminer 1990; Tavris 1992). Ehrenreich (1992) writes, 'Millions of Americans have signed on for therapies and recovery programs that promise help in rescuing the "inner child" or breaking the web of codependency' (65).

Asher and Brissett (1988) have explored the ways women become

persuaded by the addictions services industry that they are codependent. Their subjects were wives of alcoholics who themselves were enrolled in family addictions programs. The authors found that these
women indeed had accepted the label of codependent, but without
knowing just what it means. The authors summarize that 'the definitional ambiguity of codependency not only enhances the application
and stickiness of the label but also makes any individual resistance
to or rejection of the label difficult' (342). This author has observed
that when 'codependency' is applied to a client, either female or male,
it is usually done with the tone of agency authority and without any
suggestion of alternative explanations of the client's problems. Some
clients have floundered with a sense of alienation and discontent with
this label until they sometimes found, from another source, that codependency is not a valid concept.

CODEPENDENCY: RESEARCH AND MEDICINE

There have been attempts more recently to reify the idea of codependency through actual research, rather than through the previous
reliance on anecdotal impressions. However, these studies have been
marked by major flaws in research design, which invalidate their conclusions, and by interpretations that ignore obvious sex-role phenomena in the research findings, insisting instead on pathology. Perhaps
the most glaring error is that these researchers usually do not actually
try to demonstrate that codependency exists, but they *assume* that it
does (as a pathology) and pursue analysis of the results from there.
See Fischer, Spann, and Crawford 1991; Lyon and Greenberg 1991;
O'Brien and Gaborit 1992; Williams, Bissell, and Sullivan 1991; Wright
and Wright 1990 for clear examples of such errors. The study by Carson and Baker (1994) provides a good illustration of such problems.
These researchers used self-report to determine which of their subjects
had families of origin marked by alcoholism or child abuse and which
had not. The extreme stigmatization of such factors makes honesty
in self-report quite questionable (i.e., the authors may have identified
two groups of subjects, but not the groups they thought they had).
The authors tested all subjects for 'codependency,' using testing tools
that by their own account have definite validity and reliability shortcomings. They found significantly elevated 'pathology' scores among
those subjects from reported abuse or parental alcoholism backgrounds, and they use this finding to claim that therefore codepen-

dency is a valid construct to describe persons coming from such backgrounds. Even if the serious methodological problems with their work are ignored, their findings do not even begin to substantiate the grandiose claims made for codependency, as noted throughout this paper. It is interesting that the study by Fischer et al. (1992) makes the common error of assuming that codependency exists as a pathology, yet it also produces some myth-breaking data:

The results of this study challenge the widely accepted assertion that family dysfunction is closely linked to the development of codependent patterns in the offspring. Codependency was not predicted by number of addictions in the family of origin nor by the severity of the dysfunction in the family of origin. Furthermore, the results also do not support the concept that codependency is the fundamental personal dysfunction underlying all other addictions and its corollary that someone who is codependent is at greater risk for developing other addictions. Neither alcoholism nor excessive risk taking were associated with high levels of codependency. (30)

Some articles accepting the construct of codependency, or 'coalcoholism' or 'coaddiction,' are also of concern because they suggest that the research they cite supports their concepts when it clearly does not (see Coleman 1987 and Zelvin 1988).

As described previously, the core concepts of codependency have been repeatedly refuted in earlier research. Unfortunately, current publication of research on family issues in addiction seems to lean more towards poorly executed studies that feed into endorsement of 'codependency.' There needs to be an increase in publication of research that directly takes on the seriously inadequate basis of the term.

Other articles by advocates of 'codependency' are striking examples of image over substance. Sunderwirth and Spector (1992) attempt to validate the concept by discussing neurophysiology and by making a literary reference that they claim illustrates codependency. Unacknowledged in this paper is that the literature reference actually describes the feminine sex role, and that there is no evidence in human neurophysiology research to validate the alleged pathology that the authors want to substantiate. Le Poire (1992) cites only unverified myths of how 'the typical codependent' (1471) behaves, assuming actions and motivations in significant others of addicts that have never been established in solid research. She then critiques this alleged syndrome as self-contradictory and counter-productive, bringing in impressive terms, such as 'paradoxical injunctions' and 'learning theory.' It does not occur to this author that she is analysing the shortcomings of a fictional stereotype rather than reality. Morgan (1991) makes the amazing shift from commenting on 'the absence of any systematic research on codependency' (720), to listing several authors' unsubstantiated speculations on what the term means, to discussing 'codependency' as an established fact, with 'real' symptoms.

There are also attempts to reify the idea of codependency through the use of scientific-sounding phrases, such as 'the medical consequences of codependency' (Schneider 1991; see also Cermak 1986; Schaef 1986; Wegscheider-Cruse and Cruse 1990). Whitfield (1992) talks about 'primary codependence'; Gorski (1992) writes about the existence of 'child onset' versus 'adult onset codependence' and attempts to bolster his statements with his 'Codependent Classification System.' These terms have the familiar ring of medical terminology, but are not only quite vague in description but also completely without basis in responsibly executed research. The lists of supposed physical or emotional symptoms of 'being codependent' are without exception unsubstantiated (Krestan and Bepko 1990). Schaef's claim that codependency, if 'untreated, has a predictable outcome (death)' (6) is astonishingly unwarranted (see Cermak 1992 for a similar claim). If anything, such symptom lists describe the results of experiencing stress, concomitant with coping with an addict in one's life (Martin 1988; van Wormer 1989). Stress, however, is a response to a situation, not a disease.

'Codependency' is not included in the *DSM-IV* (American Psychiatric Association 1994). However, recent attempts to have 'codependency' entered as a *DSM* diagnosis (Tavris 1992) represent another effort to endorse the concept through medicalizing. Irvine (1992) and McKay (1992) analyse the ways that 'medicalizing' social problems (such as the oppression of women) serve to depoliticize and so to defocus from the social aspects of these problems, and how 'codependency,' with its pathologizing of the feminine role, fits this model. When a problem is labelled as an illness, social change is avoided (see also Asher and Brissett 1988). Hagan (1993) writes, 'Imagine what would happen if instead of saying "I'm codependent," thousands of women were saying "I'm oppressed"' (37).

The acceptance by some physicians of the label of codependency as a valid diagnosis further contributes to its popularity. With a few, it appears to be unwitting, an assumption that any term so widely accepted by addictions workers must be valid (see, e.g., Unger 1988). However, Whitfield (1991, 1992) is an example of a physician who in this regard rejects research findings. He refers to his ideas on codependency as 'healing the human condition,' and that therefore codependency is of a 'higher realm,' which makes it exempt from the scientific method of examination. Whitfield even asserts (1991) that 'blind reliance on others [implying scientific researchers] may be another manifestation of co-dependence' (46). That such statements are accepted without question by many addictions workers (as evidenced by Whitfield's popularity) is symptomatic of the naïve and even messianic attitude apparent in much addictions 'treatment' (see Babcock 1992b; Brown 1991).

To the unsophisticated reader, noteworthy phrases and the aura of research, however well or poorly executed, are impressive and convincing. This author has discussed the inadequate educational base of many addictions workers (Babcock 1992b). Haaken (1990) writes:

Clinicians who are not anchored in broad-based traditions backed by well-developed theories are tremendously vulnerable to clinical trends and popular literature that "pull it all together" conceptually ... the message is compelling because it seems to provide both the therapists who draw on the co-dependence literature and the individuals who identify with the 'disease' deliverance from the difficult task of separating out what is internal from what is external, and what is healthy and emotionally useful from what is pathological and emotionally destructive in worrisome, conflictual, interpersonal relationships (405).

'CODEPENDENCY' VS. DIAGNOSIS

One of the several serious functional problems resulting from the definitional vagueness of 'codependency' has been a retreat from diagnostic specificity. Haaken (1990) comments that 'The construct of co-dependence embraces much of humanity in a common psychopathological net ... it assimilates far too much in attempting to offer one simple construct to explain the multifarious existential, social and psychopathological bases of human emotional suffering' (405). In the uninformed worker's attempts to categorize and thus stereotype clients under the broad label of codependency, gender-role issues are ignored, but also in many cases some very real, specific emotional disorders are overlooked. Harper and Capdevila (1990) give a critique of the questionable ethics in the diagnostic inadequacy of the term. Long and Wolin (1989) do not reject the idea of codependency, but they do offer cautions about 'codependency treatment': '[these programs'] intensive, confrontational, experiential approach has produced co-dependent "casualties." A thorough diagnostic assessment is essential to responsible patient care' (42). Hearn (1991) also gives an account of the documented, dangerous incompetence of an inpatient facility claiming to 'treat codependency.'

In addition to the peril of overlooking specific psychiatric disorders, it is important for the clinician to note that a vague label like codependency also ignores variations in personality styles and life experiences. One of this author's colleagues, after having had her consciousness raised about the inadequacies of this label, (anonymously) stated about her previous use of it in therapy: 'I realize now – I was trying to force every patient into the same mold.' Gagnier and Robertiello (1991) discuss the need to distinguish between different types of dependency. Krestan and Bepko (1990) note the psychological impossibility of solutions stated or implied in the codependency construct: 'Since being affected by another is viewed as sick, a corollary assumption would be that a healthy relationship is one in which individual needs are always gratified but the self remains invulnerable from the effects of another's behaviour ... Recovered from codependency, one could magically achieve the paradoxical feat of being perfectly fulfilled in relationship without ever focusing on the other person' (220).

Burk and Sher (1990) point out the negative assumptions implicit in labelling children of alcoholics (COAs) as pathological, assumptions that they found in their research took precedence over the reality of what was actually happening for them. In this regard, it is interesting to consider whether labelling someone 'codependent' will lead to seeing her/him only in pathological terms.

COAs/ACOAs

The effects of growing up in a family with addiction are described as COA or ACOA (child or adult child of alcoholic or addict) concerns. It has been repeatedly argued by 'codependency' advocates that such a background is a breeding place for codependency. Children are alleged to be routinely damaged by growing up with addicted parents, and this history supposedly sets them up to duplicate 'codependent' dynamics in relationships with addicted partners (Gorski 1992; Mendenhall 1989). (With the increasing vagueness of the term *codependency*, the nature of these dynamics is vague. It also is now common to hear unsubstantiated claims that all sorts of troubled families can cause this alleged disorder.) Inherent in such theorizing are acceptance of the notion of pathology in COAs and ACOAs as a given, and theorizing out from that point (see Giglio and Kaufman 1990). Fisher et al. (1992), however, found that their subjects from families with alcoholic parents did not show codependency symptoms. The more thorough research findings on COAs or ACOAs indicate that, in terms of personality outcome, the results for these individuals are quite mixed. Persons from a family with addiction cannot be assumed to have emotional pathology (Beidler 1989; Fulton and Yates 1990; Jacob 1986; Tweed and Ryff 1991; Wolin 1991). Barry and Fleming (1990) report that the presence of alcoholism in their ACOA subjects, rather than the presence of any emotional disorder, determined how they perceived their current family environment. Latham and Napier (1992) found in their research that there was no correlation of their subjects' reports of level of parental drinking and the subjects' sense of social support and self-esteem. Werner (1986) has studied ACOAs who turned out to be quite resilient. El-Guebaly et al. (1993), although studying a help-seeking, clinical sample, found that the gender of ACOAs created the significant difference in how their subjects showed attachment patterns. How siblings in the same family can turn out so differently is the subject of several psychological reports (see Bower 1991).

See Burk and Sher (1988), Gallant (1990), Lewis (1990), Moos and Billings (1982), and Wilson and Orford (1978) for good summaries and critiques of COA/ACOA research. Clearly, most of this research has been done on families with alcoholism present; more needs to be done on families with members addicted to other drugs. Objections to the popularized oversimplifications and negativism about ACOA issues have even begun to reach the general media (see, e.g., McNamara 1990).

CLASS, RACE, ETHNICITY, AND SEXUALITY

Menicucci and Wermuth (1989) write that claims about pathology in family members of addicts are based on the notion of middle-class white families as the 'healthy' norm, an approach that leads to erroneous conclusions: 'the real extent and meaning of family interdependence varies across cultural and socioeconomic groups ... applications of the family systems model tend to find the family dynamics of other socioeconomic groups to be dysfunctional' (133). Inclan and Hernandez (1992) similarly describe the ways that pathologizing of closeness in the 'codependency' model ignores cultural family closeness of Hispanics. Kaufman (1980) and Walters (1990) emphasize the necessity of incorporating understanding of specific cultural backgrounds in family therapy work, noting the distortions that occur when cultural variations are ignored. The recent television film *Drugs in Black and White* (MTI 1991) argues that a family's approach to dealing with an addicted adolescent in its midst can be very different depending on whether the family is black or white. McKay (1992) writes that the dominant literature on codependency, which claims to describe family reaction to addiction, 'ignores gender, as well as the variables of race, class and sexual orientation' (8).

It is quite unfortunate that there has been subscription to the notion of codependency by some authors who profess advocacy for homosexual clients in addictions counselling (see, e.g., Finnegan and McNally 1989). Chronically oppressed groups, such as lesbians and gay men, should be especially on guard against buying into such stereotyping.

FEMINIST CRITIQUE

This author's first questioning of 'codependency' came in the early 1980s with her realization that the term's emphasis on focus on the other (as the core of the alleged disorder) actually portrays the traditional feminine sex role. 'Codependency' advocates are describing the feminine role but depicting it as a pathology rather than the result of socially enforced behaviours. More realistically, Jarvinen (1991) and Holmila (1991) discuss the ways that gender roles force women to attempt to control male drinking. It is sad and ironic that some 'women's treatment programs,' which should be concerned with the status of their clients in society, accept the concept of codependency without any informed consideration of its implication of victim blaming for their clients (see, e.g., Levers and Hawes 1990; Tracy 1991). Some articles accepting 'codependency' present their ideas in the inaccurate context of 'feminism' (e.g., A.G. Kaplan 1991; Tracy 1991). J. Kaplan (1990) calls this approach 'mangled feminism.'

The presence of the classic feminine role in a concept allegedly describing significant others to addicts makes historical sense, because, as noted above, the significant others to addicts most discussed have been female (Kaufman 1980). Indeed, another code term for codependency is now 'caretaker' (Haaken 1990), which is quite obviously the role for which women are trained. Mechanic (1976) cautions about the need to distinguish 'the appropriate boundaries between distress and culturally learned patterns of acceptable response' (33). Brown and Ballou (1992) write that psychology has a history of viewing the characteristics of dominant groups (here, males) as healthy and the characteristics of non-dominant groups (females) 'eventually as pathological' (xii). See again the Broverman et al. research of 1970.

Questions have been raised about whether gender stereotyping is rather commonly done in the medicalized diagnoses of personality disorders (Sprock, Blashfield, and Smith 1990). Thus the critique that 'codependency' is a pathologizing of sex-role pressures is congruent with other personality disorder critiques. And women have long been identified with the illness behaviour model (Nathanson 1975).

In the mid-1980s a growing movement of criticism of the notion of codependency began. Some authors, quite validly, have questioned the term on general grounds of lack of evidence and oversimplification (see, e.g., Gallant 1990; Gierymski and Williams 1986; Gomberg 1989; Haaken 1990). This criticism continues, most often on feminist principles. This author has located a number of authors in addition to herself who offer interesting variants of the feminist critique of 'codependency' (that it is a pathologizing of the feminine role): Appel (1991); Asher (1992); Asher and Brissett (1988); Fabunmi, Frederick, and Jarvis Bicknese (1985); Frank and Golden (1992); Haaken (1990); Hagan (1989); Harper and Capdevila (1990); Irvine (1992); Kaminer (1990); Kaplan (1990); Krestan and Bepko (1990); Lodl (1992); Martin (1988); McKay (1992); Mullaney (1991); Ruby (1989); Schreiber (1984); Scott (1991); Sloven (1991); Tallen (1990); Tavris (1990, 1992); van Wormer (1989); Walters (1990). This list is no doubt not complete. It is also instructive for those interested in further exploring the feminist critique to read the publications of feminist family therapists (see, e.g., Carter 1989; Goldner 1985; Hare-Mustin 1978, 1987; Tavris 1990; Walters 1990).

The similarity between 'codependency' and the traditional feminine role has been so obvious that most if not all of us making the feminist critique have come to this conclusion independently of each other. It has usually been only later that each one of us has found the others; the censorship in the addictions work field has made this connection difficult. Van Wormer's (1989) statement that 'There is a paucity of criticism in the literature (academic or popular) concerning the concept of codependency' (51) is still painfully true in published works, but not for lack of many of us trying, usually unsuccessfully, to break through the censorship. McKay (1992) writes that the mainstream addictions industry has, as a defence against the critics of codependency, 'marginalized' them.

The idea of codependency is indeed aimed mostly at women: most 'treatment programs for codependency' have more women than men as clients, and the membership of 'codependency self-help groups' is predominantly female (Haaken 1990; Kaminer 1990; Mullaney 1991). Tavris (1992) summarizes the issue: the typical 'codependent' is 'the stereotypic woman,' while the codependent-no-more person (independent, self-reliant, saying no to the demands of others) is 'the stereotypic male' (196–7). McKay (1992) challenges the image that '"Codependency" appears to be gender-neutral and is based on the implicit assumption that "co-dependency" affects both genders equally' (8). This assumption of gender neutrality of course makes 'codependency' a less obvious – and thus less easily detected – misogynistic construct than the 'disturbed personality' idea mentioned above (see also Appel 1991). Despite the claim of 'codependency' adherents that it describes the behaviours of both female and male significant others of addicts, given the shaping force of gender roles the great probability is that the two sexes cope with addicts in somewhat overlapping but predominantly very different ways. As yet that difference has not been adequately explored in research. Kane-Cavaiola and Rullo-Cooney (1991) give an anecdotal description of sex roles as they are enacted in families with addiction present. However, they ignore the sex role analysis and call these phenomena 'codependency.' Noel et al. (1991) make a preliminary investigation of family dynamics in families with alcoholics of both genders and find echoes of traditional sex roles in the marriages. That is, there are gender-socialized differences in how the partners behave, regardless of who is the addicted person and who is the significant other.

'Codependency' makes toxic even the most positive aspects of the feminine role. Fabunmi, Frederick, and Jarvis Bicknese (1985), who were among the earliest of the feminist critics of 'codependency,' write that 'the substance abuse industry declares "non-maleness" as deviant, and labels it "codependency"' (1). Goldner (1986) talks about pathologizing feminine behaviour in traditional family therapy, in terms that can apply to the current codependency movement: 'Nurturing, which everyone needs, becomes a toxic element, in the language of family therapy. Care becomes infantalizing, empathy becomes intrusiveness, and attachment becomes enmeshment' (workshop comments). Other professions have placed more positive value on necessary caretaking, which usually falls to women (see, e.g., Cantor 1983; Deets 1992). 'Codependency,' however, lumps even such activity under the less worthy label of illness.

Appel (1991) and Rosenqvist (1991) note that the idea of codependency calls upon women, not men, to change. Shapiro (1990), however, makes the following point about the comparatively problematic nature of the two gender roles: 'Perhaps the time has finally come for a new agenda. Women after all, are not a big problem. Our society does not suffer from burdensome amounts of empathy and altruism, or a plague of nurturance. The problem is men – or more accurately, maleness' (62).

In that "codependency" does view non-masculine behaviour as pathological, certainly it is an issue for the men who see themselves as engaging in feminine behaviour and so label themselves 'codependent,' joining 'codependency self-help groups' and enrolling in 'codependency treatment.' (Is this the latest way for some males to attempt to deal with anxieties about sex role security?) A note that must be added here is that considering the pervasive vagueness of the term *codependency*, it is quite questionable as to what are the real or imagined problems of anyone, female or male, who self-identifies as 'codependent' (Kaminer 1990).

BLAMING THE VICTIM

This aspect of 'codependency' merits extended discussion. Van Wormer (1989) writes, 'In labelling women "co-dependents" and blaming women for the role they may or may not play in another's chemical dependency, treatment providers are inflicting harm. Therapists are harming women in persuading them to feel guilty for being married to an alcoholic. Women are harmed in being diagnosed as showing pathology when they react normally to an extreme situation. Women are harmed when they are enrolled in lengthy treatment more for the agency's benefit than their own' (61–2). Martin (1988) similarly notes that 'labeling a woman "codependent" may be the equivalent of blaming her for a problem that has much broader psychological, political, and social ramifications' (392). Also, 'codependency' harms women by persuading them that all their problems are intrapsychic, which leaves them completely unprepared to deal with the daily pressures to accept secondary status as women. Tavris (1992) says of 'codependency,' 'It does not recognize or confront the social and economic realities in people's lives'(201).

Connell (1989) claims that those in relationships with addicts deliberately get into painful situations to feel the rush of adrenalin. This is a modification of the old psychoanalytic notion of 'masochistic woman' and equally excuses abuse of women by proposing that they actually like pain.

Beattie (1987), one of the most commercially successful advocates of 'codependency,' is blatant about the victim blaming. She states that the notion of codependency requires 'each of us to decide what part we played in our victimization' (32).

An idea similar to codependency in its victim blaming is that of 'women who love too much,' as popularized by Norwood (1986). This concept is closely related to the notion of codependency in that it similarly focuses on pathologizing 'overconcern' for others and ignores the larger reality of gender-role dynamics.

An important aspect of victim blaming is that if the victims (here, women) attempt to break out of the social construct that dictates their oppression, there will be consequences – emotionally, socially, financially, and sometimes physically (Chapman and Gates 1977; Krestan and Bepko 1990; Tavris 1992). Hagan (1989) writes about the consequences of challenging the norms of sexism: 'As a woman in this culture, when I do not defer my needs to the needs of "the man," be he husband, father, brother, teacher, or boss, I am punished ... Life is easier when I don't have needs. In fact, when I am aware of my own needs, life under oppression becomes impossible' (33–4).

Family Violence

The issue of victim blaming is especially pertinent to families with male addicts/alcoholics present. Owing to their power-down relationship to males, women involved in some way with active or 'dry-drunk' addicted males are frequently in an abusive situation. A feminist analysis would never label such a woman a 'co-abuser.' Yet that is exactly what the term *codependency* does. The tip-off is the prefix *co*, which indicates mutual involvement. In its core form, 'codependency' claims that significant others (read women) to addicts help to perpetuate the addiction – and the abuse – because of their own pathology. The National Clearinghouse for the Defense of Battered Women in Philadelphia has found that facilitators of support groups for jailed battered women often use the codependency model in 'helping' these women, who have commonly been charged with crimes as a result of their victimization (Osthoff 1992). This is surely one of the more severe examples of victim blaming.

As an answer to such thinking, this author has adapted the alternative phrase, 'enforced dependence,' from Zerin's (1983) discussion of cult victims, to describe more accurately the situation of significant others to addicts. The involuntary status of 'enforced' replaces the mutuality of 'co,' and 'dependence' refers to having to rely upon, rather than to addiction itself.

Sexual Addiction

Another especially ominous aspect of victim blaming in the use of the term *codependency* comes from its application in the area of 'sexual addictions.' For example, Young (1990) makes the unsubstantiated statement that 'codependent patterns of behavior support sex and love addictions' (256). Earle and Crow (1990), writing about sexual addiction, state that 'The spouse may play a powerful role in maintaining or ending the cycle of addiction' (94), and they freely make use of the word *codependency* in discussing this situation. Lees (1994), in a workshop accredited by nursing associations in several states for relicensure, claims the existence of 'co-sex addiction.' In that sexual addicts presumably include perpetrators of rape, incest, and sexual harassment, such thinking leads to the logical conclusion that the victims of such offences have thus 'asked for it,' owing to their own alleged pathology, which supposedly 'supports' such behaviour. In fact, this author has been informed by another addictions professional (Collins 1991) about some female adult incest survivors who had been convinced in 'therapy' to examine their own 'codependent' implication in their childhood ordeal. And indeed, we have heard it said of rape victims that 'they asked for it,' in their manner of dress or behaviour. Acceptance of the notion of codependency even provides a rationalization for sexual violence.

CONCLUSION

This review outlines history and research as they shape and refute development of the idea of codependency. The reader has been familiarized with the repetitious forms in which the victim blaming inherent in 'codependency' has surfaced for decades in psychological theorizing, and the many ways in which it has been clearly discounted. Giving this issue a higher profile may be of help in short-circuiting the current manifestation of shaming stereotyping of clients in counselling and addictions work.

REFERENCES

Alexander, B.K., and G.S. Dibb (1975) Opiate addicts and their parents. *Family Process*, 14, 499–514.

American Psychiatric Association (1994) *Diagnostic and Statistical Manual of Mental Disorders – IV.* Washington, DC: American Psychiatric Association.

Ames, G., and W. Delaney (1992) Minimization of workplace alcohol problems: the supervisor's role. *Alcoholism: Clinical and Experimental Research, 16,* 180–9.

Appel, C. (1991) 'Co-dependency': a critical appraisal of social and cultural aspects from a feminist perspective. *Contemporary Drug Problems, 18,* 673–86.

Asher, R.M. (1992) *Women with alcoholic husbands: Ambivalence and the trap of codependency.* Chapel Hill and London: University of North Carolina Press.

Asher, R., and D. Brissett (1988) Codependency: a view from women married to alcoholics. *International Journal of the Addictions, 23,* 331–50.

Attardo, N. (1965) Psychodynamics of factors in the mother-child relationship in adolescent drug addiction. *Psychotherapy and Psychosomatics, 13,* 249–55.

Babcock, M. (1991). Who are the *real* codependents? *Focus* (Aug./Sept.), 28, 44–5.

– (1992) Sexism and addicted women. Unpublished manuscript.

– (1992) Why scholarship should be more popular. *Addiction & Recovery* (July/ Aug.), 28–30.

Bargh, J.A. (1992). Does sublimality matter to social psychology? In R.F. Bornstein and T.S. Pittman (eds), *Perception without awareness: Cognitive, clinical, and social perspectives.* New York, London: Guilford Press.

Barry, K.L., and M.F. Fleming (1990) Family cohesion, expressiveness and conflict in alcoholic families. *British Journal of Addiction, 85,* (81–7).

Beattie, M. (1987) *Codependent No More.* New York: Harper & Row.

Beidler, R.J. (1989) Adult children of alcoholics: is it really a separate field for study? *Drugs and Society, 3,* 133–41.

Bernal, G., and E. Ysern (1986) Family therapy and ideology. *Journal of Marital and Family Therapy, 12,* 129–35.

Billings, A.G., and R.H. Moos (1983) Psychosocial processes of recovery among alcoholics and their families. *Addictive Behaviors, 8,* 205–18.

Binion, V.J. (1982) Sex differences in socialization and family dynamics of female and male heroin users. *Journal of Social Issues, 38,* 43–57.

Bower, B. (1991) Same family, different lives. *Science News, 140,* 376–8.

Broverman, I., D. Broverman, F. Clarkson, P. Rosenkrantz, and S. Vogel (1970) Sex-role stereotypes and clinical judgments of mental health. *Journal of Consulting and Clinical Psychology, 34,* 1–7.

Brown, J.D. (1991) The professional ex-: an alternative for exiting the deviant career. *Sociological Quarterly, 32,* 219–30.

Brown, L.S., and M. Ballou (eds) (1992) *Personality and Psychopathology: Feminist Reappraisals.* New York, London: Guilford Press.

Burk, J.P., and K.J. Sher (1988) The 'forgotten children' revisited: neglected areas of COA research. *Clinical Psychology Review, 8,* 285–302.

– (1990) Labeling the child of an alcoholic: negative stereotyping by mental health professionals and peers. *Journal of Studies on Alcohol, 51,* 156–63.

Cantor, M.H. (1983) Strain among caregivers: a study of experience in the United States. *The Gerontologist, 23,* 597–604.

Carson, A.T., and R.C. Baker (1994) Psychological correlates of codependency in women. *International Journal of the Addictions, 29,* 395–407.

Carter, B. (1989) Gender-sensitive therapy. *Family Therapy Networker* (July/Aug.), 57–60.

– (1992) Stonewalling feminism. *Family Therapy Networker* (Jan./Feb.), 64–9.

Cermak, T. (1986) *Diagnosing and Treating Co-dependence.* Minneapolis: Johnson Institute Books.

– (1992) Codependence for counselors. *Addiction & Recovery* (Nov./Dec.), 11–13.

Chapman, J.R., and M. Gates (eds) (1977) *Women into Wives: The Legal and Economic Impact of Marriage.* Beverly Hills: Sage.

Chiauzzi, E.J., and S. Liljegren (1993) Taboo topics in addiction treatment: an empirical review of clinical folklore. *Journal of Substance Abuse Treatment, 10,* 303–16.

Coleman, E. (1987) Marital and relationship problems among chemically dependent and codependent relationships. *Journal of Chemical Dependency, 1,* 39–59.

Collet, L. (1990) After the anger, *what then? Family Therapy Networker* (Jan./Feb.), 22–31.

Collins, B. (1991) Personal communication. East Stroudsburg University, Stroudsburg, PA.

Connell, S. (1989) Adrenalin: co-dependent's drug of choice. *Alcoholism and Addiction* (Oct.), 43–4.

Corder, B.F., A. Hendricks, and R.F. Corder (1964) An MMPI study of a group of wives of alcoholics. *Quarterly Journal of Studies on Alcohol, 25*, 551–4.

Deets, H.B. (1992) We all have a stake in concerns of caregivers. *AARP Bulletin* (June), 3.

Deighton, J., and P. McPeek (1985) Group treatment: adult victims of childhood sexual abuse. *Social Casework, 66*, 403–10.

Earle, R.H., and G.M. Crow (1990) Sexual addiction: understanding and treating the phenomenon. *Contemporary Family Therapy, 12*, 89–104.

Edwards, P., C. Harvey, and P. Whitehead (1973) Wives of alcoholics: a critical review and analysis. *Quarterly Journal of Studies on Alcohol, 34*, 112–32.

Ehrenreich, B. (1992) Cauldron of anger. *Life* (Jan.), 62–8.

El-Guebaly, N., M. West, E. Maticka-Tyndale, and M. Pool (1993) Attachment among adult children of alcoholics. *Addiction, 88*, 1405–11.

Fabunmi, C., L. Frederick, and M. Jarvis Bicknese (1985) The codependency trap. Unpublished manuscript. Available from the Southern Minnesota Regional Legal Services, P.O. Box 1266, Winona MN 55987.

Finnegan, D.G., and E.B. McNally (1989) The lonely journey: lesbians and gay men who are codependent. *Alcoholism Treatment Quarterly, 6*, 121–34.

Fischer, J.L., L. Spann, and D. Crawford (1991) Measuring codependency. *Alcoholism Treatment Quarterly, 8*, 87–99.

Fischer, J.L., R. Wampler, K. Lyness, and E.M. Thomas (1992) Offspring codependency: blocking the impact of the family of origin. *Family Dynamics of Addiction Quarterly, 2*, 20–32.

Fisher, G.L., S.J. Jenkins, T.C. Harrison, and K. Jesch (1992) Characteristics of adult children of alcoholics. *Journal of Substance Abuse, 4*, 27–34.

Fort, J.P. (1954) Heroin addiction among young men. *Psychiatry, 17*, 251–9.

Frank, P.B., and G.K. Golden (1992) Blaming by naming: battered women and the epidemic of codependence. *Social Work, 37*, 5–6.

Franklin, D. (1987) The politics of masochism. *Psychology Today* (Jan.), 52–6.

Fulton, A.I. and W.R. Yates (1990) Adult children of alcoholics: a valid diagnostic group? *Journal of Nervous and Mental Disease, 8*, 505–9.

Futterman, S. (1953) Personality trends in wives of alcoholics. *Journal of Psychiatric Social Work, 23*, 37–41.

Gagnier, T.T., and R.C. Robertiello (1991) The clinical usefulness of distinguishing between two types of dependency. *Journal of Contemporary Psychotherapy, 21*, 247–55.

Gallant, D.M. (1990) Current literature reviewed and critiqued. *Alcoholism: Clinical and Experimental Research, 14*, 630–1.

Gierymski, T., and T. Williams (1986) Codependency. *Journal of Psychoactive Drugs, 18*, 7–13.

Giglio, J.J., and E. Kaufman (1990) The relationship between child and adult psychopathology in children of alcoholics. *International Journal of the Addictions*, 25, 263–90.

Gilliland, B.E., R.K. James and J.T. Bowman (1989) *Theories and Strategies in Counseling and Psychotherapy.* Englewood Cliffs, NJ: Prentice Hall.

Glynn, T.J., and M. Haenlein (1988) Family theory and research on adolescent drug use: a review. *Journal of Chemical Dependency Treatment*, 1, 39–56.

Goldner, V. (1985) Warning: family therapy may be hazardous to your health. *Family Therapy Networker*, (Nov./Dec.), 18–23.

– (1986) *Is family therapy dangerous for women? Systems theory critiqued.* Presentation at Western Psychiatric Institute and Clinic, Pittsburgh, PA, April.

Gomberg, E.S.L. (1989) On terms used and abused: the concept of 'codependency.' *Drugs and Society*, 3, 113–32.

Gorski, T.T. (1992) Diagnosing codependence. *Addiction & Recovery* (Nov./Dec.), 14–16.

Haaken, J. (1990) A critical analysis of the co-dependence construct. *Psychiatry*, 53, 396–406.

Haberman, P.W. (1964) Psychological test score changes for wives of alcoholics during periods of drinking and sobriety. *Journal of Clinical Psychology*, 20, 230–2.

Hagan, K.L. (1993) Codependency and the myth of recovery. In K.L. Hagan, *Fugitive Information: Essays from a Feminist Hothead.* San Francisco: HarperCollins.

Hare-Mustin, R.T. (1978) A feminist approach to family therapy. *Family Process*, 17, 181–94.

– (1983) An appraisal of the relationship between women and psychotherapy: 80 years after the case of Dora. *American Psychologist*, 38, 593–601.

– (1987) The problem of gender in family therapy theory. *Family Process*, 26, 15–27.

Harper, J., and C. Capdevila (1990) Codependency: a critique. *Journal of Psychoactive Drugs*, 22, 285–92.

Hearn, E. (1991) What price success? *Professional Counselor* (June), 78.

Holmila, M. (1991) Social control experienced by heavily drinking women. *Contemporary Drug Problems*, 18, 547–71.

Horney, K. (1967) *Feminine Psychology.* New York, London: W.W. Norton.

Hubbard, G.B. (1989) Mothers' perception of incest: sustained disruption and turmoil. *Archives of Psychiatric Nursing*, 8, 34–40.

Inclan, J., and M. Hernandez (1992) Cross-cultural perspectives and codependence: the case of poor Hispanics. *American Journal of Orthopsychiatry*, 62, 245–55.

Irvine, L.J. (1992) The pathologizing of love: a sociological analysis of codependency. Unpublished master's thesis, Florida Atlantic University, Boca Raton.

Jackson, J.K. (1954) The adjustment of the family to the crisis of alcoholism. *Quarterly Journal of Studies on Alcohol, 15*, 562-86.

- (1956) The adjustment of the family to alcoholism. *Marriage and the Family, 18*, 361-9.

- (1962) Alcoholism and the family. In D.J. Pittman and C.R. Snyder (eds), *Society, Culture, and Drinking Patterns*. New York: Wiley.

Jacob, T. (1986) Alcoholism: a family perspective – theoretical and methodological developments. *Nebraska Symposium on Motivation, 34*, 159-206.

Jacob, T., N.J. Dunn, and K. Leonard (1983) Patterns of alcohol abuse and family stability. *Alcoholism: Clinical and Experimental Research, 7*, 382-5.

Jacob, T., A. Favorini, S. Meisel, and C.M. Anderson (1978) The alcoholic's spouse, children, and family interactions. *Journal of Studies on Alcohol, 39*, 1231-51.

Jarmas, A.L., and A.E. Kazak (1992) Young adult children of alcoholic fathers: depressive experiences, coping styles, and family systems. *Journal of Consulting and Clinical Psychology, 60*, 244-51.

Jarvinen, M. (1991) The controlled controllers: women, men, and alcohol. *Contemporary Drug Problems, 18*, 389-406.

Kaminer, W. (1990) Chances are you're codependent too. *New York Times Book Review*, 11 Feb. 26-7.

Kane-Cavaiola, C., and D. Rullo-Cooney (1991) Addicted women: their families' effect on treatment outcome. *Journal of Chemical Dependency Treatment, 4*, 111-19.

Kaplan, A.G. (1991) Co-dependency: a reexamination. *Proceedings from Learning from Women* (April), Harvard Medical School Department of Continuing Education, 31-2.

Kaplan, J. (1990) The trouble with codependency. *Self* (July), 112-13, 148.

Kaufman, E. (1980) Myth and reality in the family patterns and treatment of substance abusers. *American Journal of Drug and Alcohol Abuse, 7*, 257-79.

- (1981) Family structures of narcotics addicts. *International Journal of the Addictions, 16*, 106-8.

- (1985) Family systems and family therapy of substance abuse: an overview of two decades of research and clinical experience. *International Journal of the Addictions, 20*, 897-916.

Kogan, K.L., W.E. Fordyce, and J.K. Jackson (1963) Personality disturbances in wives of alcoholics. *Quarterly Journal of Studies on Alcohol, 24*, 227-38.

Kogan, K.L. and J.K. Jackson (1964) Patterns of atypical perceptions of self and spouse in wives of alcoholics. *Quarterly Journal of Studies on Alcohol, 25,* 555–7.

– (1965) Stress, personality and emotional disturbance in wives of alcoholics. *Quarterly Journal of Studies on Alcohol, 26,* 486–95.

Krestan, J.A., and C. Bepko (1990) Codependency: the social reconstruction of female experience. *Smith College Studies in Social Work, 60,* 216–32.

Latham, P.K., and T.K. Napier (1992) Psychosocial consequences of alcohol misuse in the family of origin. *International Journal of the Addictions, 27,* 1137–58.

Lees, A.B. (1994) The lasting scars of sexual abuse. Workshop sponsored by Carondelet Management Institute, Tucson, AZ, April.

Le Poire, B.A. (1992) Does the codependent encourage substance-dependent behavior? Paradoxical injunctions in the codependent relationship. *International Journal of the Addictions, 27,* 1465–74.

Lerner, H.G. (1985) Dianna and Lillie: can a feminist still like Murray Bowen? *Family Therapy Networker* (Nov./Dec.), 36–39.

Levers, L.L., and A.R. Hawes (1990) Drugs and gender: a women's recovery program. *Journal of Mental Health Counseling, 12,* 527–31.

Lewis, D.C. (1990) Understanding children of alcoholics. *Brown University Digest of Addiction Theory and Application, 9* (7), 8.

Lewis, M.L. (1954) The initial contact with wives of alcoholics. *Social Casework, 35,* 8–14.

Libow, J.A., P.A. Raskin, and B.L. Caust (1982) Feminist and family systems therapy: are they irreconcilable? *American Journal of Family Therapy, 10,* 3–12.

Lodl, K.M. (1992) A feminist critique of co-dependency. Unpublished manuscript.

Long, T.R., and S.J. Wolin (1989) Co-dependents: is inpatient treatment necessary? *Alcoholism and Addiction* (Oct.), 41–2.

Love, C.T., R. Longabaugh, P.R. Clifford, M. Beattie, and C.F. Peaslee (1993) The Significant-other Behavior Questionnaire (SBQ): an instrument for measuring the behavior of significant others towards a person's drinking and abstinence. *Addiction, 88,* 1267–79.

Lyon, D., and J. Greenberg (1991) Evidence of codependency in women with an alcoholic parent: helping out Mr. Wrong. *Journal of Personality and Social Psychology, 61,* 435–9.

Macdonald, J.G. (1987) Predictors of treatment outcome for alcoholic women. *International Journal of the Addictions, 22,* 235–48.

Martin, D. (1988) A review on the popular literature on codependency. *Contemporary Drug Problems, 15,* 383–98.

McKay, C. (1992) The co-dependency myth – a feminist critique. Unpublished master's thesis, Carleton University, Ottawa.

McNamara, M. (1990) Recovering from recovery. *Glamour* (Nov.), 176.

Mechanic, D. (1976) Sex, illness behavior, and the use of health services. *Journal of Human Stress, 2,* 29–40.

Mendenhall, W. (1989) Codependency definitions and dynamics. *Alcoholism Treatment Quarterly, 6,* 3–17.

Menicucci, L.D., and L. Wermuth (1989) Expanding the family systems approach: cultural, class, developmental and gender influences in drug abuse. *American Journal of Family Therapy, 17,* 129–42.

Miller, N.S., and R.B. Millman (1989) A common cause of alcoholism. *Journal of Substance Abuse Treatment, 6,* 41–3.

Moos, R.H., and A.G. Billings (1982) Children of alcoholics during the recovery process: alcoholic and matched control families. *Addictive Behaviors, 7,* 155–63.

Moos, R.H., J.W. Finney, and W. Gamble (1982) The process of recovery from alcoholism: II. Comparing spouses of alcoholic patients and matched community controls. *Journal of Studies on Alcohol, 43,* 888–909.

Moos, R.H., and B.S. Moos (1984) The process of recovery from alcoholism: III. Comparing functioning in families of alcoholics and matched control families. *Journal of Studies on Alcohol, 45,* 111–18.

Morgan, J.P. (1991) What is codependency? *Journal of Clinical Psychology, 47,* 720–9.

MTI Film and Video (1991) *Drugs in Black and White* [film]. Deerfield, IL.

Mullaney, P.A. (1991) (Mentioned in) Co-dependence label offends reader. *Addiction Letter* (Aug.), 7.

Nace, E.P. (1982) Therapeutic approaches to the alcoholic marriage. *Psychiatric Clinics of North America, 5,* 543–64.

Nathanson, C.A. (1975) Illness and the feminine role: a theoretical review. *Social Science and Medicine, 9,* 57–62.

Nici, J. (1979) Wives of alcoholics as 'repeaters.' *Journal of Studies on Alcohol, 40,* 677–82.

Noel, N.E., B.S. McCrady, R.L. Stout, and H. Fisher-Nelson (1991) Gender differences in marital functioning of male and female alcoholics. *Family Dynamics of Addiction Quarterly, 1,* 31–8.

Norwood, R. (1986) *Women Who Love Too Much.* New York: Simon and Schuster.

O'Brien, P.E., and M. Gaborit (1992) Codependency: a disorder separate from chemical dependency. *Journal of Clinical Psychology, 48,* 129–36.

Orford, J. (1992) Control, confront or collude: how family and society respond to excessive drinking. *British Journal of Addiction, 87,* 1513–25.

Osthoff, S. (1992) Personal communication. National Clearinghouse for the Defense of Battered Women, Philadelphia.

Paolino, T.J., B. McCrady, S. Diamond, and R. Longabaugh (1976) Psychological disturbances in spouses of alcoholics: an empirical assessment. *Journal of Studies on Alcohol, 37*, 1600–8.

Phillips, R.D., and F.D. Gilroy (1985) Sex-role stereotypes and clinical judgments of mental health: the Broverman's' findings revisited. *Sex Roles, 12*, 179–93.

Pitman, N.E., and R.G. Taylor (1992) MMPI profiles of partners of incestuous sexual offenders and partners of alcoholics. *Family Dynamics of Addiction Quarterly, 2*, 52–9.

Preli, R., H. Protinsky and L. Cross (1990) Alcoholism and family structure. *Family Therapy, 17*, 1–8.

Price, G.M. (1945) A study of the wives of twenty alcoholics. *Quarterly Journal of Studies on Alcohol, 5*, 620–7.

Reed, B.G. (1987) Developing women-sensitive drug dependence treatment services: why so difficult? *Journal of Psychoactive Drugs, 19*, 151–64.

Roberts, M.C.F., F.J. Floyd, T.J. O'Farrell, and H.S.G. Cutter (1985) Marital interactions and the duration of alcoholic husbands' sobriety. *American Journal of Drug and Alcohol Abuse, 11*, 303–13.

Roman, P.M., T.C. Blum, and J.K. Martin (1992) 'Enabling' of male problem drinkers in work groups. *British Journal of Addiction, 87*, 275–89.

Rosenqvist, P. (1991) AA, Al-Anon and gender. *Contemporary Drug Problems, 18*, 687–705.

Ruby, J.A. (1989) Lesbian-feminist critique of Twelve-Step programs. *Off Our Backs* (Aug./Sept.), 8.

Schaef, A.W. (1986) *Co-dependence: Misunderstood – Mistreated*. San Francisco: Harper & Row.

Schneider, M. (1991) *Medical Aspects of Co-dependency* [film]. FMS Productions, Carpinteria, CA.

Schreiber, D. (1984) Hysterectomies, mastectomies and co-dependencies. *Viewpoints: The Quarterly Publication of the Minnesota Chemical Health Association* (Winter), 1–2.

Scott, A.F. (1991) The codependency cop-out. *Family Circle*, 23 July, 140.

Shapiro, L. (1990) Guns and dolls. *Newsweek*, 28 May, 56–65.

Sisson, R.W., and N.H. Azrin (1986) Family-member involvement to initiate and promote treatment of problem drinkers. *Journal of Behavioral Therapy and Experimental Psychiatry, 17*, 15–21.

Sloven, J. (1991) Codependent or empathically responsive? Two views of Betty. In C. Bepko (ed.), *Feminism and Addiction*. Binghamton, NY: Haworth Press

Sorensen, J.L. (1989) Family approaches to the problems of addictions: recent developments. *Psychology of Addictive Behaviors, 3,* 134–9.

Sprock, J., R.K. Blashfield, and B. Smith (1990) Gender weighting of *DSM-III-R* personality disorder criteria. *American Journal of Psychiatry, 147,* 586–90.

Steinglass, P. (1976) Experimenting with family treatment approaches to alcoholism, 1950–1975: a review. *Family Process, 15,* 97–123.

Steinglass, P., L. Bennett, S.J. Wolin, and D. Reiss (1987) *The Alcoholic Family,* New York: Basic Books.

Sunderwirth, S., and J. Spector (1992) Codependency: when the chemistry isn't right. *Family Dynamics of Addiction Quarterly, 2,* 23–31.

Tallen, B.S. (1990) Co-dependency: a feminist critique. *Sojourner: The Women's Forum* (Jan.), 20–1.

Tavris, C. (1990) The politics of codependency. *Family Therapy Networker* (Jan.-Feb.), 43.

– (1992) *The Mismeasure of Woman.* New York: Simon and Schuster.

Thomas, E.J., and C.A. Santa (1982) Unilateral family therapy for alcohol abuse: a working conception. *American Journal of Family Therapy, 10,* 49–58.

Tracy, J.K. (1991) Living with an alcoholic. In P. Roth (ed.), *Alcohol and Drugs are Women's Issues,* I. Metuchen, NJ, London: Scarecrow Press.

Tweed, S.H., and C.D. Ryff (1991) Adult children of alcoholics: profiles of wellness amidst distress. *Journal of Studies on Alcohol, 52,* 133–41.

Unger, K.B. (1988) Chemical dependency in women: meeting the challenges of accurate diagnosis and effective treatment. *Western Journal of Medicine, 149,* 746–50.

van Wormer, K. (1989) Co-dependency: implications for women and therapy. *Women and Therapy, 8,* 51–63.

Velleman, R., G. Bennett, T. Miller, J. Orford, K. Rigby, and A. Tod (1993) The families of problem drug users: a study of 50 close relatives. *Addiction, 88,* 1281–9.

Waites, E.A. (1977-8) Female masochism and enforced restriction of choice. *Victimology: An International Journal, 2,* 535–44.

Walters, M. (1990) The codependent Cinderella who loves too much ... fights back. *Family Therapy Networker* (July/Aug.), 52–7.

Wegscheider-Cruse, S., and J. Cruse (1990) *Understanding Co-Dependency.* Deerfield Beach, FL: Health Communications.

Werner, E.E. (1986) Resilient offspring of alcoholics: A longitudinal study from birth to age 18. *Journal of Studies on Alcohol, 47,* 34–40.

Whalen, T. (1953) Wives of alcoholics: four types observed in a family service agency. *Quarterly Journal of Studies on Alcohol, 14,* 632–41.

Whitfield, C.L. (1991) Codependency critics shoot from the hip. *Focus* (Aug./Sept.), 29, 46–7.

– (1992) Co-dependence: healing the human condition. Presentation at Allegheny General Hospital, Pittsburgh, PA, Oct.

Williams, E., L. Bissell and E. Sullivan (1991) The effects of co-dependence on physicians and nurses. *British Journal of Addiction, 86*, 37–42.

Wilson, C., and J. Orford (1978) Children of alcoholics: results of a preliminary study and comments on the literature. *Journal of Studies on Alcohol, 39*, 121–42.

Wolin, S. (1991) Family therapy researcher criticizes recovery movement. *Alcoholism and Drug Abuse Weekly*, 20 Nov., 4.

Wright, P.H. and K.D. Wright (1990) Measuring codependents' close relationships: a preliminary study. *Journal of Substance Abuse, 2*, 335–44.

Young, E.B. (1990) The role of incest issues in relapse. *Journal of Psychoactive Drugs, 22*, 249–58.

Zelvin, E. (1988) Dependence and denial in coalcoholic women. *Alcoholism Treatment Quarterly, 5*, 97–115.

Zerin, M.J. (1983) The pied piper phenomenon and the processing of victims: the transactional analysis perspective re-examined. *Transactional Analysis Journal, 13*, 172–7.

JEANE HARPER, MA, MFCC, and
CONNIE CAPDEVILA, Lic., CAC

Codependency: A Critique

During the past decade, attempts to integrate traditionally separate approaches to drug abuse treatment and alcoholism treatment under a more cohesive body of the theoretical, research, and clinical methods have given rise to the new field of chemical dependency (CD). Until recently, the central focus of the field has been on a disease concept and treatment of CD that has historically been ignored by the mental health (MH) field because, according to Stanton (1988), it 'has not progressed concurrently, hand in hand, with the developing mental health technology.'

However, the CD field continues to expand exponentially, with a growing body of its research and theory beginning to find a place in the literature of the broader MH field. The larger body of literature concerned with CD is contained in the newly established journals of the CD field and includes what might be the largest single body of bibliotherapy ever focused on one population, which is used and distributed by the specialized treatment industry with which the field *does* progress, hand in hand.

The field's most recent direction of expansion lies in an extended focus on the family members of chemically dependent persons, generating a separate body of clinical theory and treatment for codependency. Gierymski and Williams (1986) indicated that the term *codependency* originally designated the spouse of the alcoholic and is now generalized to 'all family members and the chemical dependent's close social network.' The addition of 'family services' accompanies all but forty-five of the 1,000 CD treatment programs listed in a recent national treatment directory published by the *U.S. Journal of Drug and Alcohol Dependence* (1989).

With the concept of codependency, the gap between the CD and MH fields becomes a theoretical chasm, as their mutual focus on families does not in itself constitute a bridge. While much of the literature in the CD field incorporates the language of systemic family therapy, the language is unaccompanied by the substance of its underlying theory; nor does the industry's provision of family services imply family therapy as a formal method or the family as the target of treatment. Family therapy in CD treatment settings is actually parallel to individual treatment of a family member; and codependency is the conceptual core of assessment, diagnosis, and treatment.

Yet, no two authors in the CD field adhere to the same definition of codependency, and lacking an operational definition, the CD literature reflects only a confusing array of differing opinions as to its nature, symptomatology, etiology, and prognosis. Definitions of codependency are broad, ranging from a 'primary disease' (Young 1987; Wegscheider 1981) that 'could lead to death' (Schaef 1986) to 'an emotional, psychological and behavioral condition' (Friel, Subby and Friel 1984). As a 'family disease' (Gorski and Miller 1984), it is capable of 'relapse' and requires 'life-long attention.' Broader yet are the parameters of its symptomatology, 'spanning a spectrum from no symptoms at all to headaches to suicide' (Whitfield 1984); Beattie (1987) specified 241 characteristics that were organized into fourteen categories of behaviours. Addressing this confusion, efforts by Cermak (1986b) and others to help the CD field "be clear about what they are treating in the family program" are producing operational definitions linked to *DSM* classifications of personality disorders.

There is general consensus in the CD field on codependency as a diagnostic entity, despite acknowledgement of an imprecise definition (Cermak 1986b; Gierymski and Williams 1986) and criticism of the concept's stigmatizing effect (Asher and Brissett 1988). The significance of the concept within the CD field is indicated by the fifty-six workshops that comprised the 1989 First National Conference on Co-Dependency, which was initiated by joint CD field and treatment industry effort, and by a description of codependency (Cermak 1986b) as 'the contribution which may well turn the tables on the mental health profession.'

Despite the fragility of its construct, codependency has become a salient issue for the public and there are signals that it is perilously close to being legitimized by the MH field. Just how seductive the issue has become is illustrated in the increasing numbers of MH practitioners found to be codependency specialists and in the advent of training workshops for identifying and assessing codependent behaviours in the profession. The definitive indicator is inclusion of the concept in graduate and postgraduate academic counselling curricula.

The present degree of uncritical acceptance of this empirically unfounded diagnostic entity, within both fields, calls for an examination of the origins and development of the codependency concept. A thorough examination of the concept lays bare the skeleton of the obsolete disturbed-personality hypothesis (DPH) and the perpetuation of a consistently negative view of wives who have chemically dependent husbands. The present article examines the concept and treatment of codependency.

An emphasis on wives as the target of the codependence concept is motivated primarily by its predominant referral to them in the literature to date. It is not within the scope of this examination to address models of family therapy, other than to note that research on couples with CD problems deals with a population that is primarily composed of chemically dependent males, most often coalescing around the wife's relationship to, involvement with, or effect on her husband's chemical use (Steinglass et al. 1987; West, Hosie and Zarski 1987; O'Farrell and Cutter 1984; Moos et al. 1979). Little writing has been focused specifically on husbands as the codependent; a review by Perodeau (1984) of what little research exists found that knowledge about them is 'sketchy and inadequate.'

ORIGIN OF THE CONCEPT

'Codependent' is only the most recent metaphor used to describe family members; the terms 'para-alcoholic' and 'co-alcoholic' appear earlier in both Al-Anon and CD treatment settings. Early literature from these sources makes clear that the designations referred exclusively to wives. The more neutral and inclusive designation 'significant other' was briefly utilized and remains an option, while codependent has clearly become the designation of choice.

These mutations in terminology do not represent a conceptual evolution in the perspective on wives. Remaining consistently negative, it can be traced from roots in early psychoanalytic theory, through its incorporation into Al-Anon and Alcoholics Anonymous (AA), to its emergence in CD treatment philosophy, which is closely aligned with that of the self-help groups.

Paulino and McCrady's review (1977) of theory and treatment for the 'alcoholic marriage' cited Gaether's early clinical description of wives, who were thought to decompensate if their husbands stopped drinking. Based on a small sample of wives of late-stage alcoholics in 1939, Gaether's study found them to be 'anxious, angry, abnormally dominant and masochistic ... sexually repressed.' This description was expanded by Whelan (1953), who provided four character types based on nine wives under her observation: (a) 'the sufferer ... an unnecessary martyr who symbolically asks for crucifixion'; (2) 'the wavering wife ... who never followed through with attempts to cope with the problem' and for whom there was 'never a point of no return'; (3) 'the controller ... with a desperate need of her own, apart from any realistic connection to the alcoholism situation'; and (4) 'the punisher' who needed 'an emasculated husband to punish ... ,' while denying the intrapsychic origins of her anger.

These descriptions formed the basis for the DPH and decompensation hypothesis (DH), complementing an earlier theory of an alcoholic personality, all long since abandoned by the MH field (Jacob et al. 1978; Vaillant 1977; Edwards, Harvey, and Whitehead 1973). However, the formative descriptions of the DPH remain relevant today, providing the structure for the codependency diagnosis. The essence of Gaether's characteristics and the literal application of Whelan's types are still found in the cross-fertilized literature of Al-Anon and the CD field, which is used as educational material for family members in treatment settings.

TRACING THE DEVELOPMENT

When AA was founded in 1935, psychiatric treatment offered little help for alcoholics, and other drug use was not widespread and still confined to the unspeakable. Therefore, concepts underlying the view of wives were initiated relative to wives of alcoholics.

Wives of the founders met informally during the early days of AA's formation and their view of themselves contradicts the DPH. Given a voice in AA's first publication (Alcoholics Anonymous 1939) – 'we ask our wives to spread the message to the wives of other alcoholics' – they referred to themselves as 'grateful wives' and evidenced a spirit of generosity and appreciation for the difficult job and enormous accomplishment inherent in their husbands' recoveries. By the time these same wives formally incorporated as the Al-Anon Family Groups some twenty years later, Al-Anon's literature reflected an entirely different view, which incorporated the DPH and could be traced to religion as well as psychoanalytic influence.

Consequently, a moralistic tone and negative theme appeared early in the annals of Al-Anon literature, both introduced there by Reverend Kellerman (Al-Anon 1969), who described wives as 'the Provocatrix ... who never gives in, never gives up, never lets go, but never forgets.' Kellerman also introduced Whelan's types verbatim into the Al-Anon literature (1979), citing her as 'an authority in this field ... ' Refashioned only slightly, they appear as 'Controlling Catherine, Suffering Susan, Wavering Winnie, and Punitive Polly.' The tone and theme endure as these works continue to be reissued verbatim and CD treatment programs continue to utilize them in family treatment.

Later CD and Al-Anon publications mirrored each other, synergistically building on a core concept, central to which are the DPH characteristics. While literature from both sources disavows intentional blaming of the wife, Greenleaf's work on codependency (1984) makes an 'etiological distinction' between adults and children in order to 'spare the child any assumption of blame and responsibility,' both presumably inherent in the concept of codependency. Less central to the core concept of codependency is Whelan's (1953) attribution of 'sexual repression.' Evidence of its continuing influence, however, can be found in the claim made in *My Wife Drinks Too Much* (Al-Anon 1976b) that 'professional counselors have found ... guilt feelings in the spouse of the alcoholic are often rooted in sexual maladjustment.'

While there are some objective descriptions of wives in the CD literature and other far more compassionate tones and themes in Al-Anon literature, they are not the ones that resonate, as the foregoing do, in the following four descriptions of codependency currently competing for operational definition in the CD field.

Codependency as a Causal Implication

The same Al-Anon pamphlet that introduced the Provocatrix contains the explanation that 'a person must have the help of at least one other person to become an alcoholic ... it cannot appear, get worse, or continue in isolation from others,' leading directly to a causal interpretation of wives' behaviours. A 1980 reissue of this material, utilized by a major CD treatment/research institution, retains the label 'Provocatrice,' changing only the spelling, while updating part of its terminology to combine the American Medical Association's definition of alcoholism as a disease with a systemic concept of family behaviour. The revision places responsibility on the family, which is 'involved in a way that literally enables the [disease] to continue and become worse,' and generates the concept of enabling as an added symptom of codependency without removing the DPH and DH interpretations.

The causal implication prevails in the popular belief held by CD counsellors: 'no wonder the alcoholic drinks; who wouldn't with a crazy co-dependent spouse' (Beattie 1987). The negativity was so overt in this belief that Kellerman was later compelled to refute any such interpretation of his writings. The effect of this negativity on wives' self-esteem is witnessed in the reflection of one wife – a client in marital therapy with one of the authors (Harper) – some five years after her participation in a family program: 'it's as though the husband has this little seed, which drops into fertile soil and turns into a terrible disease ... and the fertile soil is supposed to be us [wives].'

The CD literature and Al-Anon continued to evidence variations on this theme, and by 1975 literature on drug abuse treatment (e.g., Cadogen 1975) also began to reflect a corollary of the causal implication that wives sabotage recovery: 'spouses feel guilty and sabotage treatment.' A later study (Powell 1984) on treatment of alcoholism-associated problems for the alcoholic still referred to the concern that the wife 'may refuse to let him get well, create tension and a quarrelsome environment to strike back at his progress.'

Codependency as a Disease

The genesis of this concept is unclear. There are indications that the concept springs from the DPH influence in Al-Anon, where Ablon (1974) reported that 'many women admit they are as sick or sicker than the alcoholic.' Furthermore, men were not excluded, and one of the few pieces of Al-Anon literature (Al-Anon 1976b) specifically addressed to them explains that 'denial is part of the sickness that afflicts the spouses, too.' The Al-Anon (1979) attribution more frequently refers to wives, as 'presenting a more acute problem than her [chemically dependent] husband.' CD literature (e.g., Burgin 1976) articulated this problem as 'a syndrome with an onset, pathological characteristics and prognosis – by which she is accorded the special status of the sick,' while a primary CD reference work addressed to wives (Woititz 1979) explained that 'you are sick, you have developed a disease.'

As the CD field increasingly incorporated the language of systemic family therapy, eschewing its theoretical substance in favour of prior assumptions, a confusing mixture of overlapping concepts emerged, as in 'the family disease, within each and every family member through denial and delusion' (Wegscheider-Cruse 1985) and Al-Anon's description (1976a) of a wife as the 'true patient ... of the family disorder.'

The disease concept has been carried to fantastic dimensions in the book credited with popularizing codependency outside the CD field. Schaef (1986), like Beattie, extended the parameters of symptomatology beyond all limits. Specifying codependency as 'the condition of the spouse of an alcoholic' and 'a previously unnamed disease,' Schaef listed over 100 symptoms of the disease, among which are some of the more stereotypical: relationship addiction; not trusting her own perceptions; caretaking; physically illness; controlling; distorted feelings; and fear and blaming. In Schaef's thesis, codependency is the underpinning of the 'basic addictive process' that afflicts those persons with some affective disorders, most compulsive disorders, 'all chemical dependents,' 'non-liberated men and women,' and 'most mental health professionals.'

The argument for codependency as a disease gained momentum as it proceeded from being parallel with CD to an analogous disease process and further progressed towards a definition of both as the identical disease. According to Wegscheider (1981), the codependent, with a parallel disease, is 'self-deluded just as the [chemically dependent person] is – suffering a loss of role with the [chemically dependent person's] recovery, just as the [chemically dependent person] loses a chemical.' The construction of an analogous disease process includes the supposition that codependency may end in death, as untreated CD can and often does. The codependent 'risks death' (LoVern and Zohn 1982) and her death may occur 'even before the alcoholic's' at the hands of 'the drunk who beats her' (Schaef 1986). Some CD literature (e.g., Unsigned 1980) informs wives that both she and her chemically dependent husband 'progress in their illness in similar stages.' The language implies an identical disease, which later becomes a 'mutual addiction' in Capell-Sowder's elaborate construction (1984) of codependency as an addiction to the chemically dependent partner, with the codependent 'exhibiting the same increased tolerance and loss of control.' It is noteworthy that tolerance and loss of control are two primary medical diagnostic criteria for the disease of alcoholism and appear as major indicators in the *DSM-III-R* category of 'Psychoactive Substance Dependency.'

In order to establish codependency and CD as being identical, definitional boundaries of each are made permeable. Although this is usually accomplished by expanding the boundary of codependency symptomatology to include characteristics of addiction, the reverse is true in a 1980 revision of an earlier Al-Anon publication (1969), wherein the boundary of alcoholism, per se, is no longer confined to the toxic effect of a chemical on the central nervous system and the bodily organs of the drinker but envelops the spouse as well: 'this downward spiral of [the alcoholic's] denial and [the spouse's] counter-denial is called Alcoholism.' Boundaries are also blurred (Cermak 1986a): 'it is a disservice to make large distinctions between alcoholics and co-dependents ... distinctions lead to confusion among family members regarding what is alcoholic thinking vs. co-dependent thinking.'

Codependency as Dysfunctional Behaviour

The CD field's attachment to the disease concept of codependency is evident in the failed attempts by so many authors to explain codependency in terms of dysfunctional behaviour. Most begin to describe patterns of behaviour only to conclude with a declaration of a disease entity. Whitfield's 'maladaptive or problematic behavior' (1984) becomes an indicator of 'the primary illness.' Similarly, CD literature for the family about their 'coping behavior patterns' (Unsigned 1980) loses its focus with the conclusion that 'it is not strange to call the behavior ... illness.'

When behaviour remains the focus, echoes of the DPH can be heard: Wegscheider-Cruse (1985) refers to the wife's 'obsession with her spouse and her own slavery to the sickness of alcoholism' and Brown (1985) describes wives as 'compulsively repressing feelings ... unable to see themselves as anything other than victims.' Wives have been told in the CD family treatment literature (Unsigned 1987) that they are 'preoccupied, deluded, devoting an extra share of life to the chemically dependent, hating but feeling good only when taking care of the chemically dependent' and 'obsessed with controlling other people's behavior' (Beattie 1987).

Codependency as a Personality Disorder

The disease concept of codependency, far from being abandoned, has evolved into ever more sophisticated theories of mental illness. In addition to behavioural interpretations and inferred motivations, symptomatology is ascribed to emotions, generally acknowledged to include the 'guilt, anger, fear, worry, dread, helplessness, low self-esteem, and depression' found in one group of family members (LoVern and Zohn 1982). Thus, the author's client cited earlier in her retrospective reflection, laments with some accuracy, 'It's as though the chemically dependent person has a chemical causing the problem, but *we* have something deep inside.'

Current attempts to locate wives' cognitive, affective, and behavioural characteristics within a personality disorder require several conceptual links to connect an ambiguous illness to a precise *DSM* diagnosis. One link appears in an explanation (Zink 1977) that wives' 'adaptive behaviors are not to be confused with healthy adjustment'; rather they denote 'a symbiotic relationship dependent on the alcoholic's illness to maintain [her] own precarious balance.' A link to the 'Dependent Personality Disorder' is forged with a conceptually unchanged operational definition. Making the distinction that codependency is not a 'primary disease,' Smalley and Coleman (1987) define it as an 'easily identifiable (overt) or carefully disguised (covert) learning pattern of exaggerated dependency and extreme and painful external validation, with resulting identity confusion.'

In a separate work, Coleman (1987) extends this definition to chemically dependent persons as well as spouses, singling out wives by emphasizing that 'wives are not dominant as Whelan states ... but may have elements of co-dependency ... sometimes carefully disguised as dominance, independence, and/or strong ego functioning.' This thesis appears to be little more than a sanitized version of 'the enabler ... looking too good to be true' (Unsigned 1980), making it difficult to ignore the inherent potential for an independent wife with good ego functioning to be held liable for assessment of pathology on that very basis.

Cermak (1986b) agrees that codependency 'most closely resembles' the 'Dependent Personality Disorder,' but rejects that diagnostic framework on the basis that 'it would be an oversimplification to collapse codependency into this existing category.' Instead, a *DSM* classification of 'Mixed Personality Disorder' is suggested. Codependency is so conceptually complex, in this view, that it would require four separate *DSM* categories to contain it, combining characteristics found in 'Alcoholism,' and the 'Dependent,' 'Borderline,' and 'Histrionic Personality' disorders, as well as an additional category made up of 'associated features.'

These attempts to define codependency as a personality disorder extend the diagnosis to chemically dependent persons. Applied to wives of chemically dependent husbands, as it will be, the diagnosis unequivocally binds the CD field to an unmitigated alignment with the DPH and the DH perspectives of a pathogenic wife.

TREATMENT OF CODEPENDENCY

Treatment philosophy for both partners is rooted in the experience, need, and requirements of the recovering chemically dependent partner. Therefore, treatment goals for family members are the same as those for the chemically dependent person, accurately represented in LoVern and Zohn's model (1982), as 'cessation of denial and acceptance/participation in a recovery program.' Recovery, too, is viewed (e.g., Gorski and Miller 1984) as identical to recovery from CD, requiring 'ongoing' self-help group attendance and 'periodic relapse check-ups with a professional alcoholism counselor'; only the treatment modes differ.

Treatment for family members in CD treatment programs is primarily referral to a relevant self-help group and a weekly educational lecture/discussion series. The introduction of a psychoeducational approach for families may be the real contribution of the CD field; unfortunately, the present content relies heavily on adopted, adapted, and expanded versions of Al-Anon's literature, with faulty execution of method. Education about family behaviour also draws on Satir's model of family roles (1972) but is rigidified to conform to the disease concept of codependency and is used in the service of the treatment goal of ending denial. Reification of Satir's roles and the inclusion of the enabler role (Unsigned 1980) – 'defensive, rigid and rebellious' – contradict the essence and spirit of Satir's humanistic approach.

Given the importance attached to the concept of the wife as enabler, it would be consistent to include couples therapy in the treatment of married or intimately involved, chemically dependent patients. In fact, there is a residual belief by many in the CD field that marital or couples therapy, per se, may threaten the recovery of the chemically dependent person. Brown (1985) found marital therapy to be contraindicated for the alcoholic in early recovery, a nebulous time period, while Stanton and colleagues (1982) considered the wife to be secondary in importance to the family of origin for the addict's treatment.

However, it is not uncommon for the couple to be seen conjointly once during the length of the treatment program, usually by the chemically dependent person's individual counsellor or sometimes in conjunction with the family counsellor. Technically limited to the facilitation of communication, a more important function of the session is to assess codependency in the spouse. The priority is explicit in the warning (Cermak 1986a) that 'you should never assume that codependency of individual family members is being assessed simply because the family is being seen as a whole.' With the advent of inpatient treatment for codependency, per se, Lawson and Lawson (1984) find that 'the 7-day program provides therapists with more information than it does the family.'

One reason family programs conform to a CD treatment model and philosophy may lie in the fact that during its early years of development, treatment staff was composed largely of 'paraprofessionals ... who define themselves as recovering alcoholics' (Fingarette 1988). While this description ignores the increase of those paraprofessionals who have become credentialled alcoholism counsellors, the certificate does not extend to competence in family therapy, and the codependency perspective is part of its knowledge base. Moreover, some CD treatment settings can still be found where family treatment is performed by paraprofessionals whose only qualification for counselling family members is their own extensive exposure to, and participation in, Al-Anon.

The negative tone and theme of the literature regarding wives is shared, to some degree, by most counsellors in the CD field. Describing her work as a CD counsellor in 1976, Beattie (1987) relates that she was 'given the job of organizing support groups for the wives of addicts in the program' because she had 'the least seniority and no co-workers wanted to do it.' It is reasonable to assume that such reticence stems from another popular belief Beattie 'soon subscribed to': 'those crazy co-dependents are sicker than the alcoholics.' The two beliefs referred to by Beattie have not lost popularity in CD treatment settings and are conceptually embedded in the terminology of disease, coaddiction, and 'Mixed Personality Disorder.'

While any clinical treatment approach requires the informed consent of the patient, it is safe to assume that no wife is initially engaged by obtaining her agreement to her need for treatment of a primary illness. Consequently, individual treatment for codependency begins with the implicit assignment of patient status to wives who are unaware of this fact. One wife – a professional colleague who volunteered her personal experience in a CD treatment setting – appeared with her husband for an initial assessment of his alcohol and other drug abuse and was greeted with 'So, you're the co.' She subsequently related that she was surprised, but 'thought it [codependency] might be an idea with some use.' After learning, during the second session, that anything less than complete identification with the role was viewed as her denial, the couple sought help elsewhere.

More often, initial staff contacts, written materials, and lectures begin with some degree of empathy towards a wife's confusion about her husband's need for hospitalization and offer the 'good news that chemical dependency is a treatable disease' (Unsigned 1987). Only after her attendance at lectures does the agenda change, illustrated by one counsellor's statement (LoVern and Zohn 1982) that 'all participate in the role of patient, no matter what their preconception might have been.' She learns – midway through the lecture/bibliotherapy given her, and by a shift in the staff's attitude towards her – that *she* is viewed as a patient.

Her patient status is validated by any reticence shown towards attendance at lectures and Al-Anon or any disagreement with their content. Surprisingly, no consideration appears to be given to the possibility that wives' 'resistance to treatment' may be due to their perceptions of the blame and negativity directed at them. At the same time, when wives comply with the referral to Al-Anon, the underlying belief is that she goes 'in order to learn how to better manipulate and manage' her chemically dependent partner (Young 1987).

The negative tone and theme are transferred when the CD treatment philosophy enters MH settings. Describing a 'group therapy treatment model' for family members in a Veterans Administration hospital setting, LoVern and Zohn (1982) surmised that 'telling them they are sick and to go to Al-Anon doesn't work.' Instead, these authors present an educational model that elicits from an audience of family members the admission that they 'can't live without the alcoholic' and a list of feelings experienced by them. Although 'grief' is among the many and varied emotions expressed by this group of family members, the presentation reframes these emotions as 'psychological symptoms ... the logical implications of which are mental illness.'

LoVern and Zohn's model clearly represents a purist CD philosophy regarding family members, yet their work is published in an MH family therapy journal and is recommended reading (Heath and Atkinson 1988), along with that of Wegscheider (1981), in an academic graduate course addressing 'the development and maintenance of substance abuse patterns in families.'

CONCLUSION

The disease concept of CD has benefited chemically dependent persons by reducing guilt, as well as by removing an undeserving moral stigma previously attached to them and, by association, to their families. The codependency designation has the reverse effect on spouses, and on wives especially, imposing a stigma far more encompassing than the vicarious one and exacerbating guilt for them. In so doing, the term *codependent* rightly belongs in the class of those 'semantic labels' defined by English (1981) as 'symbols of the stigmatization.' The concept is at odds with a primary obligation of the helping professions to 'first of all, do no harm' (Becvar, Becvar, and Bender 1982) and is unworthy of further attempts to verify its diagnostic status.

Previously cited MH reviews refuting the DPH note a lack of methodology implicit in the anecdotal material and impressionistic descriptions of wives. The present article confirms this in a review of the contemporary literature, and finds that to the degree methodology is lacking, what pertains is a bias so persistent as to defy the boundary of method. The methods maintaining the bias constitute an extensive methodological breach, evident in the linguistic shifts, internal inconsistencies, and contradictions within the conceptual structure of codependency, as well as in the practice of adopting theoretical language without the substance of the theory. The generation of new hypotheses, which neither incorporates nor rules out existing ones, results in contradictory levels of meaning by simultaneously disavowing the DPH and reinstating it, resulting in such educational postulations as normal feelings = sick person.

The bias is implicit in the CD field's neglect to pursue alternative directions provided over the long years it has held to a DPH perspective. An early, pivotal sociological model of wives coping with their husband's alcoholism (Jackson 1954) is given only the status of a nodding acquaintance. A critical review by Orford (1975) and suggestions for cross-fertilization from the MH material on wives, including Jackson's research, were instrumental in the CD field's provision of family services in CD treatment; however, the substance of his critique has been ignored. Omitted as either reference or guide in later works are

Nace and colleagues' alternative rationale (1982) for wives' behaviours, as well as several confrontations of the field's negative attitude towards 'women addicts or members of an addict's family" (Coleman 1981) and specifically 'wives' (Miranti-Burnett 1984).

Flawed methodology serves to validate treatment of an assumed diagnostic entity and the methods used to do so. There is every reason to question whether a wife's 'need to be a primary patient' (Brown 1985) originates with her or whether, as Becvar, Becvar, and Bender (1982) find, she is not among the population of concern and is 'controlled by the ability to serve rather than by the need for such services.' The findings of the present article call for MH professionals to reassess the ease with which the codependency concept has been accepted and to examine the premises in the clinical assessment and treatment of clients diagnosed or self-diagnosed as codependent.

The degree to which a spouse's primary-patient status is linked to the 'billions in health insurance coverage spent on inpatient and outpatient alcoholism treatment' (Fingarette 1988) cannot be discounted in attempts in the CD field to fit codependency into an existing, and reimbursable, diagnostic category. In the MH field, Becvar, Becvar, and Bender (1982) are concerned with the establishment of new dysfunctions leading to the creation of 'a formal agency and a new body of professionals.' In either case, unnecessarily extending the criteria for dysfunction tends to serve the treatment provider better than those who receive the treatment.

Existing treatment methods for codependency in CD settings should be called into question, beginning with the invisible line separating engagement from seduction or induction. The methods of addressing all family members must be challenged on the grounds that didactic presentations that metamorphose midway into diagnostics are highly questionable as a treatment method, while grave ethical concern must surround a treatment model (LoVern and Zohn 1982) that combines empirically unfounded assumptions, lecture format, and such sophisticated therapeutic strategies as 'unconscious conditioning, therapeutic binds, and indirect suggestion.' While such strategies are not common, these authors do represent a common attitude and approach to treatment provided in family services. The potential excesses in such an approach are witnessed in the condescension of Burgin's (1976) 'special status of the sick' and in Lo Vern and Zohn's chilling rationale that family members accept the attribution of 'emotional illness' because 'they fail to examine critically the label, emotional symptoms.'

An appropriate lens for viewing the CD field's efforts to postulate and define codependency is a systemic one, in particular, the theory involving levels of change. Static patterns are maintained, despite the application of problem-solving strategies when the strategies consist of changing only the rules of the game, allowing the game to remain the same. Such strategies, however novel they may be, remain at the level of 'first-order change' (Wazlawick, Weakland, and Fisch 1974). The CD field remains stuck at this level with its constant alteration of terminology, maintaining a static underlying concept of wives, and by its novel application to them of diagnostic criteria and treatment goals borrowed from CD treatment approaches.

According to this theory, changing static patterns require second-order change (i.e., changing the game itself rather than only the rules). What is necessary now is a breakthrough to a non-pathological view of wives of chemically dependent persons and a more accurate assessment of their unique problems and needs, together with a fresh approach to addressing these issues. A follow-up article to this critique is currently in progress and will describe the present authors' alternative perspective on wives with chemically dependent partners.

This article appeared in the *Journal of Psychoactive Drugs*, Vol. 22(3), July–Sept. 1990, pp. 285–92. Reprinted with permission.

REFERENCES

Ablon, J. 1974. Al-Anon family groups: Impetus for learning and change through the presentation of alternatives. *American Journal of Psychotherapy* Vol. 28(1): 30–45.

Al-Anon. 1979. *Al-Anon Faces Alcoholism*. New York: Al-Anon Family Group Headquarters.

– 1976a. *A Message of Hope*. New York: Al-Anon Family Group Headquarters.

– 1976b. *My Wife Drinks Too Much*. New York: Al-Anon Family Group Headquarters.

– 1969. *Alcoholism: A Merry-Go-Round Named Denial*. New York: Al-Anon Family Group Headquarters.

Alcoholics Anonymous. 1939. *Alcoholics Anonymous*. Alcoholics Anonymous World Services.

Asher, R. and Brissett, D. 1988. Co-dependency: A view from women married to alcoholics. *International Journal of the Addictions* Vol. 23(4): 331–350.

Beattie, M. 1987. *Co-Dependent No More*. Center City, Minnesota: Hazelden.

Becvar, R; Becvar, D. and Bender, A. 1982. Let us first of all do no harm. *Journal of Marital and Family Therapy* Vol. 8(1): 385–391.

Brown, S. 1985. *Treating the Alcoholic: A Developmental Model of Recovery.* New York: John Wiley & Sons.

Burgin, J. 1976. *Help for the Marriage Partner of an Alcoholic.* Center City, Minnesota: Hazelden.

Cadogen, D. 1975. Marital and group therapy in alcoholism treatment. In: Kaufman, E. and Kaufmann, P. (Eds). *Family Therapy and Drug Abuse.* New York: Gardner.

Capell-Sowder, K. 1984. On being addicted to the addict. *Focus on the Family and Chemical Dependency* Vol. 7(1): 14–15.

Cermak, T. 1986a. *Diagnosing and Treating Co-Dependence.* Minneapolis: Johnson Institute.

– 1986b. Diagnostic criteria for codependency. *Journal of Psychoactive Drugs* Vol. 18(1): 15–20.

Coleman, E. 1987. Marital and relationship problems among chemically dependent and codependent relationships. *Journal of Chemical Dependency* Vol. 1: 39–57.

Coleman, S. 1981. An endangered species: The female as addict or member of an addict family. *Journal of Marital and Family Therapy* Vol. 7(2) 171–180.

Edwards, P.; Harvey, C. and Whitehead, P.C. 1973. Wives of alcoholics: A critical review and analysis. *Quarterly Journal of Studies on Alcohol* Vol. 34(1): 112–132.

English, R. 1981. Stigma. In: Woody, R. (Ed.) *Encyclopedia of Clinical Assessment.* Vol. 2. San Francisco: Jossey-Bass.

Fingarette, H. 1988. *Heavy Drinking: The Myth of Alcoholism as a Disease.* Los Angeles: UCLA Press.

Friel, J.; Subby, R. and Friel, L. 1984. *Codependency and the Search for Identity.* Pompano Beach, Florida: Health Communications.

Gierymski, T. and Williams, T. 1986. Codependency. *Journal of Psychoactive Drugs* Vol. 18(1): 7–13.

Gorski, T. and Miller, M. 1984. Relapse: The family's involvement. *Focus on the Family and Chemical Dependency* Vol. 7(1): 3–14.

Greenleaf, J. 1984. Co-alcoholic/para-alcoholic: Who's who and what's the difference. *Co-dependency: An Emerging Issue.* Pompano Beach, Florida: Health Communications.

Heath, A. and Atkinson, B. 1988. Systemic treatment of substance abuse: A graduate course. *Journal of Marital and Family Therapy* Vol. 14: 411–418.

Jackson, J. 1954. The adjustment of the family to the crisis of alcoholism. *Quarterly Journal of Studies on Alcohol* Vol. 15(4): 562–586.

Jacob, T.; Favorini, A.; Meisen, S. and Anderson, C. 1978. The alcoholic's spouse, children and family interactions. *Journal of Studies on Alcohol* Vol. 39(7): 1231–51.

Lawson, G., and Lawson, A. 1984. Treating the whole family: When intervention and education aren't enough. *Focus on the Family and Chemical Dependency* Vol. 7(1): 14–16.

LoVern, J. and Zohn, J. 1982. Utilization and indirect suggestion in M-F-G therapy with alcoholics. *Journal of Marital and Family Therapy* Vol. 8(3): 325–333.

Miranti-Burnett, M. 1984. Toward a model for counseling the wives of alcoholics: A feminist approach. *Alcoholism Treatment Quarterly* Vol. 1(2): 51–60.

Moos, R,; Bromet, E.; Tsu, V. and Moos, B. 1979. Family characteristics and outcome of treatment for alcoholism. *Journal of Studies on Alcohol* Vol. 40(1): 78–88.

Nace, E.; Dephoure, M.; Goldbert, M. and Cammarota, C. 1982. Treatment priorities in a family-oriented alcoholism program. *Journal of Marital and Family Therapy* Vol. 8(3): 143–150.

O'Farrell, T. and Cutter, H. 1984. Behavioral marital therapy couples' groups for male alcoholics and their wives. *Journal of Substance Abuse Treatment* Vol. 1: 191–202.

Orford, J. 1975. Alcoholism and marriage: The argument against specialism. *Journal of Studies on Alcoholism* Vol. 36(11): 1537–1563.

Paolino, T. and McCrady, B. 1977. *The Alcoholic Marriage.* New York: Grune & Stratton.

Perodeau, G. 1984. Married alcoholic women: A review. *Journal of Drug Issues* Vol. 14(4): 703–719.

Powell, D. 1984. Treatment of impotence in male alcoholics. *Alcoholism Treatment Quarterly* Vol. 1(3): 65–83.

Satir, V. 1972. *Peoplemaking.* Palo Alto, California: Science and Behavior Books.

Schaef, A.W. 1986. *Co-dependence: Misunderstood — Mistreated.* San Francisco: Harper & Row.

Smalley, S. and Coleman, E. 1987. Treating intimacy dysfunctions in dyadic relationships among chemically dependent and codependent clients. *Journal of Chemical Dependency* Vol. 1: 229–243.

Stanton, D.M. 1988. Coursework and self-study in the family treatment of alcohol and drug abuse: Expanding health and Atkinson's curriculum. *Journal of Marital and Family Therapy* Vol. 14: 419–427.

Stanton, D.M.; Todd, T. and Associates. 1982. *The Family Therapy of Drug Abuse and Addiction.* New York: Guilford.

Steinglass, P.; Bennet, L.; Wolin, S. and Reiss, D. 1987. *The Alcoholic Family.* New York: Basic Books.

Unsigned. 1987. *Family Enablers.* Minneapolis: Johnson Institute.

Unsigned. 1980. *Chemical Dependency and Recovery Are A Family Affair.* Minneapolis: Johnson Institute.

U.S. Journal of Drug and Alcohol Dependence. 1989. *The Treatment Directory (1988-89).* Deerfield Beach, Florida: U.S. Journal of Drug and Alcohol Dependence.

Vaillant, G. 1977. *Adaptation to Life.* Boston: Little, Brown.

Watzlawick, P.; Weakland, J. and Fisch, R. 1974. *Change: Principles of Problem Formation and Problem Resolution.* New York: Norton.

Wegscheider, S. 1981. From the family trap to family freedom. *Alcoholism* January-February: 36–39.

Wegscheider-Cruse, S. 1985. *Choicemaking.* Pompano Beach, Florida: Health Communications.

West, J.; Hosie, T. and Zarski, J. 1987. Family dynamics and substance abuse: A preliminary study. *Journal of Counseling and Development* Vol. 65: 487–489.

Whelan, T. 1953. Wives of alcoholics: Four types observed in a family service agency. *Quarterly Journal of Studies on Alcohol* Vol. 14: 632–641.

Whitfield, C. 1984. Co-alcoholism: Recognizing a treatable illness. *Family and Community Health* Vol. 7: 16–25.

Woititz, J. 1979. *Marriage on the Rocks.* New York: Delacorte.

Young, E. 1987. Co-alcoholism as a disease: Implications for psychotherapy. *Journal of Psychoactive Drugs* Vol. 19(3): 257–268.

Zink, M. 1977. *So Your Alcoholic is Sober.* Minneapolis: CompCare.

JANICE HAAKEN, PhD

A Critical Analysis of the
Codependency Construct

Codependency is a mental health idiom that has achieved tremendous currency in the popular clinical literature in recent years. Books on codependency now fill self-help sections of bookstores, and therapeutic gurus promote workshops offering relief for this newly identified population of sufferers. The prototypical codependent is also described in the burgeoning literature on adult children of alcoholics (ACOA). ACOA has become part of this new psychotherapeutic lexicon as well, indicating, particularly among women, a socially recognized emotional disability as well as a prescribed course of recovery. Counsellors and therapists draw increasingly on ACOA language in their therapeutic practices and marketing tactics, for example, offering specialty counselling for 'ACOA's' or 'codependents.'

In clinical situations, the term *codependency* carries the same pitfalls as diagnostic labelling generally: the potential for reifying the patient or applying labels as a substitute for careful analysis. Diagnostic categories can also be used defensively by therapists in responding to pressures and anxieties felt in therapeutic situations, for example, a readiness to label demanding patients 'borderline.' But the term *codependency* also raises broader social questions in that it is being used increasingly by groups and individuals as a basis for self-definition and group identity.

Constituting a unique social and clinical phenomenon, the codependency literature and the many recovery groups it has spawned are of interest because they apply the Alcoholics Anonymous Twelve Step philosophy (see appendix) and the disease model of addiction to interpersonal problems, extending these ideas far beyond the 'primary addictions,' that is drugs and alcohol. With the growing public anxiety of alcoholism and drug dependence, the concept of addiction, as both metaphor and reality, has come to occupy a larger and larger terrain in American popular psychology, encompassing a broad range of social and emotional ills. The analysis presented here criticizes the codependency literature from psychodynamic and social-psychological perspectives.

Psychodynamically, the codependency literature is conceptualized in the critique presented here as containing insights consistent with current psychoanalytic theory and as paralleling the current psychoanalytic emphasis on interpersonal phenomena and character pathology. This paper describes these parallels as well as the problematic limitations and overincorporative quality of the codependency literature. The codependency literature popularizes diagnostic concepts of interpersonal conflicts by pointing to constellations of behaviour, which are conceived of as symptomatic of an underlying mental disease with an associated set of antecedent or causal deficits and a subsequent set of functional impairments. It is argued here that the extension of the disease concept of addiction, popularized by Alcoholics Anonymous, to more pervasive personality and character phenomena represents a troubling trend in the popular psychology literature.

I will be exploring implicit assumptions about gender in the codependence literature from a feminist psychodynamic perspective as well as a social-psychological perspective. I will also discuss the tendency in the codependence literature to pathologize a feminine identity based on caretaking and to oversimplify dependence conflicts.

CODEPENDENCY AND THE CLINICAL CONSTRUCTION OF FEMININITY

Codependency historically describes a feminine malady, but perhaps more basically, it describes the emotional condition of the oppressed. While some clinicians use the term *codependency* to encompass a broad range of psychopathological conditions (see Beattie 1987; Schaef 1986), it more commonly refers to an identity based on caretaking and responsibility for others. The codependent's caretaking identity is formed out of the experience of powerlessness; it is an identity forged out of the adaptive necessity of compromise, appeasement, and covert manipulation.

Codependency originates in a tendency, particularly common among daughters in 'dysfunctional' families, to overcompensate for parental inadequacies by becoming parentified and by developing an excessive sensitivity to the needs of others. The concept of the dysfunctional family, which originally referred to patterns of interaction associated with alcoholism, has gradually expanded to incorporate all family systems based on 'denial' (Middleton-Moz 1989; Ricketson 1989; Wegscheider-Cruse 1985) or 'shame-based rules' (Bradshaw 1988). This broad concept of the dysfunctional family includes a wide range of pathogenic dynamics and impoverished emotional interactions within the family, particularly where avoidance of confrontation or the inability to develop healthy means of resolving conflict predominate. Codependency refers to a set of counter-identifications with parental deficiencies.

The codependency literature expresses the pain, anguish, and helplessness, combined with an overwhelming, wearisome responsibility for others, which dominate the lives of many women. While there are stories of men in the codependence literature, for the most part they are women's stories. They are stories of women who are trying desperately to hold families together and to keep things going under seemingly impossible conditions. This literature speaks of the emotional deprivations of women, particularly in their relationship with men, and of the experience of finding gratification and a sense of strength through what Hochschild (1983) refers to as 'emotional work,' that is, managing the feelings of others.

Beattie (1987), one of the leading writers of codependency literature, understands that the appeal of her book is not only to those in the helping professions but to women who exhaustively take care of others and feel emotional deprived and depleted by these efforts. She poses the following question: 'Does endlessly taking care of other people ... mean Marlys is a good wife and mother? Or could it mean Marlys is co-dependent?' (22). Beattie describes clients who present with an array of life difficulties and a sense of confusion and feeling crazy. In responding to an illustrative client, Beattie offers the explanation that 'maybe your husband is an alcoholic, and your problems are caused by the family disease of alcoholism' (20). She goes on to explain summarily that 'now, if you ask Patty what her problem is or was, she will answer: "I'm codependent."'

Beattie defines a codependent as 'one who has let another person's behaviour affect him or her and who is obsessed with controlling that person's behaviour' (31). She goes on to describe this condition as one that results from victimization but that requires 'each of us to decide what part we played in our victimization' (32).

The theme of victimization is pronounced in the codependency literature. The assumption is that victims internalize a set of rules that were adaptive in the family of origin but cause them to recreate their victimization as adults. Subby and Friel (1984) define codependency as 'an emotional, psychological, and behavioural condition that develops as a result of an individual's prolonged exposure to, and practice of, a set of oppressive rules' (31). Schaef (1987) links racism, sexism, and homophobia to the 'addictive thinking' that creates codependency. The implicit idea here is that institutionalized oppression cultivates pathological forms of dependency whereby both victim and perpetrator, master and slave, share a common, impoverished emotional world.

While the codependency literature focuses on victimization, the typology is general enough to include anyone who is often upset or who has emotional difficulties that are manifested interpersonally. Schaef (1986) concludes that 'everyone who works with, lives with, or is around an alcoholic (or a person actively in an addictive process) is by definition a co-dependent and a practicing co-dependent' (29). Beattie lists dozens of problems and psychopathological conditions – from neurosis to personality disorder and psychotic conditions – that are all subsumed under the umbrella of codependency. Cermak (1986) views codependency as a mixed personality disorder that can be manifested symptomatically as depression, anxiety disorder, hysterical personality disorder, dependent personality disorder, or borderline condition.

While the codependency construct does not have real diagnostic discriminative validity, the popular literature that has emerged under this idiom clearly suggests that it articulates important themes in the lives of many – again, particularly of women. Its appeal lies in giving a name – a conceptual container – to a broadly defined set of emotional ills, interpersonal pressures, and conflictual dependencies, and in providing a message of hope, that is, a path to recovery.

Codependency converges with another so-called feminine malady, 'relationship addition' or 'love addiction,' popularized by Robin Norwood (1986), who is also proponent of Twelve-Step recovery groups. The codependence literature provides more clinical elaboration of this malady, introducing a broad constellation of pathological behaviours and etiological explanations associated with an identity based on caretaking and overinvolvement in relationships. While some use the terms love addiction and codependency interchangeably, the latter term refers to a more general pattern of behaviour: a personality disorder based upon excessive responsibility for others. Put still another way, the love addict is assumed to be codependent, but the codependent is not necessarily a love addict. Whereas the love addict becomes overinvolved in dyadic relationships, the codependent may manifest her/his 'disease' through a tendency to take responsibility for the feelings and well-being of others in myriad interpersonal contexts. None the less, both constructs are based on an extension of the disease model of addiction advanced by Alcoholics Anonymous to conflictual interpersonal dependencies.

The popular appeal of these constructs for many contemporary women seems to be related to the apparent contradiction between objective conditions approaching greater parity with men and a subjective lag in feelings of autonomy and independence. Old feminine ideals, including women's identification with mothering and relationship concerns, now feel ego dystonic for many women. In a society that prizes competition and narcissistic self-sufficiency, the legacy of the feminine past feels 'dysfunctional' (see Herman and Lewis 1986). The women's movement of the 1960s and 1970s involved, psychodynamically, the recovery of the powerful pre-oedipal mother of our collective, archaic past – a sense of goodness and strength that extended beyond familial concerns to a larger social ethos. With the decline of the women's movement, and a concomitant assimilation of women into the paid work force, maternal identifications for women are less apt to be experienced as an adequate internal bridge to external reality.

ORIGINS IN THE ALCOHOL AND CHEMICAL DEPENDENCE FIELD

Much of the literature on codependency comes out of the alcohol and chemical dependence field (see Schaef 1986; Wegscheider-Cruse 1985; Whitfield 1985). The term began to appear in mental health literature in the late 1970s as drug and alcohol treatment programs began to focus more extensively on 'family systems.' These programs have focused increasingly over the past decade on the role of family members, particularly parents and spouses, in maintaining the addict's self-destructive behaviour. The movement to adopt a family system perspective in the treatment of alcohol and drug abuse did open up new areas of insight into the complex social and psychological aspects of these problems.

The essential insight behind the codependency construct emerged out of the treatment of alcoholics. Family members, typically the spouse of the alcoholic, inadvertently supported the very behaviour

that they were ostensibly trying to control. By interviewing and protecting the alcoholic – for instance, lying to the alcoholic's boss, cleaning up messes, and paying unpaid bills – the spouse was compensating
for the alcoholic's irresponsibility and loss of control. However, these
very attempts at restoring control had the effect of preventing the
alcoholic from experiencing the uncomfortable consequences of his/
her own behaviour. As the spouse increasingly took over areas of the
alcoholic's life and functioning, the alcoholic's tendency to deny the
destructiveness of his/her behaviour intensified. In Al-Anon, the organization formed in 1951 by wives of alcoholics recovering in AA,
this pattern of behaviour is called 'enabling,' and historically it has
been the wife who has played this role in relation to the alcoholic
husband.

The enabling dynamic presupposes gender dynamics within the family in which women, in the role of wives and mothers, are in the ambivalent position of being both emotionally protecting and potentially
'castrating' or overpowering. As Chodorow (1989) has argued, women's
near-exclusive involvement in the care of young children creates a psychological legacy, for both men and women, of both the 'good,' all-
powerful pre-oedipal mother and the 'bad,' devouring one. Women
as mothers are associated with the regressive pleasures and fears of
early childhood, whereas men and fathers come to represent the 'reality
principle' of the larger social order. In patriarchal societies, males come
to repress their early identification with the mother and its associated
dependency longings, but they are compensated for this loss by identifying with the rights and privileges of the father, that is, in developing
a masculine sense of entitlement. The girl is required to give up her
infantile claims to the mother without the compensating right to patriarchal power and privilege that is offered the boy in his relinquishment of the same infantile claims (Janeway 1974; Mitchell 1974).

Family systems approaches to 'enabling' in the alcoholic family generally fail to address either the infantile components of family members'
fury toward the mother or the different social bases of power within
the family. In the prototypical alcoholic family, the father/husband may
be consciously or unconsciously perceived as being 'castrated' by his
alcoholism. Paradoxically, the alcoholic state can represent both an assertion of the man's masculine sense of entitlement and, ultimately,
a condition that imparts a sense of impotence, both sexually and socially. Unconsciously, the intoxicated state also permits a regressive
recovery of infantile pleasures – a rebellion against a masculine identity
based on the renunciation of dependency longings (see Chodorow

1978). For the mother/wife, the husband's alcoholism evokes twin fears of having become the 'devouring, castrating' mother in relation to her husband and of having failed to be the good, protective mother in relation to her children.

The family's belief that the mother is the 'real' villain – the one who 'enabled' the husband's alcoholism – can be overdetermined by archaic fantasies of the omnipotent mother. The family's confrontation of the 'enabler' can be based on both its recognition of the mother's *actual* ambivalent motivations (nurturant and unconsciously hostile) and its infantile rage towards her. In addition, there may be disappointment in her for failing to protect the family from the father's abusive behaviour, for instance, 'If she had responded differently to him, he would not have been so sick.'

The problem of enabling also points to moral dilemmas within the family associated with women's caretaking position. In her study of gender and moral development, Gilligan (1982) concludes that females, who identify more closely with the mother, are more likely than males to experience moral conflict in situations where they fail to provide nurturance or to maintain relational ties. In female development, the pre-oedipal tie to the mother is not as fully relinquished as it is in male development, creating a tendency in women towards more flexible ego boundaries (Chodorow 1978). In the context of moral choice, females are more apt to require moral justification for failing to respond to the needs of others, whereas males are more apt to construct moral arguments in relation to preserving social distance, that is, not 'intruding' and managing competitive strivings (Chodorow 1978; Gilligan 1982).

In the enabling situation, it is noteworthy that the woman's failure to respond to the problems of her alcoholic husband requires justification in terms of *his* need for a different response. It is understandable that many women embrace the enabling construct and experience some relief in being told that *not* to respond to the demands of the alcoholic spouse is actually more loving than to do so. The underlying feminine ideal of maternal sensitivity to others is preserved by a reframing of the moral issues.

The tendency for family systems therapists to ignore or downplay these gender dynamics may be related to a conservative tendency of the theory itself – a tendency that has informed concepts of 'The Alcoholic Family.' Family system theorists view the family as a system in much the same sense that an individual is a system – an organism constituted of interdependent parts and a set of self-regulating mechanisms. The family is conceptualized as having a distinctive personality and identity based on a personal past, and as having self-regulating mechanisms that mediate its relation to the internal and external reality, that is, that function like an ego (Steinglass 1987). The assumption here is that the family, as an organism, equally benefits from or is compromised by 'dysfunctional' patterns of interaction.

There is much that is useful in this concept of the family as an interdependent system, particularly when it allows family members to recognize their own unconscious contribution to the disturbing behaviour of another family member. From this perspective, the alcoholic or addict is no worse (or better) than the person who vicariously supports the self-destructive habit. The notion of alcoholism as a 'family disease' introduces a taboo against self-righteous condemnation of the alcoholic and points to the social context of individual pathology. Consistent with the systems approach, Subby (1987) focuses on the importance of family dynamics in potentiating alcoholism: 'I have no doubt that there are real genetic factors behind alcoholism and other forms of chemical dependency. But I don't believe that even someone who was born with all that genetic loading and as a result becomes alcoholic, would have to practice their alcoholism or addiction long before they would also have to find or create a new co-dependent system to support their alcoholism' (12).

The family system model, however, obscures differences in ego strength and power and minimizes the conflictual aims of family members. The family is a socially constructed institution, with economic and affinitive bases for both interdependence and conflict. It is quite unlike an individual organism in that the family has no superordinate ego or self that organizes its conduct. Many family systems theory models draw extensively on organismic metaphors that can blind theorists to the conflictual and socially constructed dimensions of family life and family dynamics.

Steinglass (1987) provides an analysis of the alcoholic family that draws on systems theory while challenging the tendency in systems theory to oversimplify family phenomena. He concludes that the alcoholic family is one where alcohol-related behaviour becomes central to both the family's identity and its self-regulating capacities. A central finding of his study is consistent with the shift in the alcoholism literature from understanding alcoholism as a discrete behavioural syndrome to an emphasis on interactive and personality dynamics. Steinglass found that the level of alcohol consumption per se was not associated with disturbing family dynamics or with individual pathology within the family. It was in association with social/behavioural aspects of alcoholism – that is, when alcohol use became associated with unpredictable and destructive behaviour – that the family identity became 'alcoholic.' In contradistinction to the codependency literature, however, Steinglass stresses the heterogenity of alcoholic families, pointing to the tendency in the literature to provide too narrow a typology of alcoholic family dynamics. In finding that alcohol consumption is not a simple causal variable of family distress, he concludes that what is common to alcoholic families is the focus on alcohol as the family's *explanation* for irrational behaviour.

The therapeutic interventions described by Steinglass focus initially on distinguishing between the family with an alcoholic member and an alcoholic family. This distinction suggests that an underlying set of personality variables mediates alcohol use in the family. 'Family alcoholism' suggests interactive and personality dynamics potentiated by and organized around alcohol intoxication.

While the family systems approach to alcoholism has opened up new avenues of insight and clinical intervention, it limits understanding of the emotional and interpersonal complexity of alcoholism and other addictive processes. As Scharff and Scharff (1987) have argued, systems approaches to family therapy provide means of quickly organizing the problem and actively intervening. But in doing so, they often sacrifice important clinical material of diagnostic and prognostic significance (Friedman 1980). When a hypothesized disease process with unitary symptoms and progressive stages is combined with a family typology of alcoholism, the differing and specific ego strengths, object relational capacities, and psychopathology of individual family members become obscured. For example, some alcoholics are able to sustain empathetic ties with their children, and some cannot. Some are abusive when drunk, and some are not. These are important clinical distinctions that are lost in the joining of the disease model of alcoholism with family systems perspectives.

PSYCHODYNAMIC IMPLICATIONS OF CODEPENDENCY

There are problematic implications, both etiologically and therapeutically, in the notion of an underlying congruence among addictive processes – whether those processes refer to substances or to interpersonal relationships. While a review of the debates on addiction falls outside the scope of this paper, the psychiatric literature does suggest that there are no clearly identifiable dynamics or consistent etiological factors underlying drug or alcohol dependency (Meyer 1986; Mirin 1984; Rounsaville et al. 1987). Further, regardless of how one conceives of the regressive component of chemical or alcohol addiction, there are myriad problems in extending these formulations to the interactive pressures and dependencies of relationships. In some formulations addiction implies a regressive retreat from the object relational world, with the drug becoming the substitute object. But the women who are described in the codependency literature do not achieve the euphoria that might be expected in a logical extension of addiction theory. Whatever the pathology that underlies these conflictual attachments, it exists in a world of real objects that make demands requiring some capacity for sublimation, ego functioning and normal dependency despite the pathology.

However, it can be granted that there is a certain phenomenological congruity to compulsive forms of desire, whether the object is alcohol, drugs, or people (Peele and Brodsky 1975; Simon 1982). To describe something or someone as addictive is to express the power of infantile longings and the emergence of an archaic split between exciting and persecutory objects. Falling in love has been described as an intoxicating state, and alcohol has been described as a faithful lover. In both experiences the euphoria of union contains the memory of an idealized, gratifying, comforting object, along with the heightened narcissism derived from it. It also awakens the experience of infantile ambivalence and the sense of terror and loss when the exciting, 'bad' object is withdrawn.

There is a notable congruence between the ideas voiced by the codependency literature and the interpersonal approach to psychopathology that has gained currency with the ascendance of object relations theory and self psychology within psychoanalysis (see Greenberg and Mitchell 1983). Both the psychoanalytic literature and the codependency literature stress the interactive manifestations of psychopathology and primitive mechanisms of defence, for example, splitting and projective identification. The codependency literature describes a compulsive tendency to attempt to maintain emotional stability and a sense of well-being by maintaining contact with someone who is out of control.

Inherent to this dynamic concept of codependency is the psychoanalytic notion of projective identification. Projective identification refers to interpersonal dependencies and interactive processes based on the primitive defence of splitting (for discussion, see Meissner 1980). The good self preserves a sense of goodness and wards off knowledge of disturbing, bad-object representations by maintaining contact with an externalized bad object. For the codependent, this external object is the alcoholic, drug addict, or abusive partner, who is identified with and conforms to the disturbing projections. The split-off ego functions that underlie these anguished interpersonal dependencies can be manifested by shifting valences in the dependency ties as well. The abused partner, who is initially emotionally dominated by and dependent upon the abuser, begins to assume control by taking over the ego functions of the abuser.

In important respects, however, the codependency literature differs from psychoanalytic formulations of these processes and the means of resolving conflict between good and bad self and object representations. Whereas projective identification refers to a primitive mechanism of defence central to particular character pathologies, the codependency construct is used as a label for a broad range of conditions and as a basis for individual and group identity. A key difference here is that the codependency literature fails to differentiate between extreme pathologies and those neurotic conditions that afflict people with some real object relational capacity and ego strength. There is little attention in the codependency literature given to specific developmental factors associated with greater or lesser degrees of ego integration and object relational capacity.

By focusing exclusively on pathology – for example, assuming that codependents are unable to develop emotional 'boundaries' (Schaef 1986, 48) – the codependency literature fails to identify positive identifications and developmental experiences that often co-exist with the pathology. Just as psychotherapists who focus exclusively on pathology can make the patient feel 'sicker' than he/she is, the codependency literature tends to cast the reader into a chaotic world of bad object and self representations without adequate recognition of the problems attendant on emotionally assimilating these warded-off aspects of the self.

PSYCHODYNAMICS OF THE TWELVE-STEP PATH TO RECOVERY

With few exceptions, the codependency literature promotes Twelve-Step programs or recovery groups and argues that such groups are essential to 'breaking through the denial' associated with the 'disease' of codependence. Whereas the early Alcoholic Anonymous and Al-Anon literature focused on a shared but circumscribed set of problems associated with alcoholism, the unifying basis of contemporary recovery groups such as Adult Children of Alcoholics (ACOA) is much broader and more defining of the self. The groups are organized around a self-diagnosed, shared personality disorder originating in a dysfunctional family understood in a particular way. A central basis for the appeal of Twelve-Step programs for those who identify with the codependency literature is their provision of a means of emotionally containing and conceptualizing the experience of being out of control or the experience of being with someone who is out of control.

The transformation of alcoholism and other addictions into disease categories did have its progressive aspects, permitting the moral neutralization of chemical dependency so that it could be understood psychologically and therapeutically. As long as these problems were understood to be the result of moral weakness or lack of self-discipline, the distance between the alcoholic and the rest of humanity seemed mysteriously vast and beyond human capacities to bridge.

And yet, Twelve-Step programs do offer a moral interpretation of addiction alongside the disease model. Even though the alcoholic is not seen as morally responsible for the disease, alcoholism, like Original Sin, requires spiritual redemption and divine intervention. Just as the concept of Original Sin liberates the believer from personal responsibility for his/her 'fallen state' while at the same time making the 'sinner' responsible for seeking salvation, so too the AA disease model shifts the moral ground from the alcoholism (a disease for which the alcoholic is not responsible) to the alcoholic's responsibility to seek recovery through a Twelve-Step program.

The first step in recovery groups is to acknowledge that one has lost control – that the destructive compulsion has taken over and is beyond personal attempts to regain mastery. Whatever the object of the compulsion – alcohol, food, drugs, or relationships with people – the message is that the individual feels out of control because he/she is suffering from a progressive disease, a pernicious condition that can be arrested only by following the Twelve-Step path to recovery. This requires a conversion experience in which the sufferer turns his or her life and will over to a 'Higher Power,' whose guidance is sought in the moral awakening that follows from the conversion experience.

In Twelve-Step programs, the disease concept of alcoholism operates psychodynamically much as the concept of the 'devil' does in fundamentalism. (For related discussion, see Antze 1987). What characterizes fundamentalism is not only particular ways of thinking about God and Scripture but the extent of one's belief in the devil. The devil and hell are full rivals with God in the religious cosmology. The appeal of both fundamentalism and Twelve-Step programs is similar: the hope of connecting with a source of goodness and benevolent control amid a world dominated by chaotic, destructive forces. Both belief systems permit a mystical transformation of bad feelings and experiences into good feelings of peace and well-being. God comes to represent the longed-for object of comfort and hope – the object that has failed the believer in reality but that he/she hopes to recover through faith and relinquishment of personal will. The complexity of experience is reduced to some basic unifying ideas, and anxiety is warded off by following a set of prescribed steps.

In the codependency literature, the anguish of conflictual dependence is transformed through a form of reaction formation, that is, defensive transformation of the feared or hated object into its opposite. Many codependency authors argue that conflictual attachment must yield to a state of detachment, and that 'when confronted by a foe, praise him, bless him, let him go' (Norwood 1988, 264). There is an emphasis on the transformative powers of emotional surrender as 'we allow life to happen instead of forcing and trying to control it' (Beattie 1987, 56). The disturbing sense that something important is missing – either within oneself or within one's life experience – is warded off by renouncing conflict and doubt. 'Detachment means accepting reality – the facts ... the natural order and destiny of things in this world ... We believe in the rightness and appropriateness of each moment' (Beattie, 56).

CONCLUSION

Codependency is presented in the popular clinical literature as a condition that has varying symptoms but is based on an underlying personality disease shared by all sufferers. According to the literature, it originates in all sufferers in an equivalently understood, repressive, addictive family system, it progresses in an equivalent way towards ultimate self-destruction, and it requires the same redemptive solution.

The person who attempts to hold the family together is the same as the alcoholic who abandons it; the person who depends upon drugs for a sense of well-being is the same as the one who depends upon people for the same feelings. There are no victims and therefore no perpetrators in this no-blaming world of moral equivalents. While the codependency literature does reject the repressive moral categories of the past, it provides a morally and psychologically impoverished substitute world devoid of the tensions inherent in differentiated consciousness.

The self-help groups that draw so extensively on the codependency literature do offer comfort and hope to individuals who share a common experience of feeling overwhelmed and out of control. The groups provide a place and language for talking about emotional pain in a society that provides little space for such release. Recovery groups reduce the sense of isolation and aloneness so common in American society and convey hope and a commonality of purpose through which members can transcend the limits of individual experience (Cutter and Cutter 1987).

On the other hand, the contemporary codependency literature and the recovery groups that draw on this literature pathologize caretaker dilemmas and vastly oversimplify problems of human dependency and interdependency. The message that 'codependents' must disinvest in unrewarding relationships is particularly compelling for women today, who continue to carry the traditional burdens of caretaking responsibilities and whose entry into the paid work force has, to some degree, intensified these burdens. While women have gained some measure of autonomy and freedom from enforced dependencies upon men and family life, conditions of daily life have not permitted a real emancipation from the old division of domestic and emotional labour. The old social contract between the sexes has unravelled, and as yet new forms of reciprocity and healthy interdependence between men and women have not been sufficiently realized. The codependency literature vastly oversimplifies these problems of dependency and interdependency, on both the social and the individual levels.

The construct of codependency embraces much of humanity in a common psychopathological net. While this clinical concept articulates concerns that are common to many in our society and points to the need for sociological and cultural explanations for psychopathology, it assimilates far too much in attempting to offer one simple construct to explain the multifarious existential, social, and psychopathological bases of human emotional suffering.

We do need theories and ideas that speak to core human dilemmas and to the commonalities in human emotional suffering. But as clinical work has become increasingly guided by narrowly defined specialities on the one hand, and by ad hoc eclecticism, such as codependency models, on the other, the potential for broadbased theorizing has diminished. Clinicians who are not anchored in broad-based traditions backed by well-developed theories are tremendously vulnerable to clinical trends and popular literature that 'pull it all together' conceptually. The codependency label becomes a broad conceptual container into which myriad life difficulties and internal and external pressures are placed. The message is compelling because it seems to provide both the therapists who draw on the codependency literature and the individuals who identify with the 'disease' deliverance from the difficult task of separating out what is internal from what is external and what is healthy and emotionally useful from what is pathological and emotionally destructive in worrisome, conflictual, interpersonal relationships.

APPENDIX: THE TWELVE STEPS OF ALCOHOLICS ANONYMOUS

1. We admitted we were powerless over alcohol [in groups for codependents, 'relationships' or 'people' is substituted for alcohol].
2. Came to believe that a Power greater than ourselves could restore us to sanity.
3. Made a decision to turn our will and our lives over to the care of God as we understood Him.
4. Made a searching and fearless moral inventory of ourselves.
5. Admitted to God, to ourselves, and to another human being, the exact nature of our wrongs.
6. Were entirely ready to have God remove all these defects of character.
7. Humbly asked Him to remove our shortcomings.
8. Made a list of all persons we had harmed, and became willing to make amends to them all.
9. Made direct amends to such people wherever possible, except when to do so would injure them or others.
10. Continued to take personal inventory and when we were wrong promptly admitted it.
11. Sought through prayer and meditation to improve our conscious contact with God as we understood Him, praying only for knowledge of His will for us and the power to carry it out.

12. Having had a spiritual awakening as a result of these steps, we tried to carry this message to alcoholics [or, to 'other codependents'], and to practice these principles in all our affairs.

This article appeared in *Psychiatry*, Vol. 53(4), Nov. 1990, pp. 396–406. Reprinted with permission.

REFERENCES

Alcoholics Anonymous. 3rd ed. New York: Alcoholics Anonymous World Services, 1976.

Antze, P. Symbolic action in Alcoholics Anonymous. In M. Douglas, ed., *Constructive Drinking: Perspectives on Drink from Anthropology.* Cambridge University Press, 1987.

Beattie, M. *Co-dependent No More.* Harper & Row, 1987.

Bradshaw, J. *Healing the Shame That Binds You.* Pompano Beach, FL: Health Communications, 1988.

Cermak, T.L. *Diagnosing and Treating Co-Dependence.* Minneapolis: Johnson Institute Books, 1986.

Chodorow, N. *The Reproduction of Mothering: Psychoanalysis and the Sociology of Gender.* University of California Press, 1978.

– *Feminism and Psychoanalytic Theory.* Yale University Press, 1989.

Cutter, C., and H. Cutter. Experience and change in Al-Anon family groups: Adult children of alcoholics. *Journal of Studies on Alcohol* (1987) 48: 29–32.

Friedman, L.J. Integrating object-relations understanding with family systems intervention in couples therapy. In J.K. Pearce and L.J. Friedman, eds., *Family Therapy: Combining Psychodynamic and Family Systems Approaches.* Grune & Stratton, 1980.

Gilligan, C. *In A Different Voice: Psychological Theory and Women's Development.* Harvard University Press, 1982.

Greenberg, J.R., and S.A. Mitchell. *Object Relations in Psychoanalytic Theory.* Harvard University Press, 1983.

Herman, J.L., and H.B. Lewis. Anger in the mother-daughter relationship. In T. Bernay and D. Cantor, eds., *The Psychology of Today's Woman: New Psychoanalytic Visions.* Analytic Press, 1986.

Hochschild, A.R. *The Managed Heart: Commercialization of Human Feeling.* University of California Press, 1983.

Janeway, E. On 'female sexuality.' In J. Strouse, ed., *Women and Analysis.* Grossman Publishers, 1974.

Meissner, W. A note on projective identification. *Journal of the American Psychoanalytic Association* (1980) 28: 43–68.

Meyer, R.E. *Psychopathology and Addictive Disorders.* Guilford Press, 1986.

Middleton-Moz, J. Recovery: An interview with Jane Middleton-Moz. *Journey* (1989) 1: 1–6.

Mirin S.M. *Substance Abuse and Psychopathology.* American Psychiatric Press, 1984.

Mitchell J. On Freud and the distinction between the sexes. In J. Strouse, ed., *Women and Analysis.* Grossman Publishers, 1974.

Norwood, R. *Women Who Love Too Much.* Simon and Schuster, 1986.

– *Letters from Women Who Love Too Much.* Pocket Books, 1988.

Peele, S., and A. Brodsky. *Love and Addiction.* New American Library, 1987.

Ricketson, S.C. *The Dilemma of Love: Healing Codependent Relationships at Different Stages of Life.* Pompano Beach, FL: Health Communications, 1989.

Rounsaville, B.J., Z.S. Dolinsky, T.F. Babor, and R.E. Meyer. Psychopathology as a predictor of treatment outcome in alcoholics. *Archives of General Psychiatry* (1987) 44: 505–13.

Schaef, A.W. *Co-Dependence: Misunderstood – Mistreated.* Harper & Row, 1986.

– *When Society Becomes an Addict.* Harper & Row, 1987.

Scharff, D., and J.S. Scharff. *Object Relations Family Therapy.* Jason Aronson, 1987.

Simon, J. Love: Addiction or road to self-realization, a second look. *American Journal of Psychoanalysis* (1982) 42: 252–62.

Steinglass, P. *The Alcoholic Family* Basic Books, 1987.

Subby, R. *Lost in the Shuffle: The Co-dependent Reality.* Pompano Beach, FL: Health Communications, 1987.

Subby, R., and J. Friel. *Co-Dependency, An Emerging Issue.* Pompano Beach, FL: Health Communications, 1985.

Wegscheider-Cruse, S. *Choice-Making for Co-dependents, Adult Children and Spirituality Seekers.* Pompano Beach, FL: Health Communications, 1985.

Whitfield, C. *Alcoholism, Other Drug Problems, Other Attachments, and Spirituality: Stress Management and Serenity During Recovery.* Baltimore: The Resource Group, 1985.

WENDY KAMINER

Chances Are You're Codependent Too

The *New York Times*, 11 February 1990*

Instead of a self-help section, my local bookstore has a section called Recovery, right around the corner from the one called New Age. It's stocked with books about addiction, psychic healing, and codependency – a popular new disease blamed for such diverse disorders as drug abuse, alcoholism, anorexia, child abuse, compulsive gambling, chronic lateness, fear of intimacy and low self-esteem. Codependency, which originally referred to the problems of people married to alcoholics, was discovered by self-actualization experts about five years ago and redefined. Now it applies to any problem associated with any addiction suffered by you or someone close to you. This amorphous disease is a business, generating millions of books sales, countless support groups and, in September 1989, the First National Conference on Co-dependency in Scottsdale, Ariz. Codependency "has arrived," according to a conference report; recovery is a national grass roots movement.

Codependency is advertised as a national epidemic, partly because every conceivable form of arguably compulsive behavior is classified as an addiction. (We are a nation of sexaholics, rageaholics, shopaholics and rushaholics.) "I have a feeling we're soon going to have special groups for third cousins of excessive sherry drinkers," the child psychologist Robert Coles told me. "You don't know whether to laugh or cry over some of this stuff." The codependency movement has "run amok," he said. It's a "typical example of how anything packaged as psychology in this culture seems to have an all too gullible audience."

The codependency movement also exemplifies our fears of an enemy within and the demonization of addiction and disease. What were once billed as bad habits and problems – Cinderella and Peter Pan complexes, smart women loving too much and making foolish choices about men who hate them – are now considered addictions too, or reactions to the addictions of others, or both. Like drug and alcohol abuse, they're considered codependent diseases. If the self-help industry is any measure of our state of mind in 1990, we are indeed obsessed with disease and our will to defeat it; all codependency books stress the curative power of faith and self-discipline. It's morning after in America; we want to be in recovery.

Almost everyone – 96 percent of all Americans – suffers from codependency, these self-proclaimed experts assert, and given their very broad definitions of this disease, we probably do. Melody Beattie, the best-selling author of "Codependent No More" and "Beyond Codependency," defines codependency as being affected by someone else's behavior and obsessed with controlling it. Who isn't? Another definition comes from Anne Wilson Schaef, the author of the best-selling "When Society Becomes an Addict" and "Co-Dependence: Misunderstood – Mistreated," who calls it "a disease process whose assumptions, beliefs and lack of spiritual awareness lead to a process of nonliving which is progressive."

That some readers think they know what this means is a tribute to what George Orwell considered reduced expectations of language and the substitution of attitudes and feelings for ideas. It is enough for Ms. Schaef to mean that codependency is bad and anyone can have it, which makes this condition seem more like a marketing device. Codependency offers a diagnosis, and support group, to virtually anyone with a problem who can read.

The publishing industry, which didn't exactly invent codependency, is making sure that millions of Americans discover it. Such publishers as Harper & Row, Prentice Hall and Thomas Nelson have special lines of recovery and "wellness" books. Harper's San Francisco branch, a leader in the field, lists about 80 recovery books, the majority of which are published in conjunction with the Hazelden Foundation, a leading treatment center for chemical dependency. Sales can fairly be called phenomenal: "Codependent No More" has enjoyed more than 70 weeks on the New York Times paperback bestseller list and, according to Harper & Row, sales of about 1.5 million copies. Smaller publishers are also cashing in on what appears to be an insatiable market. Health

Communications Inc., which specializes in paperback codependency books, has about 102 titles, including some best sellers. The company says that its top book, "Adult Children of Alcoholics" by Janet G. Woititz, has sold 1.1 million copies. Charles L. Whitfield's "Healing the Child Within" has sold more than 500,000 copies, and John Bradshaw's "Bradshaw On: The Family" has sold 350,000 copies. Peter Vegso, the president of Health Communications, said he expects sales for all their books to top three million this year.

What's striking about all the codependency books on the market (I've read 21) is their sameness. They may differ in levels of literacy and how they balance the discussion of codependency theory with recovery techniques. But they describe the same syndromes in the same jargon and prescribe the same cure – enlistment in a support group that follows an overtly religious recovery program (stressing submission to a higher power) borrowed from Alcoholics Anonymous. Codependency books line the shelves in bookstores like different brands of aspirin in a drugstore. As Mr. Vegso said, "A lot of people are looking at why they're not happy."

Their unhappiness begins at home, in the dysfunctional family, codependency authors stress, drawing heavily on family systems theory, explaining the way individuals develop in relation or reaction to their families. Codependency is attributed to child abuse, which makes it an intergenerational familial disease; child abuse, defined broadly to include any emotional or physical abandonment, disrespect or inadequate nurturance, begets child abuse, or anorexia and other forms of self-abuse. This is surely part of codependency's appeal. We are all fascinated by our families. No soap opera is more compelling than our own.

Codependency books lead readers back through childhood to discover the ways in which they've been abused and the "negative messages" they've internalized. Exercises, quizzes, and sentence-completion tests (for example, "I have trouble owning my feeling reality around my father when — ") assist readers in self-evaluation. You can estimate your codependency score, your place on a "worry index" or your PTSD (post-traumatic stress disorder) average. You can find your own pattern or syndrome in the usual assortment of case studies that track the children of abuse into adulthood. Readers are encouraged to reconstruct their pasts by drawing family trees that chart their legacy of disease: grandfather is an alcoholic, mother is a compulsive rescuer and Uncle Murray weighs 270 pounds; father is a sex addict, your sister is anorexic and you only have affairs with married men.

Still, encased in silliness and jargon are some sound, potentially help-ful insights into how character takes shape in the drama of family life. Codependency literature may reflect some of the often criticized self-ism of the 1970's. (Ms. Beattie dedicates "Codependent No More" "to me.") But accusing self-help authors of selfism is like accusing fiction writers of making things up, and the concept of codependency does combine concern for self with the more recent focus on family and community. The self is never viewed in isolation: codependency theory places the struggle for individual identity in the context of familial relations.

"We cannot have an identity all alone," Mr. Bradshaw writes in "Bradshaw On: The Family." "Our reality is shaped from the beginning by a *relationship*." Children in dysfunctional families are shaped by bad relationships and are improperly "individuated." (Codependents are al-ways said to suffer from "boundary" problems, confusion about where they end and other people begin.) Dysfunctional families sacrifice their members to the family system, Mr. Bradshaw suggests, in one of the more cogent explanations of codependency: *"The individual exists to keep the system in balance."*

In our culture, women have long been assigned primary respon-sibility for the family's emotional balance, and codependency is often described as a feminine disease. (Rooted in the model of a coalcoholic wife, it's commonly associated with compulsive caretaking.) As Ms. Schaef says in "Codependence: Misunderstood – Mistreated," the non-liberated woman "gets her identity completely from outside herself; [she] and the co-dependent are the same person." Although codepen-dency books sound nonsexist (the third-person masculine is used, if at all, with apology) and many of the codependents described in them are men, they speak primarily to women. Mr. Vegso estimates that 85 percent of the codependency market is female.

There are differing feminist perspectives on this mostly female phe-nomenon. Defining femininity as a disease is troubling because it over-looks the ways in which women are trapped in abuse by circumstance, not weakness. Charging codependent wives with complicity in their husbands' addictions may be, as the social critic Barbara Ehrenreich asserts, another way of "blaming women" for the crimes and failures of men. But while the view of a nonliberated woman as diseased is anathema to feminists who see her as oppressed, it's balanced by a view of liberation as healthy. Codependency theory shares some feminist ideals, often couched in New Age jargon: Mr. Bradshaw describes a good relationship as one "based on equality, the equality of two self-actualizing spiritual beings who connect at the level of their beingness."

There are, however, few such beings in this culture, male or female, Mr. Bradshaw and others agree. Women are not alone in their pathology. Men are sick in complementary ways, and society itself is addicted to (among other things mentioned in these books) the arms race, the repression of emotion, the accumulation of capital and enlarging the hole in the ozone layer. These "addictions" partly reflect what is implicitly condemned as the disease of masculinity: rationalist left-brain thinking. As Ms. Schaef explains in "When Society Becomes an Addict," the "White Male System" is addictive, and it's the only system we know.

This view of codependency as a pervasive, institutionalized disease not only provides codependency authors with the widest possible audience – everyone – it imbues them with messianic zeal. Codependency is, after all, considered fatal, for individuals, corporations and the nation. It causes cancer and other stress-related diseases, these books warn, as well as business failures, environmental pollution and war.

If society and everyone in it are addicted, self-destructing, infected with left-brain rationality, then people in recovery are the chosen few, an elite minority of enlightened, if irrational, self-actualizers with the wisdom to save the world. As Ms. Schaef confirms, the only people who can help cure our addictive system are those "recovering from its effects."

Experts themselves must thus admit that they're recovering codependents too, and codependency books tend to be partly confessional, following a model of the expert as patient taken from A.A.: "Hello! My name is Carla and I am recovering from just about every addiction known to humanity," Carla Wills-Brandon perkily reveals at the beginning of "Is It Love or Is It Sex?" Personal experience with addiction and recovery is as important a credential as professional degrees, partly because the therapeutic profession itself is considered a nest of practicing codependents. Lynne Namka, the author of "The Doormat Syndrome," advises you to choose a therapist "who has fewer psychological problems than you do."

But if they decline to cloak themselves in the power of professional expertise, these writers who've "been there" invoke the moral authority we grant survivors. Everyone wants to be a survivor, as if survivalhood were the only alternative to victimization. "QUAKE SURVIVOR RELOCATES seeks 'humanistic' male," a recent personal ad in The New York Review of Books explains. "I survived" the subway strike, the summer of '88, Hurricane Hugo, T-shirts attest. "I survived codependency," people in recovery may boast, like figures at a New Yorker cartoon cocktail party. In recovery there are no victims – of incest, drug abuse or love – there are only survivors.

The process of recovery (it's not an event, these experts repeatedly explain) brings even more than survival. The recovery "lifestyle" eventually brings rebirth. Its goal is healing your inner child – the wounded child who took refuge from abuse and deprivation in a recess of your soul.

Or perhaps the inner child *is* the soul. *"We all carry within us an eternal child,"* Jeremiah Abrams writes in his introduction to "Reclaiming the Inner Child," an eclectic anthology, to be published next month, of academic and pop essays about the child within that are alternately eloquent, intelligent, trite and incomprehensible. Inner-child theory is an equally eclectic synthesis of Jung, New Age mysticism, holy-children mythology, pop psychology and psychoanalytic theories about narcissism and the creation of a false self that wears emotions without experiencing them.

Codependency, which includes narcissism, is generally described as a failure to feel, or a failure to feel what's true. Addiction masks true feelings and the true, childlike self. Codependents are considered adult children. If some behave more like Scrooge than Peter Pan, all have a Tiny Tim within.

Inner children are always good – innocent and pure – like the most sentimentalized Dickens characters, which means that people are essentially good, and most of all, redeemable. Even Ayatollah Khomeini had a child within. Think of little Adolf Hitler abandoned in his crib. Evil is merely a mask – a dysfunction.

The therapeutic view of evil as sickness, not sin, is particularly strong in codependency theory. Shaming children, calling them bad, is a primary form of abuse. Both guilt and shame "are not useful as a way of life," Ms. Beattie writes in "Codependent No More." "We need to forgive ourselves — Guilt makes *everything* harder." This is not moral relativism; distinctions are made between healthy and unhealthy behavior. It reflects instead the need to believe that no one is unforgivable and everyone can be saved. Because within every addict there's a holy child yearning to be free, recovery holds the promise of redemption.

Its religiosity distinguishes codependency literature from the predominant personal development and relationship books of the 70's and early 80's. Books like "The Cinderella Complex" by Colette Dowling, or "How to Get Whatever You Want Out of Life" by Joyce Brothers, focus on mental, not spiritual, health; on happiness, self-confidence, love and success in the temporal world, not salvation. Codependency literature combines the pop psychology and pop feminism of these books with New Age spiritualism and some traditional evangelical ideals: addiction and recovery look a lot like sin and redemption. Addiction is often described as enthrallment to a false god; recovery leads you to the true. The suffering associated with addiction is purposeful and purifying, and it prepares you to serve: "Without my suffering, I would not be able to bear witness," Mr. Bradshaw says. Sin can be the low road to redemption, as Jimmy Swaggart made clear. Codependents take a familiar confessional pride in their disorders, as if every addiction were a crucible.

The disease of codependency is probably millennium fever. Everybody wants to be reborn, and in recovery, everybody is. No matter how bad you've been in the narcissistic 70's and the acquisitive 80's, no matter how many drugs you've ingested, or sex acts performed, or how much corruption enjoyed, you're still essentially innocent: the divine child inside you is always untouched by the worst of your sins.

* * *

This relentless optimism drove me to Kafka (that incorrigibly unrepentant codependent) and to some old-fashioned preaching. God issues a lot of negative messages (thou shalt nots), Harlan J. Wechsler reminds us in "What's So Bad About Guilt?," a sensible, if avuncular, defense of conscience and rationality. Use your intellect to make moral judgments and devise constructive punishments for yourself and others, he heretically suggests. If your husband leaves you for a younger woman, "berate him, punish him, and make his life miserable."

Of course, there is no revenge in recovery and little Old Testament justice. God issues only cloyingly positive messages – affirmations, like "You are loveable." Chanting affirmations to yourself daily is an important recovery technique. "Energy follows thought," Ms. Namka reports in "The Doormat Syndrome." "You actually become what you think." Develop a "happiness habit" by thinking happy thoughts and avoiding "worry conversations," Norman Vincent Peale advised in his 50's best seller "The Power of Positive Thinking." Imagine yourself succeeding and you will, like the Little Engine That Could.

Codependency authors are not nearly so materialistic or oblivious to social injustice as Dr. Peale, who believes most problems are caused by bad attitudes; nor do they claim recovery will be easy. But they owe him much – the reliance on simple, universal techniques to facilitate individual change and the belief that we need never be victims of circumstance, that the wounds of childhood need not be fatal. Codependency experts share with Dr. Peale the conviction that each of us carries within the power to heal ourselves, that happiness, health and wisdom are acts of will, grounded in faith.

Faith healing has long been part of the self-help tradition, as the popularity of Christian Science attests (Mary Baker Eddy was an author too). In the self-help universe, anyone can be healthy, spiritually centered, rich and thin – with faith, self-discipline and the willingness to take direction. This hopeful pragmatism is supposed to be singularly American, and we tend to be as proud of the self-help tradition as we are enamored of the notion that we are a country of people forever inventing ourselves.

But if the how-to phenomenon reflects a democratic belief in the power of will to overcome circumstances of nature and class, it's built on an authoritarian mystique of expertise that encourages conformity. Experts pretend to divulge secrets to readers, mystifying the obvious in jargon and italics. Experts are always unique (their tritest pronouncements are packaged as news), but readers are fungible, suffering the same syndromes and needful of the same cures. Self-help books collectivize the process of identity formation, exploiting readers' fears of embarking on the search for self without the aid of exercises, techniques, assurances of success and, of course, support groups.

To criticize the conformity implicit in self-help, you needn't deny the solace people find in collectivity or suggest that they are better off pursuing their addictions individually than curing them in groups. You needn't question the sincerity of recovery proselytizers or even the benefits offered by a few profiteers: we are all better off if addicts consume only books. We will all survive recovery. But what of the passivity and search for simple absolutes the recovery movement reflects?

Codependency authors say that recovery is ultimately an individual journey, but readers are not expected to find their paths or their transport techniques alone. There is little solitude and no isolation in recovery: outside your support group you're with God. Recovery requires much less than self-help; it requires self-surrender, to a higher power or cosmic truth or other nondemoninational universal force.

This isn't the narcissism commonly associated with self-help so much as submission; it isn't individualism so much as a hunger to belong. The putative message of codependency – that we are responsible for ourselves and shouldn't spend our lives heeding or pleasing others – is undermined by the medium in which it's conveyed. Merely buying a self-help book is an act of dependence, a refusal to confront the complexities of a solitary creative effort, as well as its failures.

Of course, to the extent that codependency and other self-help books discourage independent thought, they're part of a frequently bemoaned trend associated with television and the decline of public education. Intellectuals, right and left, complain about the debasement of public discourse the way fundamentalist preachers complain about sex. Still, (to complain just a little), recently the self-help syndrome has made a significant contribution to the general dumbing down of books and begun changing the relationship between writers and readers. Today, even critical books about ideas are expected to be prescriptive, to conclude with 10- or 12-point recovery plans for whatever crisis they discuss. Like politicians, writers are not generally supposed to raise problems they can't readily solve. Publishers want writers to answer questions for readers, not ask them, and popular books about ideas are often merely bromides or harangues. Reading itself is becoming, perversely, a way out of thinking.

Codependency may soon be as passé as last year's diet, but the self-help genre will always be in fashion. Self-help books market authority in a culture that idealizes individualism but not thinking and fears the isolation of being free. "A book must be the axe for the frozen sea inside us," Kafka wrote. Self-help is how we skate.

An expanded version of this article was published in *I'm Dysfunctional, You're Dysfunctional: The Recovery Movement & Other Self-Help Fashions* (Vintage Books 1992). Copyright Wendy Kaminer.

PART II

Victim Blaming and Codependency

MORRIS KOKIN, Clinical Psychologist, and
IAN WALKER

Codependency Is a Misleading Concept

Are women who develop relationships with alcoholics 'different' from other women? Are they victims of circumstance or the authors of their own destiny? Are they simply unfortunates who happen to have strayed into a web called alcoholism, or do they deliberately seek out an alcoholic mate in hopes of satisfying certain deep-rooted needs within themselves? Does such a woman really want her mate to stop drinking, or does she only say so? Does she support his efforts to stop, or does she unconsciously impede his progress and undermine his attempts?

By now you might well be asking yourself, what kind of questions are these? They are surely not serious. If anything, they seemed designed to give offence. Any woman who has ever been through the turmoil and terror of living with an alcoholic, whose hopes, dreams, and family life have been shattered by the bottle, could scarcely be blamed – in the face of such remarks – for feeling stunned, angry, and hopelessly misunderstood.

On the other hand, the question does exist: Is it just possible that such women – including those who have died at the hands of an alcoholic partner or who have chosen to taken their own lives as a desperate, final solution to their anguish – deliberately committed themselves to a relationship with a man they knew to be alcoholic or susceptible to alcoholism? Is it remotely possible that these women avoid seeking help and stay in such relationships because they are disturbed people? Is it conceivable that they derive some 'sick' satisfaction from such a relationship?

Let us look at some of the things that have been said in this area. Historically, two major psychological perspectives have dominated our understanding of wives of alcoholics and influenced societal attitudes towards them. One describes these women as villains, while the other sees them as victims. What is noteworthy, however, is that even when perceived as a victim, the wife continues to be blamed in one way or another for her own suffering as well as for that of her children and alcoholic mate.

In addition to the foregoing, a third perspective has been emerging in recent years, one that tends to describe wives' behaviour as symptomatic of illness. Many professionals no longer consider alcoholism to be a disease associated with just the drinker; they view it as a family disease – all who live with the alcoholic are said to become as sick as, or sicker than, the drinker. This so-called family disease has variously been referred to as co-addiction, co-alcoholism, or codependency.

Once the disease manifests, codependents are said to behave in a manner that is not in their own best interests and that unintentionally supports and prolongs the drinking of the alcoholic. In short, this is simply another way of saying that wives are somehow to blame for their own suffering as well as for the suffering of those around them.

In simplest terms, then, it does not appear to matter which psychological perspective one draws from. Whether victim, villain, or 'diseased,' wives of alcoholics are somehow seen as responsible, directly or indirectly, for the difficulties incurred by alcoholism.

LABELS THAT DISABLE

When we describe someone as co-alcoholic, what exactly are we saying? To my mind the implication is that the person spoken about is somehow an accessory or accomplice to the alcoholic and all the wrongdoing that his drinking may entail. A similar case might be made for the terms *co-addict* and *codependent*. Likewise, what about the word *enabler*? When applied to an unpleasant reality – such as alcoholism is – the expression takes on an equally unpleasant connotation. It is a though we were speaking about a person who 'enables' a crime to take place by averting his or her gaze.

Wives of alcoholics are consistently tagged with the above labels. In addition, they are accused of denial, lying, covering up, protecting, excusing, and defending their mates' behaviour. In fact, the terms used to describe the behaviour of these women are at best negative, at worst somewhat synonymous with the language used to describe deviant or irresponsible behaviour.

THE INFLUENCE OF WORDS

The point is simple. Words influence – they can enhance or distort the way we perceive reality. When we affix negative labels to wives of alcoholics, these women start to look negative, feel negative, and suffer negative treatment at the hands of society and professionals, who should know better.

The majority of professionals who employ these labels will insist – and legitimately – that they do not blame women for causing their mates' alcoholism. None the less, the words exert their own hidden effect. Living with an alcoholic is itself a very painful ordeal. What makes it even more difficult is that the alcoholic tends to deny his drinking problem and to project blame onto everyone and everything other than the bottle and himself, the most common target being, of course, the wife.

Because many people, including wives of alcoholics, are either un-informed or misinformed about alcoholism, they fail to understand the denial of the alcoholic. They thus tend to feed neatly into his litany of excuses and explanations. Also, since in many of his accusations there is a hint of truth, the wife is often inveigled into accepting at least some if not a great deal of the blame for his behaviour. This acceptance contributes not only to feelings of guilt and shame but also to a gradual loss of self-esteem and self-confidence.

The irony of the whole situation – and it is a tragic one – is that many therapists are inclined to interpret these feelings and consequent coping styles as illness, as we have already seen. They then attach their negative labels to the disturbance and inadvertently succeed in adding to the low self-esteem and low self-confidence that these women already have and that they, the therapists, initially set out to cure. In some sort of unintentional but convoluted way, they end up supporting the alcoholic's accusations that his drinking is related to his wife's disturbance or sickness.

One of the most questionable terms of all those applied to wives of alcoholics is 'codependency.' The expression started to become pop-ular in the 1970s, and although its origins are somewhat obscure, the concept itself is all too familiar. It is simply a new word used to dress an old idea – to perpetuate the notion that wives of alcoholics are sick people badly in need of psychotherapy.

We shall not attempt to give an exact meaning for 'codependency,' simply because there is no single agreed-upon psychological definition of it. In fact, to stretch a point, it might also be said that there are about as many interpretations of the word as there are professionals using it. Some describe it as a learned behavioural problem; others say it is a personality disorder; still others say it is something that resembles a personality disorder; and many others say that it is a disease.

According to some theorists, codependency is caused by living with or loving an alcoholic, who may be one's spouse, parent, grandparent, or close friend. Other theorists see the cause as involvement with anyone who is chemically dependent, and still others regard codependency as an innate part of an individual's make-up that responds to involvement with an alcoholic. To add to the potpourri, there are some specialists who claim that codependency may have nothing to do with growing up in any type of disturbed family environment.

The characteristics and behaviour of the individual who is supposedly afflicted with this condition are so general and all-inclusive that one wonders if there is anyone left on this planet who is not codependent. Codependents deny that they are involved with an alcoholic or that they have personal problems; they attempt to control others; they are confused and cannot express their real feelings; they feel depressed, angry, afraid, worried, and anxious; they have low self-esteem and low self-confidence, and they often develop stress-related medical complications.

One could go on and on describing the characteristics of codependents, but such a listing would probably consume a good portion of this chapter – and there is really no point to it. Though there is no single definition and both the causes and characteristics vary considerably, the concept has been employed almost exclusively in connection with wives of alcoholics. Furthermore, the way these women are affected and the way they respond to or attempt to cope with a mate's excessive drinking is described as the 'disease' of codependency.

There is so much wrong factually and morally with this concept that one scarcely knows where to begin to attack it. Describing women who are living with or married to an alcoholic as codependent suggests that all these women are the same – sharing the same experiences and consequences – yet we know that notion is absolutely not true.

Even when the effects are similar, wives tend to perceive and interpret the problem differently, and they also attempt to cope with the situation in a multitude of ways that can be very different from one woman to another. Perhaps this variation explains the numerous definitions and characteristics needed to describe codependents – so that no woman who is involved with an alcoholic will feel forgotten or left out.

A second problem with the term *codependency* is the link it establishes. Just because an alcoholic is considered to be dependent on alcohol does not make the spouse or lover co-alcoholic, co-addicted, codependent, or co-anything. Why should she not be simply who she is and be given the dignity and respect of retaining her own individuality and identity? If her mate was mentally deficient, would she be co-deficient? If he developed a disease such as epilepsy or diabetes, would she be a coepileptic or codiabetic? Is it not enough that a woman married to an alcoholic shares the agony and grief of his disease? Must we also make her share the disease in name?

CODEPENDENCY AND SICKNESS

Wives of alcoholics are emotionally affected in numerous ways – but are they really sick? The answer is almost unequivocally 'No'. In feeling the way she does and in attempting to cope in the way she does, the wife shows signs of health, not sickness. It is natural and healthy to feel bitter about a man who is destroying one's life and one's family.

It is also understandable that a wife feels worried and even pities her mate, because this is a man she certainly once loved a great deal and perhaps still does. If alcoholism were considered to be willful misconduct, then we might legitimately ask ourselves how she can feel pity for such a man. But if we say that alcoholism is an illness, then it makes little sense to criticize the woman who loves him for being concerned about what is happening to her sick husband. It is as if certain professionals are looking for any way in which to interpret the wife's behaviour as illness.

We speak about emotional and mental disturbance when an individual does not behave in a manner appropriate to a given circumstance. Here we have an entire population of women who are behaving in a manner most appropriate to their circumstances, and their actions are defined as indicative of disturbance and a need for psychiatric help. Why?

Part of the answer is that we are living in a sickness-oriented rather than a health-oriented society. In other words, by virtue of our training and diagnostic ability, we are often so busy looking for the tell-tale flaw, the hidden hint of sickness, that we fail to recognize signs of health. In short, for health we can do nothing, so we look for sickness, because we have remedies for that.

Many people who are quite normal suffer from problems in living, and wives of alcoholics suffer from a very specific problem – they are living with an alcoholic. There is no question that the experience may bring on a wide range of negative emotions. But this is surely a most appropriate reaction to a very painful and frightening problem in life. How, therefore, does this translate into codependency and thus sickness?

According to at least one author, codependency is a disease because it has a clearly identifiable onset (the point at which the individual's life is not working), it has a definable course (the continued deterioration of the individual emotionally and mentally), and if it is not treated, there is a predictable outcome (death).

If this is the basis for determining that so-called codependency is a disease, then almost anything in life is a disease – in fact, life itself is a disease. It has a clear onset (birth) and a definable course (the human being after initially growing and developing begins to deteriorate physically and mentally), and whether or not it is treated, the outcome is predictable – in fact, guaranteed. It is death.

The logic of such arguments defies comprehension.

ALTERNATIVES

The time is well overdue to stop accusing wives of alcoholics for everything and anything they do or fail to do. The name calling should stop – they are not codependent, co-alcoholic, co-addicted, near-alcoholic, or enablers; they are simply human beings living in a tremendously difficult situation that requires immediate, urgent attention. They need proper information, education, and support. They need professional services that will treat them in an understanding, sensitive manner and help to highlight how well they have actually done in their efforts to keep themselves and their families together against spectacular odds.

Tragically, this situation is unlikely to happen. There are those who will not be satisfied until they have 'pathologized' the behaviour of these women – in other words, until they have identified their behaviour as a form of disease. There is even a suggestion that codependency not only should be retained as an appropriate term, but should be adopted into the official psychiatric handbook, *Diagnostic and Statistical Manual of Mental Disorders*, as a legitimate personality disorder. We hope that this idea will be carefully reconsidered. The additional harm that this inclusion would do to wives of alcoholics is unconscionable. 'Codependency,' like its predecessors 'co-alcoholic' and 'co-addiction' and its contemporary 'enabler,' is an absolutely unsatisfactory and insidious term. Granting it further status as a disease only adds to the damage already done by the alcoholic and his bottle.

Similarly, when attempts to cope are defined as enabling, the responsibility for drinking or not drinking is turned over to the wife. Our understanding has always been that alcoholics do not need to be enabled to drink. They are quite adept at enabling themselves, whatever the circumstances, if that is what they choose to do. The alcoholic needs to assume responsibility for his disease and for doing something about it. Instead, well-intentioned theorists too often pass the buck and point the finger at the wife. Where the wife needs understanding, she receives negative labels. The unfortunate result is that all too often she is condemned even before she enters the specialist's office.

CONSTANCE FABUNMI,

LORETTA FREDERICK, and

MARY JARVIS BICKNESE

The Codependency Trap

STATEMENT

We acknowledge that some persons exhibit a recognizable dependency that consists of a 'pattern of beliefs about life, learned behaviors and habitual feelings that make life painful' (Smalley 1982) and that persons presenting this syndrome, which has been labelled 'codependency' may benefit from help. We also recognize that some family members of persons entering treatment for substance abuse may display symptoms that would indicate assessment and possible referral for assistance.

POSITION

The validity of the concept of codependency as an identifiable, treatable syndrome may be challenged both in theory and in practice.

Theory

Acculturated 'femaleness' in our society is expressed in nurturing, responsibility, reliability, obligation, and commitment. The model of 'health' intrinsic in the theory of codependency as pathology is a 'male health model'. The idea that the process of healthy or 'normal' differentiation proceeds from connectedness to separateness is a western male idea. For women, the process of differentiation typically progresses from dependence to a more relationship-oriented interdependence. Typically, women are acculturated to value responsibility to and for others more highly than they value their own rights.

All persons experience and exhibit some level of dependence – it is an element of human reality. Dependence can be observed on a continuum from a total lack of individuation (schizophrenia) to a total alienation (sociopathy) and is not a constant for either men or women. Some women manifest an extreme dependence or fusion with another person or persons. These women may benefit from assistance that helps them to balance the focus between themselves and others.

The codependency model judges that part of the 'self' that is 'female' by comparing it with the male standard of 'healthy' separateness. This model fails to acknowledge that the social orientation of women is different. Rather, it arbitrarily imposes a male-defined standard of 'healthy' differentiation and judges the connectedness of women as deviant. The relationship values of most women are different from the male ideal promulgated by the substance-abuse industry. Refusing to allow this 'difference' as normal, the substance-abuse industry declares 'non-maleness' as deviant and labels it 'codependency.'

Typically, if a woman accepts the label of codependent and attempts to adapt to a male-defined standard of 'healthy' relationship in order to 'get better,' she will be at deviance with the culturally learned understanding of self as 'woman.' This 'gender conflict' is intrinsic to the male-defined model – the 'codependency trap.'

Practice

The accepted practice of disease-model substance-abuse treatment is to assess the spouse (the wife, in particular) and other family members for codependency. In most cases, female spouses who wish to be helpful and involved in their male spouse's treatment can expect to be labelled codependent and told that they are sicker than their husbands. As an adjunct to the primary treatment of their husbands, women typically are required to attend lectures in which they are 'educated' about their 'disease.' Confrontational group sessions, couple counselling, Al-Anon meetings, 'family treatment,' and long 'aftercare' are also typical of the 'in-house' treatment packages offered by most substance-abuse treatment programs. This package deal is almost always presented as a necessity rather than an option. Should a woman in this situation reject the 'diagnosis,' the model conveniently labels the refusal as 'denial,' which is a symptom of 'codependency,' and further proof that this is a 'sick woman.' The woman is offered further incentive to accept treatment with warnings that her husband 'won't get well' unless she 'gets well.'

The criteria employed by most treatment centres for assessing codependency are so vague, broad, and all-encompassing that most woman are vulnerable to conviction. The practice of assessing women for this 'disease' during the high-stress crisis period of treatment provides additional assurance that the 'disease' will be 'discovered.' This is an inappropriate time for accurate assessment of psychological stability because the symptoms of stress reaction are very similar to many of the described 'symptoms' of codependency.

The creation of this 'disease' for women has provided a virtually endless supply of new clients for the substance-abuse industry. The financial gain inherent in positive assessment for codependency vastly increases the likelihood of indiscriminate application of this label. For the most part, the substance-abuse treatment industry and related self-help programs such as AA and Al-Anon justify their insistence that most (if not all) wives of substance abusers are codependent with vague, non-specific, claims. The anonymous nature of many programs conveniently precludes empirical research that would test their findings. Because of the non-unitary nature of concepts such as alcoholism, success, relapse, sobriety, and codependency, the veracity of existing research is questionable, when it is available.

There are, however, several studies that appear to challenge the preconception that spouses of alcoholics are sick. Paolino et al. (1976) compared the spouses of alcoholics with a norm group on the Psychological Screening Inventory (PSI) and found that there was no significant difference between the two groups, with the exception of the defensiveness scale (which, while elevated, also fell within normal range). The studies of Rae and Forbes (1966) suggest that wives of alcoholics are essentially normal people who are simply reacting to stress in a predictable way.

We have discovered no studies that measure the effectiveness of 'codependency treatment' in terms of outcomes for the person receiving treatment. There are studies that show that the more 'treatment' spouses of alcoholics receive, the greater the chance that the alcoholic will remain sober. This finding suggests that the non-abusing spouse is viewed merely as an accessory to the alcoholic, and that manipulation of the spouse is justified in terms of the sobriety goals of the alcoholic!

There are instances where the labelling of women as codependent and referral to a Twelve-Step program of treatment and/or maintenance may be dangerous as well as inappropriate. Wives of alcoholics and other substance abusers are often physically abused. Abused women often cultivate a high level of awareness of subtle changes in behaviour of the abusing spouse. This preoccupation with the spouse is a learned survival skill which enables the abused woman to anticipate and sometimes avoid situations where she (or her children) will be physically hurt. Treatment programs often write off physical abuse as symptomatic and secondary to the substance abuse in lieu of laying the responsibility directly on the physical abuser. They encourage the abused woman to 'take the focus off the abuser and put it on herself.' Physical abusers frequently continue their abusive behaviour during and after treatment for substance abuse; in many cases, withdrawal of chemicals as a coping mechanism escalates physical abuse. Physically abused women should not have their survival systems tampered with by substance-abuse counsellors, and certainly not by non-professional persons in Al-Anon and similar Twelve-Step groups. In no way should it be suggested to an abused woman that she is 'powerless' or that she is in some way 'asking for it.' Al-Anon is an inappropriate referral for most physically abused women.

The practice within Alcoholics Anonymous of encouraging members to attend Al-Anon meetings (this concept is called 'Double-Winners') is another serious concern. An increasing number of Al-Anon groups count a significant number of male 'Double-Winners' among their ranks. This concept had its beginnings in the belief that most alcoholics usually have some other alcoholic family members, and that they can benefit from Al-Anon by discovering their own 'codependent' behaviours. (Interestingly, AA meetings are not open to non-alcoholics, with the exception of an occasional open meeting.) What typically happens is that women find themselves in an Al-Anon group that is controlled by the male Double Winners. In this milieu, women are 'educated' about their 'disease of codependency' by envoys from AA who remind them that their disease is just 'the other side of the coin of alcoholism.' They are taught to repress their anger, to discover 'their part' in their spouse's addiction, to cultivate forgiveness and acceptance.

There is a prevailing attitude among general and mental health professionals and paraprofessionals that referral to a Twelve-Step program is a panacea for any and all presenting problems that are remotely related to substance use and abuse. Even those who question if it can help seem to subscribe to the belief that 'it can't hurt.' There was also a time when aspirin was considered a benign alternative to more specific treatment and a reasonable placebo when no accurate diagnosis was made. Recent research, however, has discovered serious contraindications for the prescription of aspirin – as in the presence of certain viral infections and for persons susceptible to excessive bleeding. As a result, the AMA undertook to inform its membership and the general public, through massive public service campaigns, of the possible dangers of self-medicating with this common household preparation.

Similar contraindications exist for many women who seek assistance for life problems associated with the substance abuse of family members. The mental health and substance-abuse treatment professions should consider the implications of irresponsible labelling as 'codependent,' and the danger in referral to Al-Anon and other Twelve-Step programs for some women. It is their ethical responsibility to avoid generalizations about women and other family members of substance abusers. Whatever the reason – bias, ignorance, expedience, greed – an unacceptable number of women are being crammed through the 'codependency' pigeon-hole. Every woman seeking assistance from the mental health / substance-abuse community has the right to be recognized as an individual and to receive treatment (only if necessary) that is specific to the presenting symptoms.

This article was given as a presentation at the annual conference of the National Association of Rights, Protection, and Advocacy, 1985. Reprinted by permission of the authors.

REFERENCES

Paolino, T.J., B. McCrady, S. Diamond, and R. Longabaugh (1976) Psychological disturbances in spouses of alcoholics. *Journal of Studies on Alcohol 37* (11), 1600–8.

Rae, J.B., and A.R. Forbes (1966) Clinical and psychometric characteristics of wives of alcoholics. *British Journal of Psychiatry, 112*, 197–200.

Smalley, S. (1982) *Co-dependency.* New Brighton, MN: SBS Publications.

JO-ANNE KRESTAN, MA, LSAC, and

CLAUDIA BEPKO, MSW

Codependency: The Social Reconstruction of Female Experience

Very few of us can be in clinical practice today without being challenged not only to treat alcoholism, but to treat clients whose frame
of reference for seeking treatment is to define themselves as codependent. The alternative terminology we hear is 'I'm an Adult Child
of an Alcoholic, or an Adult Child of a dysfunctional family.' The terms
are, or have become, synonymous. They reflect the client's awareness
that he or she has been affected by the addiction of a parent or other
significant member of a family or intimate relationship. Increasingly
the terms suggest that the client has been negatively affected by almost
any non-nurturing behaviour that can occur in a family. For women
more specifically, codependency suggests the process of 'losing' one's
identity to an over-focus on another person or relationship.

As clients come to us armed with a definition of their problem, they
have also usually acquired a large self-help armamentarium of materials that point to the solutions to that problem. The self-help movements as typified by such groups as Alcoholics Anonymous, Al-Anon,
and their other counterparts have been unquestionably significant in
relieving the pain associated with addiction. They have become more
successful than most forms of professional treatment in promoting
healing and change (Withorn 1986). But when embraced as a response
to so-called codependent behaviour, the self-help paradigm and its extension, the 'recovery' paradigm, have their unproductive elements.
The uniqueness of the client's individual set of life experiences tends
to become blurred within the framework of an overdefined and over-
generalized identity. One might argue that the addicted person does
need for a time to adopt the new and structured identity that the
recovery programs provide (Bepko and Krestan 1985). But loss of iden-

tity is precisely at the core of the dominant definitions of codependency. Immersion in an external structure that rigidly defines self in terms of deficits and disease seems only to perpetuate rather than to address the so-called problem.

Beyond providing a frame for our clients' sense of their treatment needs, the adoption of the language of codependency has become a social phenomenon that seems to reflect a more global search to name and articulate pain. In part what we are witnessing in the codependency movement is the emergence of a mythology for our time. It's a mythology that tells a story about our hope for redemption from our common human woundedness. Unfortunately, however, the myth is one that defines its characters as victims rather than participants in a complex relational drama. The mythical codependents have become very subtly the new social bearers of pathology. They are increasingly viewed as sick and diseased. We see a proliferation of hospital and privately based treatment programs springing up to treat them. What is less clear is the precise nature and definition of the 'disease' that's being treated.

The phenomenon that has become the codependency movement forces us to explore the power of language and story to shape our views of reality and our definitions of ourselves. It challenged us to look again at the political and economic forces that often underlie concepts of mental health and sickness. It forces renewed awareness of the concerns of the minority that most often inherits labels of pathology, that is, women.

As part of this exploration, this paper will describe the historical evolution of the concept of codependency, and discuss the dysfunctional dynamics in families that are viewed as the origins of codependent behaviour. Finally, we shall suggest an alternate language that can more effectively direct how we treat the problem in its redefined form.

THE PROBLEMS OF DEFINITION

Codependency has had an interesting evolution as a concept. It has developed from being a term of description to assuming the status of a diagnosis. The fact relates, in some ways, to its association with the disease concept of alcoholism.

When we examine the origins of the term *codependency*, we should remind ourselves that the movement originally began with the very powerful and important observation that children who grew up with alcoholic parents were affected in predictable and traumatic ways and that they had specialized needs for treatment that were going unrecognized. The traumatic nature of their experiences with parental alcoholism was viewed as being connected to their relational problems as adults. This growing awareness of the factors affecting family members who lived with alcoholism had its roots in two other important historical developments in our understanding of addiction. The first was the more widespread acceptance that addiction, or more specifically, alcoholism, was a medically diagnosable and treatable disease.

In the 1930s and 1940s, alcoholic behaviour moved from being defined as a moral evil to being 'medicalized' and subsumed under a disease umbrella of professional diagnosis and treatment (Conrad and Schneider 1980). While it is important to note that this trend had very positive consequences for our overall approach to treating and researching problems of addictive behaviour, it also raised still-unresolved controversy in the mental health field about the validity of calling addiction a disease. But nevertheless, the prevailing view that alcoholism was a physiological process that rendered the victim out of control was accepted and promoted by both the medical profession and the new self-help movements that were developed during this period.

The second related development was the growth of family systems thinking. As newer ideas about alcoholism finally began to define abusive drinking as a phenomenon that might be something other than an intractable moral failure, family systems thinkers began to view the drinker in a relational context (Steinglass, 1979). The family was acknowledged as affecting and being affected by the problems of its individual members.

In 1977, Claudia Black (1981) pioneered in promoting wider acceptance and understanding of dysfunctional patterns that children in alcoholic homes grow up with. But slowly it became commonplace to call those who lived with alcoholism, both children and particularly spouses, codependents. The idea was that while the alcoholic was addicted to the drug, other family members were also out of control in terms of the compulsive behaviours they developed in response to the alcoholic's drinking. It was not a difficult leap to decide that if the alcoholic had a disease, then so must the other people in the family. Gradually came the shift from describing a problem to ascribing pathology. Surely, part of the basis for this shift was purely economic.

If one is dealing with a disease, there is justification for establishing high-cost programs to treat it.

Just as alcoholic behaviour had become 'medicalized,' the increasing tendency to refer to codependent behaviour in the context of disease speaks to a general social tendency to render behaviour that is problematic or confusing a legitimate focus of medical treatment and control. Since codependents are primarily women, it's not surprising that this aspect of their experience, along with many others (Reissman 1983), should be brought under the aegis of the professional expert. That expert, then, supposedly has the power to cure a 'disease,' which some would argue has been created by diagnostic labels that reflect primarily the self-serving and self-reinforcing standards of the treating profession itself.

Another part of the leap to ascribing pathology to the entire family, may have been even more broadly political. Since many families in treatment were affected by the behaviour of the male alcoholic, describing the female spouse and children as also sick helped to detour responsibility away from the male alcoholic. Since defining the alcoholic husband as sick implies that the wife is somehow stronger or 'better' or more healthy threatens the balance of power in traditional families, the notion of codependency became a useful way of applying so-called family-systems principles in the interests of maintaining a cultural status quo. Women are ascribed more pathology in this culture than men, so in any situation where the male clearly has the impairment, it *must* be the case that the woman as well as her children are sick too. The codependency label, on a political level, becomes simply another tool in the oppression of women, fostering denial of male accountability.

Even a brief review of the history of the developing definitions of codependency quickly establishes the struggle to legitimize and maintain the lexicon of sickness. These definitions also point to the increasing globalization of the problem.

'Codependency is a primary disease and a disease within every member of an alcoholic family' (Wegscheider-Curse 1984).

'Codependency is a pattern of learned behaviors, feelings and beliefs that make life painful' (Smalley, as quoted in Schaef 1986).

'Codependency is an emotional, psychological, and behavioural pattern of coping that is born of the rules of a family and not as a result of alcoholism' (Subby 1984).

'Codependence affects not only individuals, but families, communities, businesses and other institutions, states, countries' (Whitfield 1984).

'A codependent is anyone who lives in close association over a prolonged period of time with anyone who has a neurotic personality' (Larsen 1983).

'A codependent person is one who has let another person's behavior affect him or her, and who is obsessed with controlling that person's behavior' (Beattie 1987).

'Codependence is a toxic brain syndrome' (Cruse 1989).

'Codependence is immaturity' (Mellody 1989).

These definitions are irresponsible and so vague as to be meaningless. If we view all behaviour as adaptive, they demonstrate how adaptive responses to stressful and traumatic situations can be pathologized in ways that are of little benefit to those needing relief from them. They are definitions that suggest that one is 'bad' for having a problem with the difficult dilemma of being in relationship with an addicted person. More recently, some students of alcoholism (Cruse 1989) have attempted to 'disease' this adaptive behaviour in the same way that alcoholism was finally defined as a disease – by suggesting a physiological basis for the problem.

The basic message of codependency implied in these definitions is a relational one – it reflects the common struggle that we all face to maintain the integrity of our separateness in the face of our need for relatedness. Most of the descriptions of codependent behaviour are a commentary on that struggle. The question is, how does one avoid ever being affected by the behaviour of another person? The culture's current obsession with codependency may be, on a metaphorical level, another version of the quest for painless relatedness. Since being affected by another is viewed as sick, a corollary assumption would be that a healthy relationship is one in which individual needs are always gratified but the self remains invulnerable to the effects of another's behaviour. Relational 'health' would be represented by a curious cross between total autonomy and perfect need gratification. Recovered from codependency, one could magically achieve the paradoxical feat of being perfectly fulfilled in relationship without ever focusing on the other person.

FAMILIES AS THE SOURCE OF CODEPENDENT BEHAVIOUR

Clearly, the definitions outlined above could apply to almost anyone whether or not she grew up with or was in any way involved with alcoholism. Another widely accepted definition of a codependent is anyone who grew up in a 'dysfunctional family.' The dysfunctional family is viewed as the source of codependent behaviour. Subby (1987), a family therapist who lectures widely on codependency, defines the phenomenon as a 'dysfunctional pattern of living and problem solving which is nurtured by a set of rules in the family system.' He says that codependency is a condition that can emerge 'from any family system where certain unwritten, even unspoken rules exist.'

What kind of family is dysfunctional? Conversely, what kind of family is normal? By whose standard is any family dysfunctional? For whom is it dysfunctional? These questions tend to cloud the issue further and to add an even greater level of complexity to any efforts to clarify the nature of the problem. To speak of 'dysfunctional family' without a context for defining the term tends to be as globalizing and pathologizing a process as creating a condition called 'codependency.'

Black (1981) summarized the three unspoken rules that she felt organized behaviour in an alcoholic family. They were, DON'T TALK, DON'T TRUST, AND DON'T FEEL. These rules reflect the intense forms of denial, repression, distortion, and emotional constriction that are the hallmark of a family affected by alcoholism or addiction.

But if these characteristics suggest dysfunction in a family, what is the corollary set of characteristics of a functional family? Most of us tend to share some common assumptions about health and normalcy. Culture bound as we are, they are assumptions that reflect the dominantly white, middle- or upper-class values.

Family therapists tend to define the functional family as one that establishes clear boundaries, clear rules and roles, and correct hierarchies of power. In the functional family, children are not expected to be adults before their time, and the parents do not act like children. In a functional family, marital partners do not detour their problems through the children. There is an absence of addiction and of any kind of internal or interactional abuse. Members of the family can talk with one another, and feelings are expressed and accepted. The family operates without denial, without secrets, without the need for shame and isolation. It is flexible enough to meet the challenges posed by the different tasks required at different developmental life stages, and it is flexible enough to reorganize and change when, for example, a new baby is born, a grandparent dies, or a child reaches adolescence. Almost everything written in the past ten years about addictive or dysfunctional families suggests that they do not function in these ways.

But descriptions or theories about the dynamics of functional families are often far different from the forms family life actually assumes in a rapidly changing culture. These definitions of 'functional' presume a family form and structure that are largely mythical, and they presume a family power arrangement that, it could be argued, was never functional. In other words, the assumptions we share about functional families are assumptions about rules, roles, and communication that exist within a larger context of gross power imbalance between men and women. That power imbalance itself is dysfunctional.

Ideas about the causes of codependency presume that there *is* such a thing as a functional family not influenced by gender inequality, and that if we could re-achieve this seemingly functional structure, codependency could become a diagnosis of the past. But think for a moment about the typical vision of a normal family. Is it still 2.5 children, daddy working, mother working part time, an Irish setter and a station-wagon? Is it two lesbians raising the children of one from a former partnership? Is it a remarried family? Is it a single adoptive father?

Many of our theories about the functional family structure assume the traditional, normative, white, middle-class family balanced around a more overtly powerful working father who has access to economic resources and many options for self-definition, complemented by a mother who is fully responsible for children and the family emotional environment. Such theories deny the enormous changes in family form and structure that have taken place in the past two decades. The impact of the divorce rate alone means that as many as four children in ten born in the 1970s are expected to spend part of their childhood in a one-parent household (Leupnitz 1988).

Fantasy, however, is notoriously resistant to fact. Despite these changes in the American family, changes that may be necessary as part of an evolutionary process, we still often subconsciously hold in our heads a kind of mythic, idealized version of the family that rarely exists today. It could be argued that it is in fact our *mythology* about what constitutes a normal family that gives rise to our notions that not living in one causes codependency. Looked at more closely, it becomes evident that the mythical 'normal' family was never functional, not for women, not for children, and not really for men, although it looked like it worked for a time for white males. We could not have avoided codependency if we had normal families. It was our so-called normal family structures that in fact set the stage for dysfunction to begin with.

IMAGES OF NORMAL FAMILIES

Often we find compelling commentaries on current social conditions in movies. The film *The Great Santini* depicts a family that by all standards would be considered both normal and normative. Santini is an air force captain, successful, powerful, all man. He drinks heavily to prove it. Lillian, his wife, is the picture of both southern and female gentility. During one scene in the film, Santini's oldest son, Ben, beats him at a game of basketball as Lillian and the rest of the family cheer Ben on from the sidelines. Santini tries to rob Ben of the victory and Lillian accuses Santini of cheating. In reaction, Santini becomes abusive. He threatens to 'kick' Lillian and bounces the basketball off Ben's head, taunting him by calling him 'my sweetest little girl.' Ben and Lillian talk about the incident later and she tells Ben that his father's abuse is really his way of saying 'I love you.'

How does this scene represent the normative American family? Surely the Santinis are an alcoholic family, a dysfunctional family. But if we look at what *is* normative about it in the context of power relations we see how this normative structure can generate codependent behaviour.

Lillian in her submissiveness and willingness to tolerate Santini's abuse can be considered codependent; Ben would probably also be defined as codependent. The structure in which that codependency evolves is one in which all the women and children sit around watching the men, the important ones, while the men compete. Mother has a covert coalition with her son, which becomes overt when she accuses father of cheating and openly roots for the son. But when she roots for the son in a way that challenges Santini's power, he ups the ante: 'Who the hell asked you anything?' He expresses his rage at the boy: 'Mama's boy ... let's see you cry.' Then he abuses Ben by bouncing the basketball off his head: 'my sweetest little girl,' the worst insult a man can give another man and a reinforcement of the myth of masculinity.

In an environment like this, where any challenge to the accepted power structure creates the potential for abuse, the roles played by Lillian and Ben are adaptive and understandable. Adult children of alcoholics and of dysfunctional families, those whom we now call codependent, learn to scan their environments constantly and to adjust their behaviour in an effort to keep the emotional climate safe. They come to believe that they are powerful enough to control the environment if only they figure it out right, that it is their job to control it. In the process they lose the sense of their own identities.

Lillian has lost so much sense of herself as a person that she does not even recognize abuse. And if Ben learns to deny his anger as she instructs, his 'codependency,' too, will be assured. It's clear that Lillian has had years of practice in being hypervigilant in her focus on others. But to call her behaviour codependency is to blame the victim.

Like most women, Lillian has been socialized to be emotionally central in the family, codependent, and responsible for relationships. She caretakes the relationship between Ben and his father, reframes her husband's intentions in a way that the most elegant of strategic/systemic therapists might do: 'what happened today won't matter in five years ... he does what he does because he loves you and wants you to be the best ... he's out there practicing in the rain because he's admitting that he's getting older ... it's the only way he knows how to say I'm sorry.'

The Santinis are the normative white American family. The men are socialized to be competitive, dualistic, impulsive, 'Top Guns.' The women are socialized to be other focused and responsible for sustaining all family relationships.

The film *On Golden Pond* tells a similar story about a 'normal' family. As Jane Fonda talks about the hostile and distant relationship she had with her father, Katherine Hepburn, as her mother, explains her father's behaviour to her daughter. The mother, in effect, makes apologies, interprets his behaviour for him. Without the extreme exaggerations created by the alcoholism in the Santini story, the scene is almost identical.

In both cases, the women never question their centrality in family life, their expertise on relationships. They automatically take the emotional responsibility for explaining and interpreting the men to the children, thus maintaining the men's immobility in dealing with emotional relationships.

This same scene is played out on a very small scale in many of our lives in the following vignette: we call home and when our father answers the phone, he immediately, without really talking with us, says, 'just a minute ... I'll get your mother.'

What is going on in these three family scenes and how does it relate to codependency? What is going on is business as usual. It is, in general,

a woman's prescribed role to tend to relationships, to focus on relationships, to make sure all relationships work, to put the needs and
feelings of the other ahead of her own. And a woman inevitably loses
her relationship with herself in the overresponsible focus on the other.
Women are programmed this way in the 'normal' version of family
life, and if they grow up in an overtly dysfunctional family, they are
taught to do more of the same. In the process men have been crippled
in their capacity for emotional relatedness. Why call this socialized
behaviour codependency? Why use the language of sickness for behaviour that has been celebrated as normal all along? As we recognize
that family form and structure are changing, we need to acknowledge
that the 'normative' family of time-honoured tradition was perhaps
never functional. If it were, it wouldn't need to change.

CLINICAL ALTERNATIVES TO THE LANGUAGE OF CODEPENDENCY

Our clinical model for intervention with codependency developed in
response to our work with families affected by addiction (Bepko and
Krestan 1985). We assume that the key dynamic to interrupt in the
alcohol-affected family is the reciprocal one that evolves when one
person is overresponsible and the other underresponsible. Briefly, we
view the problem as one of a complementary imbalance. If one person
does too much either functionally or emotionally for another, that
second person becomes increasingly underresponsible for his own
well-being and inevitably maintains and perpetuates overresponsibility in the other. The two play reciprocal roles.

   Alcoholics, by the very nature of the addictive process, exaggerate
the overresponsible/underresponsible dichotomy. Overresponsible behaviour has come to be called codependency. But to talk in terms of
extremes of over- or underresponsibility is, we feel, a much more effective and less blaming language. It points to the need for behavioural
change rather than suggesting the need for recovery from a 'disease.'

   Since overresponsible behaviour is the natural growth of women's
socialization in this society, living in an addiction-affected system naturally exacerbates it. Hypervigilance about emotional climates, if not
carried to an extreme, is considered necessary and appropriate behaviour for women. We call what has been termed either enabling or
codependent behaviour overresponsible behaviour.

   The overresponsibility that women are trained to assume is not confined to the emotional arena of life. They are also taught to perform almost all of the other services that maintain family life but in a way that makes it appear that they remain in some way dependent on men.

In men, codependency may refer to female qualities that have been learned in response to a particular role in a given family. For example, many men who grew up in addiction-affected families learned to be nurturing, but in an inappropriate way. Focusing on the needs of others became a survival role and many men learned it only because of the absence of a female sibling in the system. The man who learns to be emotionally overresponsible is behaving in a stereotypically female way. Codependency is still a term thought to be more applicable to female behaviour. Men may *do* codependent things, but women *are* codependent.

REBALANCING POWER AND RESPONSIBILITY

Clinically, as we move to restore what we consider to be an appropriate distribution of responsibility within the family system, both functionally and emotionally, we are inevitably challenging old normative structures. In working with alcohol-affected systems it is traditional to assess and change those patterns that enable the drinking to continue. It is understood that if the wife of an alcoholic is told not to make excuses for her husband with his employer, she's being asked to stop enabling his alcoholic behaviour. But if one intervenes further and asks her not to pick up his dirty towel from the bathroom floor or not to referee the relationship between him and his children, one may be inciting social revolution. Calling his employer, picking up the dirty towel, and refereeing the relationship with the children are, in fact, the same behaviours within different contexts. They are all overresponsible behaviours. If she keeps calling the employer with excuses, we know the alcoholic won't get sober. But are we willing to look at what might happen if she stopped picking up the dirty towel, buying the Mother's Day card for his mother, and managing his relationship with his children? Quite simply, the old normative structure would break down.

In one example Nancy, the wife, had been asked to stop haranguing her husband Mike, who is twenty-eight days sober, about filing the income tax that has gone unfiled for three years. Nancy works for the government. Her anxiety is understandable. But the more she prods

Mike, the more he resists. Nancy has great difficulty understanding why she needs therapy and why her prodding and 'nagging' of Mike results in such reactivity on his part.

Is Nancy codependent? Is she controlling? Is she helpful? Mike feels controlled. But Nancy feels so focused on what Mike is and isn't doing that she feels her only reason for needing therapy is to understand why Mike behaves the way he does.

Since she's so focused on Mike and so affected by his behaviour, Nancy could be defined as codependent. But it is perhaps more clinically useful to call her overresponsible and to see her overresponsibility and his underresponsibility as co-created and maintained in a context in which the rule is that she *should function as overresponsible for him but in a way that lets him save face.* If she took over filing the taxes for him rather than telling him how to do it, she would be even more overresponsible but Mike would be less upset. Overresponsibility for a woman is sanctioned, but only if acted out in a way that maintains the myth that Mike is not accountable for his underresponsibility. But when Nancy nags and controls, pointing attention to his underfunctioning, in the current lexicon of disease, she is called codependent.

In response to Nancy's overresponsibility, Mike behaves in a reciprocally underresponsible way that leaves him feeling incompetent. The alcoholism masks the incompetence. But these imbalances in responsibility, exaggerated by alcoholism, are reinforced by a socialization that trains men and women to assume one set of behaviours while displaying another. So Nancy is socialized actually to manage many, if not most, of the details of her life with Mike, but she is also to show dependence. And Mike is socialized to rely on Nancy for his total emotional life, but to display autonomy. Mike appears to be very passive, but in fact, he has spent years doing what he's been taught to do as a man – deny his feelings. Nancy and Mike are trapped in their reciprocal roles by their mutual family socialization and by the larger societal rules that define gender-appropriate behaviour and that maintain gender inequality.

To upset this inequality of responsibility clinically, we first ask that couples make lists of all the functional and emotional responsibilities it takes to run their life together. The lists are typically very similar to this sample one from one couple in treatment. One partner's responsibilities were as follows: 'child care, house repairs, cleaning, laundry, decorating, dry cleaners, paying bills, problems with tenants with our rental properties, problems with local real estate, dental appointments, doctors visits, chauffeuring, buying presents, buying cards, re-pair people, school contacts, income tax preparation, car repairs, shop-ping, food preparation, cleaning of all types, reminding ... for example, insurance, car inspections, taking care of dogs and cats.' Emotional responsibilities were listed as: 'getting in the middle between spouse and children, buffering bad feelings between family, reminding each family member of each other's needs, attempts to get spouse to talk about what's going on with spouse, attempts to smooth over tension, make sure no one feels bad or sad.' The other partner's list was: 'fi-nancial, children's physical needs provided for with money, driving the car, shielding problems from spouse, avoiding conflict and con-frontation.' It would be a correct assumption to guess that the longer list is the wife's and the second list, with financial concerns being foremost, is her husband's. Responsibilities in couples don't always break down this way, particularly when the woman is alcoholic, but these represent the typical lists of female and male.

Extremes of over- and underresponsibility also develop in gay and lesbian couples when addiction is involved. But since these relation-ships tend to be more egalitarian (Blumstein and Schwartz 1983), the implications are somewhat different.

The clinical point is that the normative family structure in hetero-sexual relationships is a codependent structure. If one works towards a redistribution of the codependent structure through equalizing the distribution of responsibilities, a blow is struck at the heart of that codependent structure, but another is struck at what is considered normal for the white, middle-class American family.

When we work towards this redistribution of responsibility within the family, we assume that women and men must both give up in-appropriate responsibility for others and take appropriate responsibility for self. For a woman, relinquishing overresponsible behaviour may create a crisis of 'emptiness' for a time because her entire sense of self has been, in many cases, predicated on being *for* others (Miller 1976; Gilligan 1982). Men are typically asked to give up overrespon-sibility for work in some way. As an example, a psychiatrist recently sought consultation because of concern with his relationship with his mother. She was flying in from the west coast for a family therapy session, and although he was seeking help because of issues in his relationship with her and had initiated the idea of the therapy session, he insisted he could not take time off from work to pick her up at the airport. He had assumed that his wife would have to do that. The intervention, of course, was to insist that he rearrange his work schedule to pick her up himself. On his drive to the airport, and as he sat waiting for her delayed flight, he encountered a good deal of anxiety and depression that his busy schedule usually shielded him from.

In intervening to redistribute responsibility, it is critical that we not ask women to give up overresponsibility for their relationships in ways that shame them for being nurturing or that rob them of all responsibility. Equally, it is important not to ask men to rebalance their work lives in ways that shame them for trying to be good men.

FOSTERING RELATIONAL RESPONSIBILITY

As we better equalize responsibility within the family and replace an overfocus on others in women with a healthy focus on self, it is also crucial to maintain a concept of relational responsibility. Treatment must have as its goal the fostering of appropriate responsibility for self at the same time that it maintains a focus on concepts of relational responsibility and emotional responsiveness to others. If, for women, recovery from 'codependency' means recovering from female socialization enough to care about oneself as much as one cares about relationship, that is a needed correction. But if recovery for men points in the direction of being even more self-focused and of further devaluing the need for mutual caring and connectedness, it may represent an overcorrection.

One of the greatest dangers of the codependency movement is that in its attempt to restore appropriate responsibility to the individual, it espouses in some instances a very linear and blaming view of relationships that does not assume the mutual responsibility of both partners for the successes and failures of relatedness. Concepts that have to do with focusing on self rather than the other are often misapplied so that people stop being overresponsible, but they also stop taking appropriate responsibility for their part in relationships. They forget that the antidote to overresponsibility is responsiveness, not a failure to be responsible at all (Bepko and Krestan 1990). If the movement perpetuates an illusion of perfectibility by suggesting that if one recovers perfectly, then one has painless relationships, it simply maintains the errors and illusions of a patriarchal culture that promotes a false belief in the value of total independence and autonomy and fails to recognize the need for healthy interdependence.

EXPECTATIONS OF CHANGE

The following brief story illustrates the potential for misapplication of the ideas of codependency, a misapplication that ignores a process view of change.

A man involved in a long-term relationship with a woman began to experience serious conflicts with her. He had not been in the habit of asking directly for her time or attention; he had simply made assumptions that she would focus on his priorities and agendas. Over time, she tended to withdraw her focus on him and his needs, and he learned that he needed to be more direct in asking for what he wanted from her. When he did, she often said no and got angry as well. He went to his codependency group and asked why, when he asked for his needs to be met, he was ignored and abandoned. He was told that it was because he picked people who were not capable of giving.

In focusing on the inability or the refusal of his partner to give, both he and his group were ignoring a process view of change. By asking for something directly, this man was changing the rules of his relationship system, and the first thing any participant in a relational system does when confronted with change is directly or indirectly to insist that things change back to the way they were. If this man listens to his group and cuts off emotionally from his partner without understanding the ways in which he has changed his own part in the system, the system itself if not going to change. It may not anyway, but he needs to act with the understanding that change is a process, and that a first negative response does not make her a villain or him a 'sick codependent' who chooses the wrong kind of people.

There is a dangerous underlying assumption in the message that the group gave to this man, which is the myth that simply having a need entitles one to get it met. The recovery movement, Adult Children of Alcoholics, and its sister programs espouse the need to recover childhood. But here the movement poses further difficult questions regarding responsibility. How can one be an 'adult child' – what kind of responsibility is then appropriate? Can one really have unmet childhood needs met as an adult? Too often 'recovery' from codependency in this sense can seem like an abandonment of responsibility and an exercise in blaming or in being victim.

Clinically then, in an attempt to create more functional families, we need to challenge the distribution of responsibility and power that exists in the normative American family. A 'functional' family needs to meet the needs of women, of children, and of men. Codependency needs to be redefined as overresponsibility and overresponsibility needs to be understood as a positive impulse gone awry. Relational responsibility needs to coexist with responsibility to self, and the feminine emphasis on feeling needs to be acknowledged and celebrated, while the feminine focus on relationship needs some redirection without its being pathologized. The codependency movement possesses the potential to direct our attention to a redressing of the gendered imbalances between the male and female sensibilities within us. We hope that redressing can occur in a way that doesn't overcorrect for the female tendency to focus on relationship. If that overcorrection occurs, our social mores will simply return us to the old narcissistic position, *I have to get my needs met*, and it is codependent to care about your needs.

CONCLUSION

This discussion has focused on the codependency movement as representing the creation in language of a syndrome that is difficult to treat because it is so global and vague in definition. It's a movement that tends to perpetuate society's tendency to pathologize behaviour that is typically defined as female, as women's work.

The codependency movement is probably best viewed as a fascinating and compelling example of the evolution of a social phenomenon. It speaks to the power of our descriptions of reality to invent reality and to invent disease for economic and political gain whereby certain segments of society profit from treating others whose experience is controlled by being defined as sick. It speaks to our tendency to over-identify with negative and pathologizing views of ourselves. And it speaks to our tendency to think in generalized extremes that fail to acknowledge contradiction, complexity, distinction.

There is unquestionably some pattern of behaviour and feeling that characterizes the experience of many people who have felt the negative power of an addictive process somewhere in their lives. An understanding of these patterns can only inform and enhance our clinical work. But our understanding so far remains at a fairly elementary, unresearched level. The codependency movement can be credited with bringing these patterns to our attention and awareness, but it has also created another set of problems.

The language of codependency blames people, women in particular, for assuming a social role that has previously been viewed as normative and functional. It takes what was once considered healthy and defines it as sick. In the process it fails to acknowledge that change needs to occur at the level of social belief, attitude, and expectation. The patterns of behaviour that we see today as 'codependent' are symptoms of the damage done by adherence to constricting and patriarchal definitions of normative family structure. But the language of codependency personalizes the problem and locates it in individuals instead of acknowledging that the problem or 'sickness' is in the larger structure itself.

'Codependency' proposes a change in individual behaviour that doesn't take the process of relationship into account. It overdefines as sick some qualities that are necessary to the maintenance of relationship. It ignores the concept of relational responsibility.

Finally, the myth of codependency may need some revision. We need to create a new story about mutual responsibility and about relational responsibility. We need a story in which the characters are no longer constricted by rigid parameters of maleness and femaleness. We need a story in which power is balanced, and we need a story in which victims are replaced by wounded but responsible heroes and heroines. In the new story, those heroes and heroines view themselves not as sick reactors, but as courageous actors on the ever-demanding, complex stage of life.

This article appeared in Claudia Bepko, ed., *Feminism and Addiction* (Haworth Press: 1991), pp. 49–66. Reprinted with permission.

REFERENCES

Beattie, M. (1987) *Co-dependent no more.* New York: Harper/Hazelden.

Bepko, C. and J. Krestan (1990) *Too good for her own good: Breaking free from the burden of female responsibility.* New York: Harper and Row.

– (1985) *The responsibility trap: A blueprint for treating the alcoholic family.* New York: Free Press.

Black, C. (1981) *It will never happen to me.* Denver, Colorado: M.A.C.

Blumstein, P. and P. Schwartz (1983) *American couples.* New York: Morrow.

Conrad, P. and J. Schneider (1980) *Deviance and medicalization: From badness to sickness.* St Louis: C.V. Mosby.

Cruse, J. (1989) *Painful affairs: Looking for love through addiction and co-dependency.* Deerfield Beach, Florida: Health Communications.

Gilligan, C. (1982) *In a different voice.* Cambridge, MA: Harvard University Press.

Larsen, E. (1983) *Basics of co-dependency.* Brooklyn Park, MN: E. Larson Enterprises.

Leupnitz, D. (1988) *The family interpreted: Feminist theory in clinical practice.* New York: Basic Books.

Mellody, P. (1989) *The roots of codependency.* Audio tape produced by Listen To Learn Tape Library, Phoenix, AZ.

Miller, J.B. (1976) *Toward a new psychology of women.* Boston: Beacon Press.

Reissman, C.K. (1983) Women and medicalization. *Social Policy, 14, 1.*

Smalley S. (1986) Quoted in Anne Wilson Schaef, *Co-dependence: Misunderstood – mistreated.* San Francisco: Harper & Row.

Subby, R. (1984) Inside the chemically dependent marriage: Denial and manipulation. In *Co-dependency: An emerging issue.* Pompano Beach, FL: Health Communications.

– (1987) *Lost in the shuffle: The co-dependent reality.* Pompano Beach, FL: Health Communications.

Steinglass, P. (1979) Family therapy with alcoholics: A review. In Kaufmann and Kaufmann (eds). *Family therapy of drug and alcohol abuse.* New York: Gardner Press.

Wegscheider-Cruse, S. (1984) Co-dependency: The therapeutic void. In *Co-dependency: An emerging issue.* Pompano Beach, FL: Health Communications.

Whitfield, C. (1984) Co-dependency: An emerging problem among professionals. In *Co-dependency: An emerging issue.* Pompano Beach, FL: Health Communications.

Withorn, A. (1986) Helping Ourselves. In Conrad and Kern (eds) *Sociology of health and illness,* second edition. New York: St Martin's Press.

PHYLLIS B. FRANK, MA, and

GAIL KADISON GOLDEN, MSW

Blaming by Naming: Battered Women and the Epidemic of Codependency

Codependency is an increasingly popular term for describing an expanding population of individuals. This concept, originally identified by drug and alcohol counsellors, was formulated to describe those individuals who make relationships with substance abusers, 'enable' them, and fail to leave them even after it becomes clear that the relationship is a damaging one (Rockland County Department of Mental Health 1989–90). It appears as if the partners of the substance abusers have a peculiar addiction; that is, they are addicted to a person who has an addiction. The codependent analysis indicates that these people seem to *need* to be with someone (an abuser) who does not function in a healthy way and cannot or does not meet the codependent person's needs.

The problems of codependent individuals are defined as clearly rooted in deficits of early nurturing, such as abusive or neglectful parenting (ibid.). For example, codependent behaviour seems to be found among many adult children of alcoholics.

From the original notion that people who marry and remain with substance abusers have their own illness, the concept of codependency is beginning to enlarge (ibid.). It is now an ever-widening theory that is commonly used to describe anyone who is coupled with an abusive partner. The current definition of codependency reads: 'a pattern of painful dependency on compulsive behaviour and approval seeking in order to gain safety, identity and self-worth' (ibid.). This includes all who are coupled with anyone who is viewed as an addict or as compulsive. Then does it also include any person in a marriage that is less than adequate? Are all who stay in these inadequate marriages, where their needs are not met, codependent?

Any label that includes more than half the population raises serious clinical questions. An immediate concern is applying the concept of codependency to battered women. Calling a woman who is living with a batterer a codependent is tantamount to victimizing her again. The prefix 'co' implies shared responsibility for the abuse, which directly opposes an important segment of the work with battered women – clarifying that women are not responsible for the violent behaviour of their abusers (Frank and Houghton 1987).

One can readily see how the codependent label might be used to diagnose or explain the situation of a woman who is being abused and does not leave her partner. The implication here is that if a woman were healthy, she would not be coupled with an abuser. Codependency suggests that her staying is caused by some early deficit, first in her environment and then, as a result, in herself. It intimates that a woman finds or even seeks out a violent partner whom she may continue to try to please, change, and protect, and whom she may not leave.

Research on battered women makes it clear that any woman – whether she had alcoholic or non-drug-abusive parents, is privileged or impoverished, has or lacks self-esteem – can find herself with an abuser. Having a good childhood is not an insurance policy against coupling with an abuser (Schulman 1979).

Men who assault their partners know that they can, and they have done so, often for years, with complete immunity. Most men who abuse their partners believe that it is justifiable and appropriate behaviour. Women brought up in the same atmosphere share these beliefs. Societally and culturally, abuse of women has been condoned and sanctioned as men abuse their power to control what they believe to be theirs. Because the structure of our patriarchal history has supported the concept of male entitlement vis-à-vis wives, all women have been and continue to remain at risk of coupling with an abuser, even those who are 'healthy,' who do not have deficient early nurturing.

Many complex variables may determine whether an abused woman will leave her partner. These include, but are not limited to, the legal response to this crime within her community, the number and ages of her children, economic factors, availability of shelter and community support, willingness of family and friends to help, and her employability (Frank and Houghton 1987). The extent of the danger to the woman and her children is another factor. More battered women are killed when they leave their abusive mates than when they stay (U.S. Department of Justice 1983). As for self-esteem and psychological background, current research indicates that all aspects of both categories are represented in the battered and non-battered populations of women (University of the State of New York 1982). An additional factor indicates that self-esteem is destroyed by battering, but is not a cause of it (Pence 1985).

Our sense of value certainly depends on how well we were loved and nurtured in childhood. That sense of value, however, depends equally on the situation we find ourselves in and on the messages our culture delivers about our worth. Certainly battered women come to a relationship with a history. They are, however, like all women, living in an oppressive and violent society that consistently gives messages that a woman's physical and emotional well-being is largely insignificant (ibid.).

Consider a battered woman who is doing more caregiving than her partner, is providing most of her family's physical and emotional nurture, and is receiving little for herself. Are we looking at a codependent woman or are we looking at a woman socialized to disregard her own well-being, to care for others, and to assume responsibility for the behaviour of a partner? Are we now calling the results of traditional feminine training, including getting one's identity from one's husband, with which society has persecuted women for generations, an illness in the woman? A term like *codependent* obscures the reality of the situation that we often are dealing with: a system of oppression for which the woman is not responsible but to which she is struggling to find a response.

Terms like *posttraumatic stress disorder* are more illuminating and accurate in that they do not burden an already suffering human being with a slightly masochistic diagnosis suggesting complicity in one's own misery. The term *incest survivor* acknowledges a syndrome of trauma and pain, while also recognizing the person's strength and drive towards health. It also locates the responsibility for the suffering squarely outside the individual.

Social workers must be careful, when they feel they have happened upon a term that is descriptive of a problem, not to begin using the term in a manner that may compound the problem.

This article appeared in *Social Work*, Vol. 37(1), Jan. 1992, pp. 5–6. Reprinted with permission.

REFERENCES

Frank, P.B., and B.D. Houghton (1987) *Confronting the Batterer: A Guide to Creating the Spouse Abuse Educational Workshop*. New York: Volunteer Counseling Service.

Pence, E. (1985) *Criminal Justice Response to Domestic Assault Cases: A Guide for Policy Development*. Duluth, MN: Domestic Abuse Intervention Program.

Rockland County Department of Mental Health, Alcohol and Substance Abuse Services (1989–90) Volunteer Counseling Service training seminars, New York.

Schulman, M.A. (1979) *A Survey of Spousal Violence against Women in Kentucky*. Washington, DC: U.S.Government Printing Office.

University of the State of New York, State Education Department (1982) *Addressing Domestic Violence: A Guide for School Personnel*. Albany, NY: Author.

U.S. Department of Justice (1983) *Report to the Nation on Crime and Justice: The Data*. Washington, DC.: U.S. Government Printing Office.

PART III

The Therapeutic Implications of Codependency

KATHERINE VAN WORMER, MSSW, PhD

Codependency: Implications for Women and Therapy

The family can be viewed as a study in interconnectedness. One member's disease affects every other member of the family. Alcoholism as an illness becomes a family illness; family treatment under these circumstances can be highly effective.

Sometimes the spouse of the alcoholic suffers from a too intense emotional involvement with the alcoholic. Treatment in the area of assertiveness and emotional detachment may be beneficial. I object to the tendency today, however, to label such an individual *codependent* (or enabling or self-destructive). My arguments are two-fold: there is no actual entity that can be called codependency, and this label is currently used in a discriminatory way against women.

There is a paucity of criticism in the literature (academic or popular) concerning the concept of codependency. The primary purpose of the present paper is to provide a conceptual critique of a concept that has gone unexamined. The concern of the critique is less with the particular word, *codependency*, than with the concept that this word conveys.

The secondary purpose of this article is to examine, from a feminist point of view, the blatant blaming and labelling of women that is taking place under the guise of helping those 'who love too much' (Norwood 1985). Basic arguments presented are aimed at both proponents and critics of the concept as well as the large body of persons who use the term innocently, without an awareness of the connotations.

The first task of the paper is to examine the meaning of the term *codependency*. Attention will be paid to both the original and the popular conceptualizations. Secondly, the paper will take a historical view of codependency and show that use of this label has socio-political roots in sexism and oppression of women. Data will be presented from the literature of psychiatry and chemical dependency treatment to support the basic arguments. The third portion of the paper looks at victim-blaming, in this case blaming the spouse for the treatment s/he is receiving. In this regard, the teachings of Al-Anon (non-professional) and of family systems theorists (professional) are considered. Fourthly, the economic aspect of codependency treatment is discussed. The conclusion considers the implications of non-sexist therapy for spouses of alcoholics.

THE DEFINITION OF CODEPENDENCY

Literally, *codependency* means one who is with, alongside, the (drug) dependent person. The original term was the non-pejorative *co-alcoholic* utilized by Wegscheider (1981) and Black (1982). Codependent replaced the more limited term, *co-alcoholic*, to logically correspond to the all-inclusive term *chemically dependent*. These widely used concepts served, in the early 1980s, to denote the psychological stress and torment experienced by the alcoholic's or chemically dependent person's spouse. Codependency was conceived as a logical reaction to living with a chemically addicted individual. Because the term *codependency* so closely resembled the term *dependency*, some confusion between codependency as a reactive condition and dependency, as in 'the dependent personality,' may have occurred.

The parallel term *Enabler* (often capitalized) has been widely used in the alcoholism treatment field to refer to a family member who, in trying to protect the alcoholic, has actually impeded recovery. The Enabler is characterized as resistant, angry, and self-righteous. Given proper confrontation, 'she (the Enabler) will come to acknowledge her contribution to the family illness' (Wegscheider 1981, 175).

From the mid-1980s to the present, the concept of codependency has been expanded, developed, and popularized. The emerging term *codependent* has gone beyond the mere situational connotation of the earlier term *Enabler*. The codependent, unlike the Enabler, is seen to be suffering from a character disorder. While the Enabler may make a bad situation worse, the codependent actively seeks out a bad situation.

The definition of codependency with which this paper is concerned is a composite definition found in current literature, especially in Schaef (1986). Codependency, according to this definition, is a disease that is manifested by a tendency to enter into addictive relationships.

Origins of the disease are found in early childhood, where dysfunctional patterns of behaviour were learned. In Schaef's usage of the term, the 'co' part of codependency is no longer an essential ingredient, apparently.

Similarly, Cocores (1987), medical spokesman for Fair Oaks Hospital, has spelled out the diagnostic criteria that he would like to have included in the future edition of the *Diagnostic and Statistical Manual of Mental Disorders (DSM-IV)*. The proposed criteria for 'the co-addiction disorder' include: remaining in an intimate relationship without seeking treatment, being preoccupied with the doings of the substance abuse, neglecting one's personal needs, and trying to protect the substance abuser. These recommendations stem from a survey of fifty (mostly female) spouses of chemically dependent persons. Until this disorder is introduced, Cocores recommends the diagnosing of co-addiction disorders as obsessive-compulsive disorders and adjustment disorders.

More significantly, the revised edition of the *Diagnostic and Statistical Manual of Mental Disorders (DSM-III-R)* (APA 1987) introduced the controversial term *self-defeating personality disorder* to describe a disorder in which a person persists in behaviour that does not allow him or her to reach his or her goals. Because of the controversy that ensued over the inclusion of this diagnosis, however, the description is placed in the appendix as a 'proposed diagnostic category needing further study' (ibid., 367). Nevertheless, inclusion in the prestigious *DSM-III-R* in any capacity lends legitimacy to the concept.

The mass media have devoted undue attention to the phenomenon called codependency. The term as used in the popular press has emphasized codependency as an *active* rather than a *reactive* condition. Recent titles proclaim the new orientation: 'Willpower Can Break Co-Dependency Chain' (Pursch 1986); 'Loving Till It Hurts' (Kelly 1986); 'Codependency and Compulsive Addictive Behavior' (Stevens and Young 1985). A leading addictions journal carries the article, 'Do Liberated Women Drive Their Husbands To Drink?' (Harrell 1986).

In consumer magazines and books, the codependency concept that arose in alcoholism treatment has been extended to assign women to sick relationships. Terms such as *love addiction* and *sex addiction* are roughly synonymous with the generalized usage of codependency.

My own experience in chemical dependency treatment confirms that the codependency framework is widely applied with regard to family members. It is especially widely used as a descriptive label for *female* clients married to alcoholics. Where I formerly worked, many of the staff attended workshops on codependency; we all counselled clients whose chief complaint was their unhealthy relationship with an alcoholic spouse. This is a legitimate treatment concern. I am increasingly alarmed, however, at the extent of the labelling that is used against clients with relationship issues, and at the anti-female and anti-victim bias accompanying this labelling. The remainder of this paper will examine this bias in its practical and theoretical context.

CODEPENDENCY AND ALCOHOLISM

Years ago 'the predisposing personality' theory argued that the wife of the alcoholic had chosen to marry an alcoholic to satisfy deep unconscious needs, perhaps of dominance or dependence (Royce 1981, 120). Four types of alcoholic wives were characterized by the names of Controlling Catherine, Wavering Winnie, Suffering Susan, and Punitive Polly (Whalen 1953).

The codependency label is more subtle: males as well as females may suffer from codependency. References in the literature, however, are made more frequently to the *female* spouse of the male alcoholic than to the *male* spouse of the female alcoholic. Cappell-Sowder (1984), in her article, 'On Being Addicted to the Addict,' makes no pretense of talking about men: 'This article will attempt to make this relationship clear and to help co-dependents define their own symptoms and clarify means by which they can establish their own recovery programs. (Note: For purposes of this article the alcoholic will be referred to as "he," the co-dependent as "she" or "spouse.")' (14).

Statistically, there are many more wives than husbands of alcoholics. It is estimated that while nine out of ten women will stay with an alcoholic spouse, nine out of ten men will not (Kinney and Leaton 1978). This fact, coupled with the significantly higher number of alcoholic males than females in treatment, ensures that the typical alcoholic spouse is portrayed in the literature as a woman.

When a woman, consistent with her socialization to be nurturing, remains loyal to her alcoholic spouse, she is a ripe candidate for the codependency label. The characteristics of codependency, in fact (e.g., sensitivity to others' needs, vulnerability, dependency), are essentially exaggerations of women's prescribed cultural role. The wider society places a premium on autonomy and independence (Kaplan 1986). The high frequency with which the codependency label is used for female clients is suggestive of an overlap between the central dynamics of codependency and key dimensions in the sex-role socialization of women.

Codependency has become another in a long line of concepts (e.g., hysteria, histrionic personality, masochism) that have been utilized by treatment providers to categorize the problems of women. The most recent addition to the list is the term *self-defeating personality disorder*. Proposed by the American Psychiatric Association to be included in *DSM-III-R*, this term met with heated resistance that was unprecedented. Critics of the proposed 'self-defeating' label, according to Franklin (1987), found the category sexist and victim blaming. 'The high potential for misuse against women' was cited as the major objection to inclusion of this category (APA 1987, xxvi).

BLAMING THE ALCOHOLIC'S SPOUSE

Paralleling the institutionalized sexism of the wider society is the tendency to blame the women victims of crime, disease, and poverty. Victim blaming is the culmination of the American belief that there is a just world, that you control your own destiny, and that individual responsibility reigns (Lerner 1980).

Alcoholics have historically been blamed for their affliction. Efforts are being made today by mental health professionals to understand that their alcoholic clients are suffering from a disease. This same degree of sensitivity, unfortunately, is not applied to the spouses of alcoholics.

An extreme position is that a man may be driven to drink by his wife. This position has received a great deal of publicity and comment in the alcoholism treatment field. Many of my male clients endorsed this position because it constituted a rationale for drinking.

The articles that were carried in the mass media derived their information from a study in a reputable addictions journal. Harrell (1986) researched the issue of effect of marital and work roles of dual-career spouses on men's drinking. (He did not research the question of societal pressure on women's drinking patterns.) Using apparently sophisticated empirical analysis, Harrell found that women drive their husbands to drink if their husbands are of a 'masculine' orientation. The author, in this study, furnishes a causal model purporting to show

that where there is conflict over the dual-career lifestyle, liquor consumption increases. Harrell, in his research, confused association (of
male consumption, traditionalism, and marriage to working wives) and
causation. Moreover, an alternative and more likely interpretation was
not considered: the fact that the wives of these traditional men were
driven to seek work because of their husbands' lifestyle. That this
article was published in the *International Journal of the Addictions* without
any editorial comment or controversy is indicative of the ease with
which spouses of alcoholics may be blamed for the illness.

The following section of this article will explore two very different
areas where victim blaming is embodied in the teachings of the literature. The first of these is the teaching of Al-Anon, the self-help
group for spouses of alcoholics. The second place where victim blaming
emerges is in the family therapy literature that utilizes the systems
approach.

Al-Anon

Al-Anon is an active and thriving organization for families of alcoholics
which helps them cope with the family illness. Membership is 80 per
cent female. I have sent numerous clients to Al-Anon, clients for whom
the emphasis of self-growth and independence would have been beneficial. The complaints of some of my female clients, however, has
alerted me to the content of the Al-Anon literature that is a cause
for concern. *One Day at a Time* (1987) is the bible of Al-Anon. The
dual emphasis on overcoming personal shortcomings and maintaining
the marriage 'in sickness and in health' could clearly arouse guilt feelings in already troubled women.

The message for 19 February typifies the general theme and tone
of *One Day at a Time*: 'As she overcame her fear of her husband, self-
pity yielded too. She stopped involving herself in his disasters and
taking part in arguments that used to end in violence. Her husband
was compelled to face his own problems, and happily, he learned to
face them in AA' (50). The same text is at once encouraging the woman
to take care of her needs *and* blaming her for her husband's abuse.
By equating the husband's drinking with the wife's irritating behaviour, Al-Anon implies that the spouse of the alcoholic shares responsibility for her husband's disease. Similarly, the message for 9 May
states: 'The suffering is real, but we wonder how much of the hurt
is self-inflicted' (130).

Family-Systems-Based Therapy

The systems theory approach has revolutionized much of the thinking within social work and alcoholism counselling. Hartman and Laird (1983) speak of a conceptual revolution that has replaced the psychodynamic model of causation with a paradigm that is multicausal. In its attention to wholes, patterns, and social roles, systems theory has enriched mental health and family treatment considerably.

Whereas individual problems were once seen as rooted in the individual psyche, today individuals are seen within the context of the family. Individual problems are viewed as outgrowths of disturbed family communications rather than family problems seen as the result of individual disturbances. Early systems theory located the root of mental illness in a faulty communications system. When one member of the family is ill, the entire family system's communication may be put in jeopardy.

My argument with systems theory is the seeming disregard for the location of the illness inside the mind or body. There is a disregard here also of the disturbance that occurs in family organization where there is a disturbance of *individual* family members. With schizophrenia, alcoholism, and incest, alike, the cause of the dysfunction is placed by systems theorists in the aberrant family interaction patterns alone. Treatment, accordingly, is directed towards the family organizational structure.

The key issue of contemporary family systems theory is how individual symptoms are functional for the family as a whole. The basic assumption of this approach is that the 'acting out' of the individual pays dividends for the family system, often by distracting the family from the real problem. Some general quotes from leading family therapists illustrate the nature of the logic.

On schizophrenia: 'This theory considers schizophrenia to be the product of several generations of increasing impairment with lower and lower levels of differentiation until there is a generation that produces schizophrenia' (Bowen 1978, 264).

On alcoholism: 'The feelings of despair and hopelessness that are generated by a neglected child are the seeds of future alcoholism' (Lawson, Peterson, and Lawson 1983, 112).

On incest: 'Only within the past decade has incest been viewed as an expression of undue tension within the family unit' (Deighton and McPeek 1985, 406).

In general: 'Symptoms in any member of the family, whether social, (e.g., child abuse, delinquency), physical (e.g., depression, schizophrenia) or conflictual (e.g., marital conflict) are viewed as evidence of dysfunction in the family relationship process' (Helm 1970, 342).

Systems theory as applied to the violent and/or alcoholic family may be extremely disparaging of non-alcoholic members. Viewed from the context of female oppression and powerlessness, the family therapy approach to male alcoholism and female dependence is at best ineffective and at worst destructive.

The systems approach is very compatible with the shift in focus from the alcoholic to the 'codependent' person or the 'codependent' family. The earlier concept of Enabler, in fact, was a term used by Wegscheider (1981), a former student of systems theory under Virginia Satir. The conceptualization of the systems orientation is also compatible with the Al-Anon focus on the non-drinking spouse.

Bowen (1978), among the most renowned of systemic family therapists, believes that the key to sobriety for individual family members is through improvements in family communication patterns: 'When it is possible to modify the family relationship system, the alcoholic dysfunction is alleviated, even though the dysfunctional one may not have been part of the therapy' (117).

The claim is made that an individual's problem drinking is an adaptive function for the family. Evidence indicates, however, that family functioning and cohesion are enhanced, not exacerbated, through the alcoholic's recovery. Moos and Moos (1984) report favourable results among families of alcoholics who had undergone treatment when compared with a matched sample control group. Billings and Moos (1983) found that the level of stress that existed in families of alcoholics was strongly reduced upon sobriety.

THE ECONOMICS OF CODEPENDENCY

Chemical dependency is a billion-dollar-a-year industry (Fingarette 1988). The medicalization of alcoholism has reaped enormous benefits in terms of revenue for diagnosis, research, and treatment. Today there is a parallel trend to medicalize codependency. The process of medicalization consists of defining codependency as a disease, providing a list of specific criteria for diagnosis of the disease and the provision of intensive and expensive treatment to combat the disease. Codependency today is currently being redefined in terms of a disease, not to parallel the spouse's chemical dependency, but as a disease in its own right.

DSM-III-R is the leading source of diagnosis for insurance company reimbursement. The implications of the debate concerning the proposed introduction of the category, 'self-defeating disorder,' thus are economic as well as academic (Franklin 1987). The alcoholism treatment industry would have a great deal to gain through the inclusion of a category endorsed by the American Psychiatric Association. The present relegation of the new category to the appendix undermines insurance reimbursement to some extent.

Schaef (1986) has written a book that is widely read in alcoholism treatment circles. Called *Co-Dependence: Misunderstood – Mistreated*, this book has a decidedly para-professional (as opposed to professional) point of view. That codependency is a disease in its own right is the major contention of this book. Codependency is a disease, according to Schaef, that preceded the alcoholism in the spouse. Focus should not be on the addict (husband) but rather on the codependent. 'It is important to recognize,' states Schaef, 'that it is their disease they (co-dependents) are sliding into, *not* the disease of the alcoholic' (1986, 13).

Increasingly, one sees in the alcoholism treatment literature, reference to the *disease* of codependency. This concept has important medical/treatment implications. Diagnosis of this disease is on the basis of marriage to an alcoholic. As therapists downplay the impact of the daily cruelties in marriage to an alcoholic spouse and focus instead on the client's 'illness,' there are *two* potential clients where before there was only one. New inpatient treatment centres are now treating spouses of alcoholics for up to six weeks. The 'creation' of this 'disease' for women, according to Fabunmi, Frederick, and Jarvis Bicknese (1985), has provided a virtually endless supply of new clients for the substance abuse industry. Troubled family members are extremely vulnerable to accepting the need for intensive treatment. Some of the emerging therapy groups for codependents encourage self-blame and accepting responsibility for the spouse's drinking. If a woman is resistant to the mission of the group, the group may pounce on her: 'You're not in tune with your own codependency. You are in a state of denial' (ibid., 2).

Utilization of the disease concept of codependency constitutes a confusion of cause and effect to a dangerous degree. When one member of the family is alcoholic, other members develop symptoms that parallel the alcoholic's physical/mental decline into the symptomology of the disease. This same confusion of cause and effect is ubiquitous throughout the codependency literature. Victims are blamed for the problems of their spouse's disease. Systems theory and Al-Anon literature focus on behaviours associated with progression of the alcoholic's disease and then view the effects of the disease as the cause of its progression.

CONCLUSION

The framework of codependency had its conceptual origins in the prestigious school of family systems theory. Today the term has been both popularized (for mass consumption) and medicalized (for mass treatment). The position of this paper is that it should be reconceptualized. There is simply no scientific basis to indicate that those married to alcoholics show pathology (Hyman 1987; Royce 1981).

In labelling women 'codependents' and blaming them for the role they may or may not play in another's chemical dependency, treatment providers are inflicting harm. Therapists are harming women by persuading them to feel guilty for being married to an alcoholic. Women are harmed by being diagnosed as showing pathology when they react normally to an extreme situation. Women are harmed when they are enrolled in lengthy treatment more for the agency's benefit than their own.

Codependency is overwhelmingly defined as a female affliction. Because of the key importance of relationship issues for women and because of their intense loyalty 'in sickness and in health,' women are amenable to being labelled and to treatment.

Victim blaming, family systems blaming, confusion of cause and effect, all are aspects of the 'blame-the-codependent' syndrome. Failure to address the pathology in the family member who is ill is a failure to recognize that the functioning of the whole may be jeopardized by the diseased part of that whole.

A serious shortcoming of the codependency literature is its failure to address the social and political context in which women are living today and have lived formerly. The powerlessness that is falsely labelled 'dependency' is the reality of survival in the alcoholic/addict home. Women have adapted to abuses in order to survive and to enable their families to survive. Such women are suffering not from codependency but from what might be called 'the survivor's syndrome.' Their symptoms, the battle scars, should be respected accordingly.

This article appeared in *Women and Therapy*, Vol. 8(4), 1989, pp. 51–63. Reprinted by permission.

REFERENCES

American Psychiatric Association (1987) *Diagnostic and statistical manual of mental disorders* (3rd ed, revised) *(DSM-III-R)*. Washington, DC: American Psychiatric Association.

Billings, A.G., and R.H. Moos (1983) Psychosocial processes of recovery among alcoholics and their families. *Addictive Behaviors, 8*, 205–18.

Black, C. (1982) *It will never happen to me*. Denver, CO: M.A.C. Printing and Publications Division.

Bowen, M. (1978) *Family therapy in clinical practice*. New York: Aronson.

Cappell-Sowder, K. (1984) On being addicted to the addict. *Focus on Family and Chemical Dependency, 1*, 14–15.

Cocores, J. (1987) Co-addiction: A silent epidemic: *Psychiatry Letter, 5*, 5–8.

Deighton J, and P. McPeek (1985) Group treatment: Adult victims of childhood sexual abuse. *Social Casework, 66*, 406.

Fabunmi, C., L. Frederick, and M. Jarvis Bicknese (1985). *The co-dependency trap*. Presentation at the annual conference of the National Association of Rights, Protection and Advocacy.

Fingarette, H. (1988) *Heavy drinking: The myth of alcoholism as a disease*. Berkeley, CA: University of California Press.

Franklin, D. (1987) The politics of masochism. *Psychology Today, 21*, 55–7.

Harrell, A. (1986) Do liberated women drive their husbands to drink? *International Journal of the Addictions, 21*, 385–91.

Hartman A.D., and J. Laird (1983) *Family centered social work practice*. New York: Free Press.

Hazelton Center, MN (1987). *One day at a time*.

Helm, P. (1970) Family therapy. In G. Stuart and S. Sundeen (eds), *Principles and Practice of Psychiatric Nursing* (p. 342). St. Louis: The C.V. Mosby Co.

Hyman, V. (1987) Some thoughts on co-dependency. *Hazelden Professional Update, 5*, 3.

Kaplan, A. (1986) The "self-in-relation": Implications for depression in women. *Psychotherapy, 23*, 234–42.

Kelly, M. (1986) Loving till it hurts. *Minneapolis/St. Paul* (winter), 112–16.

Kinney J., and G. Leaton (1978) *Loosening the grip*. St Louis: C.V. Mosby.

Lawson, G., J. Peterson and A. Lawson (1983) *Alcoholism and the family: A guide to treatment and prevention*. Rockville, MD: An Aspen Publication.

Lerner, M. (1980) *Belief in a just world*. New York: Plenum Press.

Moos, R.H., and B.S. Moos (1984) The process of recovery from alcoholism. *Journal of Studies on Alcohol*, 45, 11–18.

Norwood, R. (1985) *Women who love too much: When you keep wishing and hoping he'll change*. New York: Pocket Books.

Pursch, J. (1986) Willpower can break the co-dependency chain. *St. Paul Pioneer Press Dispatch* Dec. 16:20.

Royce, J.E. (1981) *Alcohol and alcoholism*. New York: The Free Press.

Schaef, A. (1986) *Co-dependence: Misunderstood – mistreated*. Minneapolis: Winston Press.

Stevens, S., and R. Young. (1985) Co-dependency and compulsive behavior. *Focus on Family and Chemical Dependency*, 8, 18–19.

Wegscheider, S. (1981) *Another chance. Hope and health for the alcoholic family*. Palo Alto, CA: Science and Behavior Books.

Whalen, T. (1953) Wives of alcoholics: Four types observed in a family service agency. *Quarterly Journal of Studies on Alcohol*, 14, 632–41.

RAMONA ASHER, PhD, and

DENNIS BRISSETT, PhD

Codependency: A View from Women Married to Alcoholics

That alcoholics are sick has become a common assumption in the alcoholism rehabilitation industry. That people who live with the alcoholic are also sick is fast becoming another taken-for-granted component of the conventional treatment ideology. Concepts such as alcoholically diseased families, co-alcoholism, and codependency have emerged in an effort both to describe the interaction between alcoholics and their significant others and to account for the problems experienced by these significant others. 'Co-dependency is described by concerned and enthusiastic supporters as a *primary* disease present in *every* member of an alcoholic family, which is often *worse* than alcoholism itself [and] has its own physical manifestations and is a treatable *diagnostic* entity' (Gierymski and Williams 1986, 7). In this paper we focus on the notion of codependency as it is applied to women married to alcoholics.

Two approaches have dominated that traditional understandings of alcoholism and marriage: 'One emphasizes the "psychopathology" of wives of alcoholics, while the second takes the view that the behaviour of wives may be understood as the reactions of "normal" women to the crisis or stress occasioned by their husbands' excessive drinking' (Orford et al. 1975, 1254). While acceptance of the traditional psychopathology model appears to be waning,[1] investigators such as Jackson (1954, 1956, 1962), Lemert (1960, 1962), Lazarus (1960), and Orford (Orford 1975; Orford and Guthrie 1968; Orford et al. 1975, 1976) have provided significant cumulative evidence that many of the problems experienced by the wives of alcoholics are a function of their coping with and adjusting to the problem of alcoholism in their spouses. The wife's behaviour is portrayed as being essentially determined by the 'fact' of alcoholism in her spouse. 'The ... theory is that the wife's behaviour is determined by the situation in which she finds herself relative to the stages of the husband's alcoholism. This implies that the stages of alcoholism in the husband cause reasonably predictable changes in the wife's behaviour.' (James and Goldman 1971, 373).

These changes in personality and behaviour of the wife have long been viewed in traditional Al-Anon thought as indications of her role in enabling the alcoholism of her mate. Only recently has the notion of enabler been medicalized into the concept of codependency, or co-alcoholism. Codependency/co-alcoholism is viewed for the most part as an objective condition with a determinable, although not yet completely specified, etiology and sequelae. 'Co-alcoholism can be defined as ill *health* or maladaptive, problematic, or dysfunctional behavior that is associated with living, working with, or otherwise being close to a person with alcoholism. It is manifested by a spectrum of symptoms, signs and problems that range from a lack of symptoms to headaches to suicide' (Whitfield 1984, 16). That these symptoms, signs, and problems often are construed as coping strategies and adjustive mechanisms underscores the view of wives of alcoholics as people whose personality and behaviour are essentially responses to the stresses incurred in an alcoholic marriage.

In challenging the notion of codependency as an objective condition, we emphasize the social construction and application of this condition. We recognize that the wives of alcoholics, like all persons everywhere, are in one sense reactors to the world in which they live. We think it important to recognize, however, that they are also actors who have a hand in fashioning the very world in which they live: 'human beings interpret or "define" each others' actions instead of merely reacting to each others' actions. Their "response" is not made directly to the actions of one another but instead is based on the meaning which they attach to such actions. Thus, human interaction is mediated by the use of symbols, by interpretation, or by ascertaining the means of one another's actions' (Blumer 1962, 157). In this context, codependency is viewed not as an inevitable consequence of being married to an alcoholic but rather as one possible way of making sense of, and living in, an alcoholic marriage. The wife is 'seen as an integral part of the interaction process, capable of making both helpful and harmful decisions about her husband's drinking and its effect on her marriage and her psychological well-being' (Wiseman 1975b). Wiseman (1975a) has reported that at least some wives of alcoholics function in a manner incompatible with what is typically considered a codependent lifestyle. They are able to fashion a separate and rather contented life for themselves while remaining married to an alcoholic. Becoming codependent, then, may be construed as one of a number of life alternatives for people married to alcoholics. It involves an active process of assuming a new identity rather than a simple recognition of an already determined pre-existing condition. A critical element of this identity work is that persons married to individuals who are labelled deviant (n this instance, alcoholic) are often considered deviant themselves. Building on Lemert's (1951) work on secondary deviance and the special problems of everyday life incurred by stigmatized persons, Jacqueline Wiseman notes that significant others 'might be called "alterdeviants" or "co-deviants" because of their close relationship to the deviated person with whom they must deal and from whom they also assume a reflected stigma' (Wiseman 1975a, 172). These codeviants, as a result of these relationships, also face problematic decisions in everyday life. Wiseman notes that 'the wife of an alcoholic is certainly an exemplar of this stigmatized identity by association' (Wiseman 1975a, 172).

In this paper, then, we emphasize the wife's role in adopting a new identity as a means of interpreting and comprehending her thoughts, feelings, and behaviours as well as those of her husband. We do so by analysing the subjective responses of the wives to their life experiences following the entry of their husbands into treatment. A significant element in this process is the wives' affiliation with certain segments of the alcoholism rehabilitation industry. The identity of codependency is both proffered and legitimized by those persons in the treatment industry to which the wife turns for counsel and assistance. At point of entry into this system, the women are confused, bewildered, and upset. Becoming codependent enables many of them to refashion their current life situation, reconstruct their troubled past, and establish a new and promising future.

METHODOLOGY

The primary data for this study are taped interviews with fifty-two wives of men diagnosed and treated for alcoholism. All fifty-two women in the study are residents of the seven-county Minneapolis-St Paul metropolitan area, married (includes separated or divorce pending) and participants in one of three area family programs for spouses of alcoholics. Each woman was interviewed three times using a standardized interview guide: (*a*) when she initially entered the family program; (*b*) at seven months following her program participation; and (*c*) at fifteen months following her program participation. This retrospective-prospective study focused on the wife's process of defining alcoholism in her husband, the wife's process of constructing an identity and lifestyle for herself, and the possible contingencies that the wife may have taken into account fashioning these ongoing definitions. The interview guide was developed by the authors and covered: (1) the beginning and escalation of problems associated with drinking; (2) attitudes and motives expressed by the wife and her husband about their marriage and his drinking; (3) the wife's social networks and activities; (4) family drinking histories of both husband and wife; and (5) the wife's plans for the future; and in the latter two interviews, questions about responses to (6) the family treatment program and (7) Al-Anon or other activities in which the wife participated. The senior author pretested the interview and conducted all three waves of interviewing starting in August 1981 and finishing in June 1983. In preparation for this study, the senior author engaged in participant observations in a five-day residential family program for relatives and close friends of chemically dependent persons, and also conducted a twelve-week participant-observation study of weekly Al-Anon meetings.

The study sample was obtained by first screening the women upon entry into a family program on the basis of geographic region, marital status, and diagnosis of husbands' alcoholism. Members of the sample range in age from nineteen to sixty-eight, with a median age of thirty-four years. Their education range is from less than high school to the master's degree; the largest group (*n* = 20) are high school graduates and the second largest group (*n* = 16) have some college education. The majority of the women work full time outside the home (*n* = 32), while about one-third are full-time homemakers (*n* = 15). Approximately 75 per cent of the women were living with their husbands at the time of the first interview (*n* = 39), while about 25 per cent were married but living apart from their husbands (*n* = 13). The number of years married ranges from less than one to thirty-six years, with an average of 11.8 years of marriage and an average of 2.3 children. Twenty-seven of the women were Protestant and all but two were Caucasian. Only a few women had participated in Al-Anon prior to entering the family program. Background characteristics are summarized in table 1.

TABLE 1
Background characteristics of sample

Characteristic	Number	Per cent
Age		
19–28	13	25.0
29–34	14	26.9
35–39	13	25.0
40–68	12	23.1
Education		
Less than high school	4	7.7
High school graduate	20	38.5
Vocational or technical beyond high school		
or some college	19	36.5
College degree	7	13.5
Master's degree	2	3.8
Employment		
Managerial professional	11	21.2
Technical, sales or administration	11	21.2
Service occupation	4	7.7
Operators, fabricators, laborers	6	11.5
Homemaker	15	28.8
Student	3	5.8
Part time / temporary	2	3.8
Present living arrangement		
Living with husband	39	75.0
Not living with husband	13	25.0
Years married		
1–3	13	25.0
4–8	15	28.8
9–17	12	23.1
18–39	12	23.1
Religion		
Catholic	23	44.2
Protestant	27	51.9
Other	2	3.9
Race		
White	50	96.2
Non-white	2	3.8

Our interest in the notion of codependency serendipitously emerged during the course of this broad field study. Our curiosity was piqued by the frequency with which the women in our sample spontaneously used the term *codependency* to describe themselves and their behaviour. Their use of the term was very matter of fact, yet they floundered for definition and explanation when probed by the interviewer as to its meaning in their lives. It was in an attempt to understand this hiatus between taken-for-granted existence and the problematic meaning of codependency that this exploratory paper emerged. Using the interview responses (and the respondents' own words as much as possible), we discuss both the nature of codependency and the process of taking on a codependent identity from the respondent's point of view. We then attempt to trace out some of the personal and societal implications of using the concept of codependency to explain the life situation of women married to alcoholics.

WHAT IS CODEPENDENCY?

In analysing the interview responses, we were most struck by the matter-of-fact nature by which the women accepted the reality of codependency. To them codependency was something that obviously and objectively exists in the world. Although not all the women totally embraced the concept for themselves, nearly all of them accepted its existence as part of the taken-for-granted world in which we live. In spite of considerable conceptual and behavioural ambiguity, which is discussed later, there did appear to be two dimensions of codependency that were, in the responses of the women, rather common. The first of these was the general theme of caretaking: 'It means baby sitter to me. That's what it means. Helping somebody that just can't stand on their own two feet, over and over again. You know, it's just like pushing a little kid. That's what it meant to me. I often wonder how I could be so strong and supportive of his bad condition and I was falling apart, you know. Ya, that's what it means to me, a real baby sitter.'

The notion of focusing one's life on the chemical dependency of the husband – of somehow being affected (e.g., 'I was thinking that it's someone that's affected by someone else's problem') especially by enduring interaction with a chemically dependent person – is a second common theme in defining codependency, even when one is not exactly sure of the causal linkage in this association: 'I guess the codependent is living with an alcoholic or chemically dependent. And kind of coming to his defense and trying to cover up for his drinking which doesn't ... help him any. And I guess I was doing that.'

In general, the women in this study subscribe to the prevailing professional orientation that codependency is an 'objective fact' of life that is reflected in their reactions to their husbands' drinking behaviour. However, in stark contrast to this widespread acceptance of something called 'codependency' in their lives, there is little consensus on the part of the women regarding its specific nature and manifestation. In other words, although the women often were able to see themselves or others as codependents, they did not seem to know what, in fact, codependency specifically entailed.

How deeply one's self is involved in codependency was open to question. Some women noted general changes in attitudes and behaviours, such as: 'To me, codependency means you have some type of relationship with a chemically dependent person. And because of this relationship, you have developed attitudes or behaviour that are not necessarily very healthy. It can just be the attitude of hating drinking, which isn't all that healthy you know — I mean you're able to still function as a so-called normal human being, but inside there's some attitudes and feelings that you're not aware of or come out in different ways because of your relationship and focus on this chemically dependent person.'

Another woman described codependency as involving a more profound change in one's self: 'To me, a codependent is a person that has lived [with] or has been affected by an alcoholic, to the point where you have changed yourself. You know, where you have stopped being the person that you once were. And you start losing it ... your self-confidence, your self-esteem, your feelings of worth ... your identity ... you know, who you are.'

Besides this uncertainty and variability regarding the degree of self-involvement in codependency, the women were also unsure as to whether codependency is an endogenous characteristic or an exogenous social role. Although many women expressed this type of ambiguity, one woman in particular is exemplary. She first described codependency as a trait innate to a person: 'the way I see it is that there's a measure of dependency that's already part of that person who is not the user. Some traits, characteristics that really have fed into, oh, for instance, the dependency on people or dependency on getting one's needs met through reacting to other people or just getting hooked into being dependent upon people is the really, kind of way I see it. And you get kind of hooked into an alcoholic's behavior and you depend on that for getting your needs met.' Yet her additional comments point to the definitional ambiguity of codependency when she described it as a social role acquired during early adolescent socialization:

I think that, I came to discover that in some ways I was being raised to fit that codependency position ... I was being trained in such as, you know, cooking meals, have meals ready on time, making your man happy, you know ... meeting his needs was training me to put mine secondary. So when it came to a point of marriage, I hadn't put a lot of time into thinking about what marriage was all about or what I wanted out of marriage or how I wanted to fit my goals and plans into a relationship of marriage with another person ... he knew what he wanted. He wanted somebody that was going to support, follow, do as, you know, he says, and all that, and I didn't have any way of combating that.

Upon being asked if codependency is similar to what a psychologist might call 'passivity' or 'passive-aggressiveness,' and whether the terms used were different because of a client's going to either a chemical dependency counsellor or a psychologist, this same woman differentiated the two by saying: 'I think there's some difference because if you're going to a psychologist or someone for counseling and they point out certain behaviors seem to fit into the realm of what we call a passive-aggressive or manic-depressive or something like that ... but when you've labeled a person codependent and part of their behavior comes from reacting to someone who has what is called a disease of chemical dependency, what we're talking about over here with the psychologist is not really a disease, I mean it's symptomatic of some dysfunction perhaps but not necessarily a disease so I think it's quite different.' It is important to note that this same woman has conceptualized codependency as an innate personal trait, as a learned social role, and implicitly as a disease or, at the very least, disease linked.

Another aspect of definitional ambiguity that emerged in the women's responses was whether or not codependency is distinctive to alcoholic-complicated relationships. Although the idea of codependency was usually first encountered in the context of alcoholic-complicated relationships, the women frequently generalized its apparent symptoms to other types of relationships and to styles of interaction in general: 'See, I think that there are people that did not have alcoholism involved that are codependent … I mean you've got people that are insecure, okay. Might not have anything to do with alcoholism at all. They're just basically insecure. And so what they're doing then is reaching out to another person to take care of, okay.' Another woman commented on this point: 'And part of it is the codependent personality. They're, like I said, people pleasers, they walk to the ends of the earth for you. I'd have been a codependent regardless. And I don't know if – like I said, I don't know if I am still or not. I think women that are in abusive homes, without alcohol, are codependents. Anyone that would be the lesser person in a relationship instead of equal, I think, has codependent tendencies. So it's a real broad word.'

The question of whether codependency is something that is relatively temporary or permanent was also an issue to these women. In other words – as the saying goes of the alcoholic – is the spouse, also, 'once a codependent always a codependent?' Many respondents were reluctant to accept a lifelong identification with the label of codependency. At the same time, it is rather common knowledge that Al-Anon encourages a lifetime involvement, with the expectation that one can always keep learning and growing. One woman in particular exemplifies this ambivalence: 'Well I guess if you say we never graduate from Al-Anon, then I would have to say I'm codependent. I don't think I have the behavior of a codependent anymore. I think that codependent behavior is pretty well gone. I think I flip into it every now and then. You know, I think I get into the old behavior, you know, once in a while, I guess when I do then I would have to say that's my codependent behavior.'

There appears, then, to be a good deal of diversity and ambiguity between and within the respondents' characterizations of codependency: whether or not it involves a profound change of self, whether or not it is an innate personal characteristic or a socially acquired role, whether or not it is a disease, and whether or not it is a temporary or permanent state of being. Yet it is generally felt that whatever it is, it does exist. One woman perhaps put it into the proper perspective: 'Codependency just has a sphere of different things that kind of fits under one. It's a big word and it has … a lot of different things that would be involved in that.' The degree of definitional ambiguity is nicely underscored by the private therapist of one of the women. On the one hand, the therapist teaches about codependency and uses the term as an identifying concept, yet on the other hand, she undermines the utility of even using the term itself: 'There were about six or seven of us in the group ... We had all seen the therapist on an individual basis besides, so we knew her, she knew us – she knew our situations, talked about you know, just the dynamics of codependency, but by the time we were done with it, she didn't even like to use that word, but she did talk about how codependency is a thing unto itself.' One might question whether a term that is so broadly and variably conceptualized need be taken very seriously or if its use would result in any patterned consequences. Yet as we will see, it can have some very serious implications for those who come to view themselves as codependent.

It is not surprising that there is wide variability in self-identification with the label 'codependent' among the women in this sample, ranging from a precarious 'Well I guess so, I'm not so sure' to a resolute 'Oh, absolutely.' Ambivalence in self-identification is clearly heightened by certain life changes. The variable identification is particularly notable as the women view themselves, their home life, or spousal interaction changing over time. Responding to a question of whether she considers herself codependent, one woman replied: 'I don't now; no, I don't now. I don't know if anyone else had observed that in me but I don't feel that I am now. 'Cause now, like I say, I speak freely and say what I feel too; that takes away from that codependency a little bit. Where I was afraid, you know, I kind of just went along with the ride.'

Although the term *codependency* appears in mass media sources and is often discussed in some Al-Anon groups, the first time it was encountered and elaborated upon for these women was usually during the family programs in which these respondents participated. Thus, when asked if she knew where she got the word *codependent*, the response of one woman that typified the experience of many others was: 'Ya, through the family program. Not knowing what it was, really, before; I think I had heard the term, of course, but not realizing that I fit into that so well.' Similarly, another woman described part of the process of coming to view herself as codependent:

They said that the spouse is probably every bit as sick as the alcoholic. I thought well, naa, I'm alright. But as time went on, and this is something that I got out of [the family program] now that I think about this. They had on the blackboard, on one side of the blackboard, had all the symptoms that the alcoholic has. And on the other side of the blackboard, they had all the symptoms of the spouse or the codependent. And I couldn't believe that because I had every symptom except I think two of them. And I hadn't seen that before, it was something new to me. And I was surprised at the number of symptoms that I had had over the years.

The 'they' referred to here is significant; for 'they' appear as those who know, those who give credence to codependency as an emerging self-identification, reiterated in the specialized lectures and exercises during the family program.

Well, when you're co-anything, you're like in partnership or you're parallel, right. And they say a codependent has the same personality traits, I guess that's the phrase I want, as the alcoholic. You know, there's the controlling, there's the low self-esteem, and then all the different personalities that all the little people take. I call them little people because of the lecture I heard, you know, you can be a scapegoat, the hero, the lost child, this type of thing ... We're reactors; so is a chemically dependent person ... it's like you're the target and ... it's like you're the target and you just keep getting the arrow shot at you [other people] bounce them off or they put up a shield. But in codependency, I think, you take everything and then maybe, depending on your personality, you take a little bit differently than somebody else.

The woman who recognized codependency symptoms in herself from the blackboard list was asked to give an example for one such symptom. Behaviour initially not seen by her as codependent none the less fit descriptively with the newly learned symptom of it. Thus, the listed symptoms and the concept of codependency came to have new and retrospective interpretive meaning: 'Like the denial. The lying for him, although I didn't think about it like that. He just went, well had gone down to get gas in the car, course that was like two, two and a half hours earlier, and maybe his brother or somebody stopped by for him ... [and I'd say], oh well, he went down to get gas in the car, he went to the bank, or he went to the post office, you know, and just, let's see, what else was it. I never called in for work for him though ... oh, what were some of them. Well of course the denial. Not wanting to go places.' Notice, here, the reinterpretation of previous behaviour in the light of a new framework – in this case, an emerging conceptualization of codependency. Goffman's (1961) insightful discussions of case histories in the moral careers of mental patients high-light this act of retrospectively elaborating experiences such that they serve as an account or explanation for taking on a new identity. Essentially, our observations of these women point to an emerging identification of self as codependent with a concomitant reconstruction of biography that establishes the plausibility of being codependent. The importance of the introduction, elaboration, and sharing by legitimated persons or authorities of this new identity and biography should not be lost here. It is also noteworthy that the definitional ambiguity of codependency not only enhances the application and stickiness of the label but also makes any individual resistance to or rejection of the label difficult.

This new framework within which one's emerging view of self appears to fit not only provides a measure of identity based on what one does, but also provides a measure of identity based on what one doesn't do. In other words, not only does the presence of certain behaviours (or traits, or symptoms) indicate codependency, but also the absence of certain other behaviours indicates codependency. For example, the inability to remove oneself from a distressing situation was offered as self-evidence of codependency by one of the women:

I'm trying to take care of myself more and not concentrate so much on living around the alcoholic, my whole life revolving around him. But yet I see the same vicious merry-go-around of alcoholism, that you stay on until you make decisions. There's a little book on it, it's called *Alcoholism and the Merry-go-round* or something ... some people can just keep going around on the merry-go-round all their lives. But eventually I guess what would happen, you know, say in another year down the line, if he's still using and I'm still on the merry-go-round, I think it would be hard to take care of yourself, hard to go to meetings and hard to be okay. You eventually should be getting worse too. But it's like deep down, like I had said last time, there's something in me that doesn't want to live this way and feels that there is more to life. But then there's something too that says, well, doesn't give me the go-ahead, chicken, my dependency I spose, on him.

Another part of the process of identifying oneself as codependent is utilizing the concept as a way of understanding similar behaviour of others, as illustrated by the following comments: 'I have a girlfriend right now who's going through it, and I have so tried to get her into what I'm in and have her learn what I have learned. I've tried to give her ... what help I can, but she has to see for herself, just like I did. And she needs not only help from her friends but from other people too, and when they say you're sick, you're sick. And you are sick, that's all there is to it. And I can see how sick she is and I know I was just as sick. You know, and I can see the hell that she's going through and I know I went through the same thing. And I wouldn't wish that on anybody.'

Another part of the process of identifying and validating oneself as a codependent, for a few women, included enrolling in codependency support-therapy groups. One woman's account of her experience in such a group in which she was 'definitely ... extremely so' helped was:

the co-dependency group I was in, I took with my private therapist, who I'd been in therapy with since about the time he went into treatment ... we'd met once a week for a couple of months over the winter. And it was so noticeable in me that I had, my friends were able to tell that I was just so up after going to this Wednesday meeting, it was so, it was noticeable in other people, the effect that it could have on me ... she talked about, I don't even know how to put the words on some of it but like how, two came together and both were empty and tried to be one and couldn't fulfill each other, and how you need to be a whole yourself before you try to do that.

Pressure to identify with the label 'codependent' may come from a significant other as well as professional personnel. Sometimes, the alcoholic husband may encourage his wife's participation and adaptation by subtle suggestions: 'He's thrown in hints a couple of times that the person that lives with an alcoholic is just as sick as the alcoholic himself. So I don't know, I think in his heart he'd probably still want me to go to Al-Anon.' This may be accompanied by feelings of guilt on her part. 'I probably should. But I just feel like my time with [the baby] right now, I don't think that I'm that bad, I mean we don't bicker and fight a lot, we get along okay. So unless it got to the point where we just weren't getting along anymore, then I would take the time to go and do something about it. But since we're doing alright, I feel that my time is better spent being here at home. As long as I'm working.'

A woman may also develop guilt feelings in choosing not to participate in Al-Anon: 'at first I had guilt dealing with not going to Al-Anon and, well, I did use the literature at first but I don't now. I think I have problems having guilt feelings that I should be doing these things, even though I didn't feel the need ... and I don't feel that need anymore ... I just don't feel the need ... so why make myself go if, you know, I have a lot of other things to occupy my time and I, you know, I'm not saying that in the future I may not find I need that, I don't know. Anyway I keep that available you know, but if I don't feel the need, then why feel guilty about it?'

Still other women see codependency as a lifetime affliction and its link with Al-Anon membership as both beneficial and obligatory: 'sure I get tired sometimes of going, or I get to the feeling like I don't want to look at it anymore. But there's been too much good stuff come out of it. And maybe I'm being judgmental, saying that some people just don't, they aren't using it right ... But Al-Anon is just a blessing ... like one gal put it, she said, "This is my medicine. I don't quit taking it just because I feel good. I take it because it's prescribed for a certain amount of time." Well for us, we'll be in recovery for the rest of our life, as will the alcoholics.'

In general, women married to alcoholics and who are exposed to the ideology of the treatment industry are faced with the task of reconciling their ongoing view of themselves (past, present, anticipated) with an apparent collective representation of codependency. Included in this identity-work are varieties of definitional ambiguity, guilt-enhancing interaction, and self-assessments. An interesting element in the interplay of codependency identity-work and its definitional ambiguity stems from the ideological differences between the dictates of therapeutic family programs and the teachings of Al-Anon. As C. Wright Mills (1959) cautions, people's personal troubles take place in and are influenced by larger issues of social organization and culture. An aspect of the larger culture of any social problem is the ownership of it – what social organizations exercise expert or legal claim over the problem? Paradoxically, lay association of the term *codependent* with Al-Anon is disputed by some Al-Anon groups. The senior author attended a panel discussion during which a speaker representing Al-Anon explained that the word *codependent* is a 'therapy term, not an Al-Anon term,' and that the Twelve Traditions of Al-Anon explicitly proscribe the use of any teachings other than those formally contained in the Twelve Steps of AA/Al-Anon and the AA/Al-Anon Slogans. She went on to say that codependency is an outside term and that Al-Anon groups (such as her own) that strictly adhere to Al-Anon teachings discourage the use of the word *codependent* by members. These larger organizational inconsistencies would only seem to reinforce the conceptual ambiguity of the concept of codependency.

In sum, then, these women tend to engage in retrospective reinterpretation of their lives with their alcoholic husbands, using these reconstructions legitimated by family problem personnel as self-evidence of their codependency. This new awareness of codependency is extrapolated not only to their own daily lives but to those of others around them. Pressure to conform to the label and to take the path of least resistance to the labelling process comes from formal and informal sources, yet some women do resist this process. The guilt that may accompany this resistance may be indicative of the pressure against it.

DISCUSSION

Following Mills's (1959) caution to locate personal troubles within the wider historical context of societal issues, we suggest that the process of becoming codependent is the result of a convolution of the illness metaphor and labelling process. It is our contention that this convolution is a twofold process involving, on the one hand, a deviantizing of the wife's behaviour by others and self, and on the other, the medicalization of this alleged deviance.

The labelling perspective emphasizes the social processes of designating and labelling deviance, especially the interactions between the labeller and the labelled (e.g., Becker 1963; Erickson 1962; Kitsuse 1962). To the extent that women married to alcoholics are viewed as non-normative in their behaviour and there are attempts to rehabilitate them, they are recipients of deviant designations. 'Human behaviour is deviant to the extent that it comes to be viewed as involving a personally discreditable departure from a group's normative expectations, and it elicits interpersonal or collective reactions that serve to "isolate," "treat," "correct," or "punish" individuals engaged in such behaviors' (Schur 1971, 24).

The possible emergence of a label, such as 'codependent,' as a defining feature of the wife is suggested by Lofland's (1969) claim that when categories of a set of dimensions begin to cluster, one of the clustered categories – a pivotal category – is treated as the significant feature of a person being dealt with and defines who the person is. He views this as a historically variable phenomenon related to the interests of moral entrepreneurs, suggesting that 'the imputation of actors as deviant can have as much or more to do with who is coding with what category under what circumstances than with simple discernment of specially differentiated deviant persons' (Lofland 1969, 144).

The notion of deviance in the wife of the alcoholic is closely related to the notion of illness largely through what has been called the medicalization of the deviance process (e.g., Conrad and Schneider 1980). Conrad and Schneider expand on the idea of illness as a metaphor popularized by Szasz (1961) by citing a general societal trend away from deviance designations (badness) towards medical interpretations (sickness) in the areas of madness, drunkenness, opiate use, child delinquency, hyperactivity, child abuse, homosexuality, and criminality. Medical designations are conventionally treated as if they are rational, scientifically verifiable, and morally neutral. As the authors caution, however, they are social, political, and moral designations. Indeed, illnesses represent human judgments of conditions in the natural world and, as such, are social creations.

We have examined a situation in which the commonly used, yet notably ambiguous, concept of codependency applied to women married to alcoholics, becomes even more evasive as we attempt to clarify and extract the meaning imputed to it by its users. Briefly, we observed two common definitional themes: (1) notions of caretaking and pleasing others, and (2) affliction by association with a chemically dependent person. On the other hand, we were able to isolate a number of rather pronounced differences of opinion regarding the nature and substance of codependency: (1) whether codependency involves a substantial alteration of oneself, (2) whether codependency is an innate personal characteristic or a learned social role, (3) whether codependency is unique to alcohol-complicated relationships, (4) whether codependency is a disease, and (5) whether codependency is a temporary or permanent condition. Most of the women in this study employed at least the general perspective of codependency as a way of understanding their own biographies, personal life situations, and the behaviour and attitudes of others with similar biographies and situations. The assumption of the identity 'codependent' appeared both to mitigate the stigma of their association with an alcoholic husband and to render comprehensible many problematics in their everyday lives.

It would seem that three primary factors account for the widespread acceptance of the identity 'codependent' on the part of these women. Surely, the promotion by the alcoholism industry of the inevitability of being codependent by virtue of being married to an alcoholic is the underlying organizational element. Most of the women simply accepted the existence of codependency as a taken-for-granted feature of any alcoholic marriage. They did not question the ontological status of the condition and were unable to disclaim their identification with the status since their husbands already had been labelled alcoholics. As well, the very definitional ambiguity of the concept allowed the women to pick and choose among the varied characteristics of codependency. They could, so to speak, choose the kind of codependent they wanted to be. For some, the assumption of the identity 'codependent' involved a lifelong commitment to a fundamental change of self. To others, it resulted in a relatively mild alteration of behaviour, attitude, and identity. While we might question the validity of a concept that allows such ease and range of applicability, it is difficult to deny its utility in providing a personal frame of reference for understanding certain difficulties in these women's lives. Finally, it is the nature of these difficulties themselves that provided a nurturing context for the assumption of the identity. The fact that these women were confused, bewildered, and upset by the circumstances in their lives certainly increased their receptivity to ideas that would resolve their difficulties. But it is not only their willingness, or even eagerness, to think and act differently that is significant. It is also the very anticipation that their lives would change by their participation in the family program and Al-Anon that very importantly facilitated their assumption of the identity 'codependent.'

There is little question that in assuming the identity of codependency, the women in this study were better able to comprehend their thoughts, feelings, and behaviours as well as those of their husbands. However, the nature of this comprehension is somewhat troubling. On the one hand, the traditional passive role of women vis-à-vis men is reinforced. Conventional perspectives on women married to alcoholics, not unlike historical perspectives on women in general, place women within a framework of relative passivity. In the case of codependency, women are said to be reacting to their husbands' progressive alcoholism. Ironically, as these women actively seek a new understanding of their alcohol-complicated relationships and construct new lifestyles, the perspective they encounter from professionals helps to perpetuate the image of being passive and reactive. When a woman takes on the identity of codependent, she is accepting the fact that who she is depends on to whom she is/was married. Discovering that she is codependent is an acknowledgement that her behaviour and attitudes have been formed by her association with an alcoholic. Aptly, her husband is the dependent; she only the codependent. It is true that exposure to this perspective may help her to see that more initiative and independence are required for change in the future[2], however, it instils a self-ownership of one's passivity a priori.

One final disconcerting feature of the perspective of codependency is its close association with the perspective of medicalization. To become codependent in this society is increasingly to become sick. Our inquiries into the manner in which women negotiate the reality and relevance of codependency in their lives reveal that the process occurs within the context of a twofold labelling process. This labelling involves, initially, a deviantizing of the women's identity and life situation and, subsequently, a medicalization of this alleged deviance. While this does not necessarily force a return to the old model that women married to alcoholics are psychopathological, it would be well to bear in mind Susan Sontag's observations regarding the two hypotheses involved in the expansion of the illness metaphor: (1) that every form of social deviation can be considered an illness, and (2) that every illness can be considered psychologically. 'These two hypotheses are complementary. As the first seems to relieve guilt, the second reinstates it. Psychological theories of illness are a powerful means of placing the blame on the ill. Patients who are instructed that they have, unwittingly, caused their disease are also made to feel that they have deserved it' (Sontag 1978, 55–6).

IMPLICATIONS FOR FURTHER RESEARCH

Characteristic of exploratory studies, this investigation has generated more questions than answers, raising several issues that deserve further inquiry. Because this sample included only women, we are led to ask what the experiences of male spouses of alcoholics might entail. Long-term longitudinal data on the relation between self-definition of codependency and subsequent behaviours and life experiences would also enhance our understanding. A fuller grasp of the prevalence and scope of both formal and informal labelling of codependency would help us to assess better the initiation, application, resistance, acceptance, and rejection of the label. As we have illustrated, it is primarily in the formal intervention programs for family members of alcoholics that the spouse is likely to be labelled codependent. However, 'the manifestations of co-dependency are protean, its criteria unclear and its boundaries vague' (Gierymski and Williams 1986, 12). We suggest that a straightforward program that encourages the wives of alcoholics to think more constructively about their life situations without involving the illness/disorder model inherent in the idea of codependency would be both more time- and cost-effective. It would also soften the stigma of their participation in an alcoholic marriage and avoid the pitfalls that have been associated with the rampant medicalization of human problems (Conrad and Schneider 1980). At the very least, 'it would seem that the vast Al-Anon network of self-help groups – together with treatment-center family programs and other low-cost, short-term, group-oriented, supportive and educational services – can address the needs of those family members who do not require medical and psychiatric intervention. Those who do require such interventions can still find care without the premature introduction of a syndrome for which there are inadequate theoretically established boundaries and meanings, and which lacks convincing empirical support' (Gierymski and Williams 1986, 12).

On a more macro level, we can ask what benefits accrue to the treatment establishment by urging disease status for spouses of alcoholics. Too, the dynamics and politics of organizational and institutional ownership or avoidance of the label may shed light on larger sociocultural issues, such as problem 'maximization' and 'deflation' (Room 1984) in the alcoholism industry. If we draw any one point from these questions and our own initial inquiry, it would be that more thorough articulation and examination of the social construction of codependency are called for.

This article appeared in *The International Journal of Addictions*, Vol. 23(4), 1988, pp. 331-50. Reprinted with permission.

NOTES

1 However, the increasing medicalization of the idea of codependency, as we will see, may in fact eventuate in the re-establishment of a psychopathological model.

2 Our thanks to James Orford for noting this possibility.

REFERENCES

Becker, H.S. *Outsiders*. New York: Free Press, 1963.

Blumer, H. Society as a symbolic interaction. In A. Rose (ed.), *Human Behavior and Social Processes*. Boston: Houghton Mifflin, 1962.

Conrad, P., and J. Schneider. *Deviance and Medicalization*. St Louis: C.V. Mosby, 1980.

Erickson, K.T. Notes on the Sociology of Deviance. *Soc. Probl.* 9: 307–14, 1962.

Gierymski, T., and T. Williams. Codependency. *J. Psychoactive Drugs* 9: 7–13, 1986.

Goffman, E. The moral career of the mental patient. In E. Goffman, *Asylums*. Garden City: Doubleday, 1961.

Jackson, J.K. The adjustment of the family to the crisis of alcoholism. *Q.J. Stud. Alcoholism* 15: 562–86, 1954.

– The adjustment of the family to alcoholism. *Marriage Family* 18: 361–95, 1956.

– Alcoholism and the family. In D.J. Pittman and C.R. Snyder (eds), *Society, Culture, and Drinking Patterns*. New York: Wiley, 1962.

James, J.E., and M. Goldman. Behavior trends of wives of alcoholics. *Q.J. Stud. Alcoholism* 32: 373–81, 1971.

Kitsuse, J.I. Societal reaction to deviant behavior. *Soc. Probl.* 9: 247–56, 1962.

Lazarus, R.S. *Psychological Stress and the Coping Process*. New York: McGraw-Hill, 1966.

Lemert, E.M. *Social Pathology*. New York: McGraw-Hill, 1951.

– The occurrence and sequence of events in the adjustment of families to alcoholism. *Q.J. Stud. Alcohol* 21: 679–97, 1960.

– Dependency in married alcoholics. *Q.J. Stud. Alcohol* 23: 590–609, 1962.

Lofland, J., with L. Lofland. *Deviance and Identity*. Englewood Cliffs, NJ: Prentice-Hall, 1969.

Mills, C.W. *The Sociological Imagination*. New York: Oxford, 1969.

Orford, J., and S. Guthrie. Coping behavior used by wives of alcoholics: A preliminary investigation. *International Congress on Alcohol and Alcoholism* Abstract 28: 97, 1968.

Orford, J. Alcoholism and marriage: The argument against specialism. *J. Stud. Alcohol* 36: 1537–63, 1975.

Orford, J., S. Guthrie, P. Nicholls, E. Oppenheimer, S. Egert and C. Hensman. Self-reported coping behavior of wives of alcoholics and its association with drinking outcome. *J. Stud. Alcohol* 36: 1254–676, 1975.

Orford, J., E. Oppenheimer, S. Egert, C. Hensman, and S. Guthrie. The cohesiveness of alcoholism-complicated marriages and its influence on treatment outcome. *Br. J. Psychiatry* 128: 318–29, 1976.

Room, R. Alcohol and ethnography: A case of problem deflation? *Curr. Anthropol.* 25: 169–91, 1984.

Schur, E.M. *Labeling Deviant Behavior.* New York: Harper and Row, 1971.

Sontag, S. *Illness as Metaphor.* London: Penguin, 1978.

Szasz, T. *The Myth of Mental Illness.* New York: Hoeber-Harper, 1961.

Whitfield, C. Co-alcoholism: Recognizing a treatable illness. *Fam. Comm. Health.* 7(2): 16–28, 1984.

Wiseman, J. An alternative role in the wife of an alcoholic in Finland. *J. Marr. Fam.* 37: 172–9, 1975(a).

– *Social forces and the politics of research approaches: Studying the wives of alcoholics.* Paper presented at Conference of Women and Their Health: Implications of a New Era, University of California at San Francisco, August 1–2, 1975(b).

JANE SLOVEN, LCSW

Codependent or Empathically Responsive? Two Views of Betty

INTRODUCTION

An important part of our task as therapists is to choose a theoretical framework through which to view the problems our clients present. Choosing one theoretical framework over another is similar to the use of a camera lens. One can choose a telephoto lens, sharpening the focus on just one part of the picture, or one can choose a wide-angle lens and capture the larger picture. The choice of a lens in treatment not only influences our clients' perceptions of their problems and of themselves, it also determines treatment choices and treatment outcomes.

This paper explores the marital problem of one couple by comparing and contrasting two different lenses that are focused on the experience of the female partner in the marriage. One lens is the popular concept of 'codependency.' Codependency is a descriptive label that emerged from the field of chemical dependency treatment. It has been adopted by many therapists and clients to refer to women in relationships with addicted or otherwise dysfunctional partners. It focuses very specifically on the women in these relationships and their behaviour.

The contrasting framework is the evolving concept of 'Self in Relation,' a psychological theory of development that has emerged from the work of feminist psychotherapists at the Stone Center for Developmental Services and Studies at Wellesley College. Its focus is broad and inclusive of many aspects of women's lives and relationships.

These two theories, or 'lenses,' provide ideal points of comparison in demonstrating the ways that one's perspective on female experience can radically affect the course of treatment.

Definitions of codependent behaviour attempt to establish a paradigm of disease. They pathologize women's experience, labelling a woman's traditional 'other focus' as unhealthy while ignoring its value to human relationships. This lens ignores the social, political, and economic factors that contribute to women's highly developed skills in these areas.

In contrast, self in relation theory explores the development of women's sense of self and hypothesizes that *healthy* development occurs for women in the context of relationship. This theory values and honours the skills of empathy and attention to connection in relationship. This wider lens incorporates social, political, and economic factors into psychological assessment.

Self in relation theory is inherently feminist in perspective, while codependency theory is not. This paper will demonstrate that while the goals of treatment conducted from either perspective are very similar, the means of achieving those goals has a radically different impact on a woman's experience of herself and on the ultimate integrity of any relationship she seeks to sustain. The theoretical stance of self in relation can be integrated much more consistently with feminist family therapy practice.

CASE HISTORY

Betty came to see me on the recommendation of her family physician. Betty was experiencing chronic back pain and neck pain. Recently, she had begun to have episodes of spastic colitis, an illness that was common in her family. At sixty-five, Betty presented as an intelligent, attractive, upper-middle-class woman.

Betty was employed as the office manager for a medium-size legal firm. She managed an office staff of five and personally oversaw all the billing. She had had the position for fifteen years, received excellent reviews, felt secure, and obtained great satisfaction from her work.

The problem, Betty said, was her marriage. A year previously, her husband, George, had told her he was in love with another woman. Although he had been acting oddly, Betty was unprepared for this as an explanation. They had been married for forty-five years, had three grown children, and had lived in the same comfortable community for most of their adult lives. Betty was stunned. She had felt George might have been experiencing a mid-life crisis: he was moody, unpredictable, and often working late; nevertheless, Betty had expected the problem to pass.

George had asked for a divorce and was not willing to discuss his feelings. Betty went to visit her oldest daughter. When she returned, George told her he had changed his mind and wanted to stay married. He said he was finished with the affair and loved Betty. Otherwise, he wouldn't discuss what had occurred.

Betty felt greatly relieved but confused. She sought a therapist. She and George began conjoint sessions. Betty felt that the therapist sided with George. 'He said I'd just have to get used to George seeing and talking to Hazel (his former lover) because Hazel ran one of the corporate subsidiaries and there was no way to avoid contact if George was to do his job.' Betty was threatened by the continuing contact. George would not change jobs; the therapist supported George's position on the issue. Betty felt she and George argued uncontrollably in the sessions and left them as unresolved and in conflict as they began. She and George dropped out of treatment after two months.

Three more months passed, and Betty and George were still fighting. They got along for a few days, but when Betty tried to talk to George about her feelings or to ask him to talk to her about his, they'd erupt into conflict. George didn't want to talk, according to Betty. He said, 'What's done is done,' and he was not explaining anything. Betty couldn't understand why George had had the affair or why he had ended it. She felt that without an understanding of the problems in the marriage that had led to the affair, they would be unable to create a secure marriage for the future. She was plagued with the question, 'Why? Why the affair? Why end the affair and return?' As George continued to refuse to discuss it, Betty became more obsessed with her questions. She would pursue George with these questions, and George would withdraw further. Betty would cry herself to sleep, and George would sleep in his daughter's old room.

When Betty first came to see me, she said George refused to return for couples counselling and she was unable to continue living as she'd been living. Betty's existence had been focused around her husband and family and now, since the kids had grown and had families of their own in other cities, her day-to-day life focused on her husband and her job. She was fine at work but dreaded returning home at night. She felt old, unattractive, and uninteresting when she was with George. Betty's sense of herself was deteriorating; work was the only place where she felt self-assured.

In looking at Betty's family history, I learned that she was one of five children. As the oldest, she was responsible from an early age for caretaking, since her mother was often dysfunctional owing to colitis attacks. Betty felt her mother asked to be taken care of by everyone and appreciated little. Betty idealized her father. What affection and attention she received came from him. She described her parents' relationship with each other as distant and unaffectionate. Betty took care of her siblings from an early age and had close relationships with three of her sisters but a distant relationship with her youngest sister, who was closest to her mother and had always received much of her mother's attention, according to Betty. Betty had been aligned with Dad, while her youngest sister had been aligned with Mom. Something in the mother-daughter relationship hadn't worked, and Betty still carried feelings of rejection and resentment. She felt no matter how hard she tried, she could never satisfy Mom, and no matter how little her youngest sister did, it was always more than enough.

In sessions, Betty had great difficulty focusing on herself. She spoke repeatedly of George, his behaviour, her inability to understand his motivations for the affair or for deciding to end the affair, the ensuing arguments, her frustration. She began to consider divorce. Betty could easily focus on her concerns about George, but when asked what *she* felt, she said she felt confused, she didn't understand why George had the affair, she didn't know how she could feel comfortable in the marriage if she didn't know why he strayed or why he stayed. Betty didn't feel he was paying attention to her, she didn't feel he really cared about her or for her. Betty couldn't focus on what *she* felt about herself or what she *needed*, aside from George's saying that he loved her and needed her and had had the affair because he was temporarily deranged.

George was invited in for one session. He seemed a self-possessed, rigid man. He spoke of his desire to stay in the marriage and his difficulty understanding Betty. He felt the affair had ended and there was no need to discuss it. He said he had no feelings about it. George also said he couldn't understand Betty's emotional reactions to him; he felt she was emotionally ill. Betty had described George as impervious to her questions about motivation and feelings. It appeared clear that George was not able to experience his own feelings and so was unable to empathize with Betty's.

Considering the factors involved in this case, I wondered which lens to choose. Would a framework defining Betty's behaviour as 'codependent' work well for her, or would a framework of 'self in relation' be more appropriate? What would be the consequences of either choice?

CODEPENDENCY THEORY

The concept of codependency evolved out of the chemical dependency field. Substance abuse counsellors working with alcoholics and addicts often found that as their 'primary' clients got better, others in the family got worse. They noticed that spouses, oldest children, and other family members seemed as 'addicted' to overfunctioning for the chemically dependent person as the chemically dependent person was to the substance. It became clear that the behaviours of family members were organized around the behaviour of the chemically dependent person. The intractability of this focus was labelled as its own disease process, co-alcoholism, para-alcoholism, and then codependency. This allowed everyone in the family to have a 'disease' from which they could 'recover.' The Twelve Steps of AA and Al-Anon could then be utilized by codependents as a way of learning to live their own lives, regardless of the behaviour of the chemically dependent person. As children of alcoholics began to receive attention and treatment, and adult children of alcoholics began to identify the consequences of growing up in alcoholic families, the concept of codependency grew. The establishment of the National Association for Children of Alcoholics (NACOA) increased national awareness.

The definition of codependency, however, shortly began to be applied to a variety of people. Anyone who grew up in a family with 'dysfunction' and rigid rules could be classified as 'codependent' regardless of the presence or absence of chemical dependency. Different definitions of codependency evolved. One early and popular definition was supplied by Melody Beattie: 'One who has let another person's behavior affect him or her, and who is obsessed with controlling that person's behavior ... The heart of the definition and recovery lies not in the *other person* – no matter how much we believe it does. It lies in ourselves, in the ways we try to affect them: the obsessing, the controlling, the obsessive "helping," caretaking, low self-worth bordering on self-hatred, self-repression, abundance of anger and guilt ... other centeredness that results in abandonment of self' (1987, 31–2). Another definition, which focuses on the style of behaviour, was offered by Sharon Wegscheider-Cruse (1985): 'A specific condition that is characterized by preoccupation and extreme dependence (emotionally, socially and sometimes physically) on a person or object. Eventually, this dependence on another person becomes a pathological condition that affects the co-dependent in all other relationships' (1985, 2).

Many varied definitions have appeared; all describe similar traits, including external reference (being other-directed), dishonesty, control, perfectionism, fear, rigidity, judgmentalism, inferiority/grandiosity, self-centredness, and not dealing with feelings in a healthy way (Schaef 1986, 42). Codependents have also been described as having difficulty experiencing appropriate levels of self-esteem, setting functional boundaries, owning and expressing their own reality, taking care of their adult needs and wants, and experiencing and expressing their reality moderately (Mellody et al. 1989).

George is not chemically dependent, yet Betty has let his behaviour become the focus of her daily life. She is 'externally referent.' *Her* behaviour can be defined as obsession with controlling *his* behaviour. She's worried he will get reinvolved with Hazel. Her behaviour can be defined as controlling – questioning him constantly, calling him at work, driving by to see if his car is there. Her sense of her own self-worth at this point is abysmally low, and at times she feels intense self-hatred. She has an abundance of anger and rage and guilt about those feelings. Her focus on George results in abandonment of her own needs and of her sense of self. Betty is anxious, she somatizes, she feels victimized, she is exhausted, angry and confused, all characteristic codependent traits (Beattie 1987, 37–9).

But, she's been in a marriage for forty-five years, and George has had an affair which he has been loath to discuss. Is her need to feel good in relationship with George pathological? Is her need for him, her unhappiness at the change in status of her marriage evidence of unhealthy characteristics of codependency springing out of her own emotional insecurity? Some of Betty's reactions are normal, expectable reactions to this situation, but Betty isn't able to work through her feelings and move on, and the feelings are heightened by George's recalcitrance and unwillingness to engage in dialogue and full disclosure of his feelings to Betty. None the less, Betty's inability to see her own deterioration and to honour her own needs, her inability to detach, and her increasing obsession with George could clearly be labelled codependent behaviour.

Treatment Implications of a Codependency Model

If I choose to view this situation through a codependency lens, how does treatment proceed and how is Betty asked to view herself? A comprehensive treatment format for codependency has been outlined by Timmen L. Cermak in *Diagnosing and Treating Codependence.* His format labels the four stages of treatment as: 'Survival,' 'Reidentification,' 'Core Issues,' and 'Reintegration.' Treatment first involves accepting the label of 'codependent,' which requires a breakdown of denial. 'Codependents place a premium on maintaining their behaviour as voluntary. While this appears to be in direct contradiction to the compulsivity which runs their lives, it makes sense if it is perceived as a *denial of limitations.* Codependents take pride in believing that they can always draw on their willpower to tolerate one more disappointment. This belief creates the illusion that they are in control while everything around them is out of control' (Cermak 1986, 70).

After accepting the label, other expected accomplishments in treatment involve taking responsibility for the perpetuation of one's own problems and dysfunctional behaviour; accepting one's limitations; recognizing that one's life has become unmanageable as a result of trying to control the uncontrollable; giving up the illusion of power and grieving its loss; exploring compulsivity; developing independence and autonomy; and finally, integrating a sense of personal power and self-worth. This model of treatment has been adapted from the traditional approach to alcoholism, a crucial element being the acceptance of alcohol abuse as a disease over which one is powerless. The use of Al-Anon and CODA meetings, along with the Twelve Steps and sponsorship, is part of treatment.

Cermak's stages and treatment recommendations can neatly fit Betty's dilemma. Some of the treatment goals are ones that most therapists would choose even without this framework. Stage one requires forming an empathic connection with one's client, obviously essential to any successful treatment approach. Phase two focuses on looking at one's limitations, that is, what one is able, realistically, to effect, and what one cannot effect. This is a usual part of goal setting in most treatment frameworks. Working on communication processes and skill development in this area is integral to most treatment models. Working with a client to help her/him to identify and feel feelings and to begin to grieve losses is, again, generally accepted treatment. One may or may not look at how one avoids grief by labelling behaviours 'compulsive.' One normally will explore patterns of behaviour that have been tried and have not worked to bring about change.

One of the initial and important solutions for codependency involves 'detachment,' trying to separate ourselves emotionally from problems that cannot be controlled. Operating from a codependency model of treatment would involve referring Betty to Al-Anon to try to help her detach from her focus on changing George. The Al-Anon daily book, *One Day at a Time*, speaks to this issue eloquently: 'When we hear an Al-Anon member say, "detach from the problem," we may think rebelliously: "How can I detach from my own wife or husband? Our lives are bound together and I am involved whether I want to be or not." That is true, but there are kinds of involvement that can only make our difficulties worse. We make trouble for ourselves when we interfere with the alcoholic's activities, trying to find out where he is, what he's been doing, where the money went. Suspicious searching and prying will only keep us in a state of turmoil, make the situation worse instead of improving it' (1985, 131).

The choice of a referral of Betty to Al-Anon would involve substituting George's name for alcohol, so that she could remain aware that she is powerless over *his* choices and behaviour. Although George was not drinking, Betty's feelings and behaviours could be seen as organized around *his* behaviour. A support system composed of others in similar difficult situations is central to Twelve-Step programs such as AA, Al-Anon, and CODA (Codependents Anonymous).

Treated from a codependency model, Betty would be expected to explore the ways in which she had exacerbated her problems, such as looking in George's pockets, checking to see if his car was at the office when he said he was working late, pursuing him to talk when he said that he didn't want to. Betty would evaluate these behaviours in the light of her own compulsivity. She would begin to understand what factors in her own behaviour create and maintain this obsession, and she would learn how to stop these behaviours. Betty would be encouraged to call people in the program when she felt the compulsion to pursue George. She would be encouraged to rely on her 'higher power' and to 'let go and let God.' She would have inspirational literature to read at such times, along with a variety of meetings where she could speak of her difficulties to a supportive audience.

In therapy sessions, she would focus on her feelings, and therapy could incorporate cognitive, behavioural, and family systems techniques. Betty would explore her family of origin, looking at the dysfunctional family rules and the ways in which other family members may have engaged in compulsive behaviours to avoid feelings. Betty might be seen in group, with other women who define themselves as codependents. Group therapy would provide support for expressing feelings, for growth, and for change.

There is tremendous support within this context for women undergoing change. Self-help groups provide free support meetings, available day or night, weekday or weekend, lots of literature, many other people available to accept one unconditionally. These aspects of support-group involvement can be immensely healing. Combined with therapy, it is a powerful treatment. Its wildfire-like spread among the population attests to its magnetism and easy applicability.

What this model requires, however, is that Betty define herself as a person who has a disease, 'codependency,' and is now in recovery. She becomes not simply a woman who has suffered a loss of faith and trust in her life partner, but the framework requires that she define her responses for the past year as emanating from a disease process that has affected her for years and stems from a dysfunctional family of origin. She must develop a sense of acceptance about her limitations and accept responsibility for *creating* unmanageability in her life.

Working in the codependency framework requires that Betty accept that these problems emanated from her denial of limitations, her exercise of willpower, and her need for control. The framework requires that the focus be on Betty and her compulsivity. The model minimizes the centrality, power, and importance of a shift or loss in Betty's most primary relationship – her marriage. It minimizes the interactional patterns that contribute to Betty's feelings of self-worth and her desire to *know* what she can expect. It places the locus of the problem in Betty. This model negates the impact of relationship and context on feelings and behaviour. It is normal to be affected by those we relate to. This isn't only Betty's problem, it is also George's and the marriage's problem. Betty cannot resolve the problem simply by detaching.

Betty's experience is also affected by the real difficulties she would face if she chose to leave George. Betty's income is half of George's income. For her to leave him and start life over as a single woman in her mid-sixties with one-third of their combined income puts her at a serious economic disadvantage. Her religious beliefs do not permit divorce. She would also face the last years of life suddenly without her life's partner, socially, economically, and physically vulnerable to the consequences of aging. The changes in lifestyle would be difficult and would involve further loss and pain. George also has a higher chance of remarrying, and those social consequences cannot be ignored.

Inherent in the codependency model is an oversimplification of the existential issues we all confront. The fact that 'much of the universe lies outside our ability to influence it by force of will' creates a sense of fear and inadequacy in anyone who chooses honestly to confront the nature of human existence. A sense of loss and a fear of personal inadequacy are certainly not pathological ways of responding to such realities. Turning such responses into a simplistic formulation of individual pathology denies the social and universal forces that affect all of us as human beings in a complex world. We are powerless to change much of what affects us daily and much of what is crucial to our well-being: the quality of our air, water, food, the influence of corporate, military, and political forces on our lives, the security of our banking institutions, the safety of our streets in inner cities. There is a reality to the experience of powerlessness in these arenas and it is often an adaptive response to take control of people and issues we have a better chance of influencing. Looking at the latter without the former distorts the nature of reality.

SELF IN RELATION THEORY

A theory that clearly incorporates culture, gender, social, economic, and political factors into psychological development has emerged from the Stone Center at Wellesley College. Essentially, recent research has differentiated development of the 'self' for women from development of the 'self' for men. Traditional theory on self-development now appears to be gender specific to men. Surrey distinguished self in relation from traditional theory in an early (1985) working paper. She has said that current theory places great emphasis on separation as an important aspect of individual development, separation from mother in early childhood, separation from family in adolescence and separation from mentors in adulthood (Surrey 1985).

These staged periods of separation have been conceptualized as crucial in order for individuals to develop a sense of autonomy, independence, and a clearly defined sense of self. While these stages may accurately reflect male development in this culture, a self in relation model suggests that women's development takes place differently; for women the self is 'organized and developed in the context of important relationships' (ibid.). Relationships, not stages of separation, become the primary goal of development and other aspects of self are seen as developing in this context. Interpretations that make separation central to psychological health incorrectly interpret women's development. If separation is seen as the 'hallmark of maturity,' women's focus on connection and relationship will inevitably be defined as 'other' and pathologized (Stiver, 1985).

The Stone Center Papers chart an evolving theory of women's psychological development. Basic themes include the importance of empathy, explorations of the ways empathy develops, and a focus on the connections between people in the process of psychological growth (Surrey, Kaplan, and Jordan 1990). Empathy has been described as a 'cognitive and emotional activity in which one person is able to experience the feelings and thoughts of another person and simultaneously is able to know his/her own different feelings and thoughts.' (Jordan 1984). This capacity has not been a focus of psychological theory, nor until now has it been valued for the high levels of 'cognitive and emotional integration' needed to develop it (Miller 1986). Jordan has stated that for women empowerment and self-knowledge flow from the experience of mutual empathy.

Treatment choices in a self in relation model are myriad. One can utilize individual, group, couple, or family therapy styles, as long as treatment is focused on issues of mutual relatedness and empathic connection. In this model development of autonomy and separation would not be the hallmarks of health; rather, the capacity to experience empathy and the development of skills to enlarge this capacity would be central to treatment. The relationship developed with the therapist would encourage empathic connectedness and would model relationship capacity as an indication of healthy development.

From a self in relation perspective, Betty's problem would be viewed as a failure in empathic relatedness. Because empathy is an interactional experience, the problem is defined as an interactional failure, not as an individual one. Betty may contribute to a breakdown of empathy because of her anxious, overresponsible behaviour. She cannot empathize with George's thoughts and feelings, however, because he is unable or unwilling to express them. He seems equally unable to experience her thoughts and feelings.

From the perspective of male socialization, there are several factors that contribute to George's failure of empathy. Men's development does not focus on relationship skills but on separation, autonomy, and independence. Skills for nurturance and empathy are not highly valued aspects of male development in this culture. When George is asked to utilize those skills of connectedness, his developmental deficits are obvious.

There are numerous consequences of empathic failure. When one feels distress and attempts to communicate it, then experiences an absence of empathy, the distress deepens. Feelings of fear and anger arise from the lack of responsiveness. This mix of feelings creates confusion. If the interaction can be corrected and one's feelings are ultimately accepted, one becomes less frightened and less isolated. The capacity to redo the interaction creates a sense of competence. The failure to make connections on a continuing basis with another person creates a profound sense of loss and inadequacy. Feelings are experienced as unacceptable and the self is experienced as inadequate.

Other consequences can include feeling immobilized, feeling that taking action will get one into trouble, loss of self-esteem, and fear that one's feelings and behaviour might result in further cut-off and isolation. If disconnection continues, the person seeking contact may try to change herself. The inability to affect the relationship is extremely damaging; the ability to affect the relationship by reconnecting is extremely empowering (Miller 1988).

Betty and George recognized that they had experienced a profound disconnection when George asked for a divorce. The relationship had obviously already suffered from multiple lapses of contact, which laid the groundwork for George to seek intimacy elsewhere. George's request for a divorce, however, made the depth of this estrangement overt. At this point Betty reacted with shock, fear, and anger. When she tried to communicate these feelings to George, he was closed to discussion. Betty felt confused, increasingly frightened by her feelings, and incompetent emotionally. The more Betty tried to engage George and failed, the more incompetent and frustrated she felt. She experienced a deep sense of loss and personal inadequacy. She feared that future attempts to pursue would cause George to leave her, yet she felt a growing sense of isolation from him.

The fears one experiences as a consequence of empathic failure when a longstanding relationship becomes threatened are a normal and realistic response to loss. The process of trying to reconnect in any way possible is understandable. Betty recognized that at sixty-five she cannot become a younger woman (Hazel is thirty-five), but she has struggled with finding a way to become more 'acceptable' to George.

Alexandra Kaplan has talked about women's tendency to take responsibility for any relational failures. She feels that this tendency
often leads to depression in women and that this accounts for the
significant ratio differential for depression in women and men. 'As
women in general experience failure or frustration in their attempts
at effective connection with others, they, themselves, take responsibility for the relational failure assuming that if they were "better" they
would not have such problems' (1984, 3).

Other issues have arisen for Betty as she has contemplated her
choices. Betty has thought of leaving George, but she has concerns
about the impact on the extended family. She fears the consequences
of emotional upheaval for her daughters, their marriages, and her
grandchildren.

When women contemplate the use of power on their own behalf
and for their own interests, many of them equate the prospect with
destructiveness and selfishness – characteristics that they cannot rec-
oncile with a sense of feminine identity. Moreover, they feel that the
use of power may lead to 'abandonment, which threatens a central
part of women's identity that affirms the need for relationships with
other people' (Miller 1982, 1).

The importance of relatedness to Betty, the value she places on connections, presents a major conflict. If she leaves George in order to
focus on herself, she may be seen as selfish and destructive. She may
see herself as selfish, which will be intolerable, and she clearly is concerned about the damage to her daughters and their families.

The Treatment Implications of a Self in Relation Approach

If the lens of 'self in relation' is chosen for Betty's treatment, couples
therapy would be recommended. This is an interpersonal issue, as well
as an individual issue for both Betty and George, and it has implications
for the extended family. Obtaining George's agreement to participate
in conjoint counselling is crucial in order to give Betty and George
assistance in making and maintaining relational connection. George's
relational skills are very likely limited. Betty would be asked to deal
with the reality of George's skills and limitations as well as with her
own limited ability to change him. Therapeutic intervention must assist
George to develop a greater capacity for empathy and connection while
supporting and affirming Betty's desire and capacity to create the same.
Her skills at relatedness and her capacity for empathy would be iden-

tified, validated, and supported. Their relationship would be explored, with particular emphasis on failures in empathy or mutual relatedness. Both of their histories in other relationships would be explored. If they are unable to redefine the relationship, the context will exist to bring in extended family members to help grieve the end of the marriage. If George will not enter treatment, individual work could proceed with Betty, with an exploration of the relationship disconnection and realistic options for future choices. This lens values and validates Betty.

The self in relation model would focus upon relatedness and movement in relationship as opposed to control or self-sufficiency. The focus is on looking to the meanings people have attached to their pain and how those meanings have affected their understanding of life experience (Jordan 1989). Utilizing both Betty and George's histories of relational failures, exploring and grieving past losses, and connecting these histories with their present reactions to each other would be part of the therapy process.

The Effects of the Choice of Lens

The choice of a codependency lens versus a self in relation lens would have a marked impact on Betty's treatment and on her view of herself. Goals of therapy in a self in relation model are not the 'attainment of a state of harmony and happiness' but rather the development of an openness to learning and growth as well as the capacity to tolerate tension and conflict so that connections can be retained (Jordan 1989). Sometimes, however, a fact of relational life is that mutuality and empathic connections fail. People change, and those with whom we have been intimate close up to us. Fear, sadness, denial, and attempts to reconnect are not pathological. A self in relation model would say 'suffering becomes a cause for joining others in alleviating pain and developing compassion. This is very different from experiencing suffering as a personal injury which reveals personal insufficiency' (ibid., 4).

The danger of using a codependency model lies in the facile equation of focus on relationship with symptoms of illness – 'defects of character.' This attribution feels to many women like 'personal insufficiency.' The focus on attaining a state of serenity may short circuit not only the development of skills in tolerating tension and conflict, but the realistic and adult expectation that life at times involves tolerating pain. It is crucial for women to learn to accept limits without pathologizing them.

In a self in relation model of therapy, Betty could experience her feelings in a context of mutually responsive relationship and any failures of empathic connection could be examined. As an adjunct to therapy, work in a Twelve-Step program could be helpful to Betty if she could disregard the concept of disease. Betty could use the program to explore what behaviours of George were beyond her control as well as to develop other mutually enhancing relationships. Therapy would validate her desire and capacity for connection. These interventions differ from use of a codependency model in one very crucial aspect: a codependency model could too easily view relational needs and skills as pathology and tell Betty she has to recover from her compulsive need to connect. This distinction results in a profoundly different perspective in Betty's view of herself.

In either framework, Betty can learn to change what can be changed, accept what cannot be changed, and move on. The crucial difference is whether she will see herself as recovering from an illness or as a woman who appropriately places value on connecting empathically yet may need to let go to trying to have contact with someone who has become unavailable. If the relational connection with George cannot be restored, then Betty needs help to grieve the loss.

THE IMPLICATIONS FOR FEMINIST FAMILY THERAPY PRACTICE

Feminists have pointed out that male values permeate concepts like fusion, enmeshment, individuation, differentiation, and boundaries (Goodrich, et al. 1988, 19). Feminist family theory emphasizes that 'the family' exists in a culture that is patriarchal. The ways in which our society defines male and female roles support and encourage power differentials rooted in gender. Feminist family therapy explores and exposes these characteristics; it asks therapists to increase their own awareness and to explore such issues in therapy with clients. It presupposes that we critically examine the ways in which our treatment supports inequitable hierarchies and power imbalances. It asks us to address economic dependence, independence, or parity. Feminist family therapy looks at stereotypes in gender, relationships in families, relationships in society and in treatment. It asks us to look at our expectations, suppositions, and language. Traditional interpretations of mental health and development are explored for value biases. The use of language is crucial to our awareness of gender bias. Sex differences often become exaggerated through the use of pejorative labels that focus on individuals and ignore the social structures that contribute to the widespread unhappiness of women in relationships (Hare-Mustin 1978). This is a crucial factor in choosing a lens for treatment.

With these issues taken into account, codependency theory seems based in traditional gender-biased values, stressing the importance of individuation, self-orientation, and boundaries. Context appears limited to family, ignoring important culture-based factors. Women's development of other-focus and desire for connection are associated with poor boundaries and are pathologized. A client treated via a codependency model will be labelled 'diseased' for her culturally predetermined gender-associated traits.

Self in relation theory is more closely consistent with feminist family therapy values and goals. Women's development of a sense of self within the context of relationship can be valued as well as being seen in context as influenced by economic, social, and political factors. The importance of women's skills in seeking and maintaining empathic connectedness are validated as important means for sustaining human life, relationships, families, and the changing fabric of society.

This article appeared in Claudia Bepko, ed., *Feminism and Addiction* (Haworth Press 1991), pp. 195–210. Reprinted with permission.

REFERENCES

Al-Anon (1983) *One day at a time.* NY: Al-Anon Family Group Headquarters.

Beattie M. (1987) *Co-dependent no more.* Center City, MN: Hazelden Foundation.

Cermak, T.L. (1986) *Diagnosing and treating co-dependence.* Minnesota: Johnson Institute.

Goodrich, T.J., C. Rampage, B. Ellman, and K. Halstend (1988) *Feminist family therapy: A Casebook.* NY: W.W. Norton.

Hare-Mustin, R.T. (1978). *Family process.* A Feminist approach to family therapy. 17: 181–94.

Jordan, J. (1984) *Empathy and self-boundaries.* Work in Progress, No 16. Wellesley, MA: Stone Center Working Paper Series.

– (1989) *Relational development: Therapeutic implications of empathy and shame.* Work in Progress, No. 39. Wellesley, MA: Stone Center Working Paper Series.

Kaplan, A.G. (1984) *The "self-in-relation": Implications for depression in Women.* Work in Progress, No. 14. Wellesley, MA: Stone Center Working Paper Series.

Mellody, P., A.W. Miller, J.K. Miller (1989) *Facing codependence*. New York: Harper & Row.

Miller, J.B. (1982) *Women and power*. Work in Progress, No. 82–01. Wellesley, MA: Stone Center Working Paper Series.

– (1986) *What do we mean by relationships?* Work in Progress, No. 22. Wellesley, MA: Stone Center Working Paper Series.

– (1988) *Connections, disconnections and violations*. Work in Progress, No. 33. Wellesley, MA: Stone Center Working Paper Series.

Schaef, A.W. (1986) *Co-dependence: Misunderstood – mistreated*. Minneapolis: Winston Press.

Stiver, I.P. (1985) *The meaning of care: Reframing treatment models*. Work in Progress, No. 20. Wellesley, MA: Stone Center Working Paper Series.

Surrey, J.L. (1985) *Self-in-relation: A theory of women's development*. Work in Progress, No. 13. Wellesley, MA: Stone Center Working Paper Series.

Surrey, J.L., A.G. Kaplan, and J.V. Jordan. *Empathy revisited*. Work in Progress, No. 40. Wellesley, MA: Stone Center Working Paper Series.

Wegscheider-Cruse, S. (1985) *Choicemaking*. Florida: Health Communications.

PART IV

The Political Implications of Codependency

BETTE S. TALLEN, Ph D

Codependency: A Feminist Critique

I live in a community where codependency is big business, where women have had in-hospital treatment for it, where many belong to Codependents Anonymous, where therapists advertise in the women's community as specialists in codependent treatment. Many women have described themselves to me as codependent. Last year, when the Women's Studies Department in which I work offered a one-credit workshop on codependency, we were so flooded by student demand for the course that we had to schedule a second section. This is all in a community of less than 40,000 people. Moreover, the more I talk to other women around the country, the more I realize none of this behaviour is all that unusual. Books on codependency are best sellers, not only in feminist bookstores but on national best-seller lists. Women-only and lesbian-only codependent groups abound. Treatment centres for women advertise in newspapers as well as on TV.

Codependency is an idea whose time has come. Sharon Wegscheider-Cruse defines codependents as 'all persons who (1) are in a love or marriage relationship with an alcoholic, (2) have one or more alcoholic parents or grandparents, or (3) grew up in an emotionally repressive family.' Feminists and non-feminists alike embrace the concept of codependency to describe a phenomenon that, according to Wegscheider-Cruse, affects 96 per cent of the population (Wegscheider-Cruse, as quoted in Schaef 1986).

Startlingly few critiques of the concept of codependency have emerged from our lesbian and feminist communities. We have no sustained analysis of the history of the term and have had little or no discussion of the political implications of using it as a method of understanding women's lives. Recently, I heard a woman describe another woman who is dying of cancer as only sick because she was codependent (cancer being one of several fatal diseases that codependency causes, at least according to Anne Wilson Schaef.) I was enraged, both as a cancer survivor and as a teacher of courses on women and health. I know only too well about the environmental and political issues that are critical to any discussion of cancer. African-American women and men suffer from and die from cancer in far greater numbers than do white people. Women continue to die from drugs such as DES. Are we all codependent? Or are we all suffering from a system that systematically targets certain groups as expendable? What do we as women gain from explaining aspects of our lives as stemming from codependency?

Who is a codependent person? Who gets to say? Who has the appropriate credentials and skill to label someone 'codependent'? The list of symptoms of codependency sounds like a catalogue of our lives. Anne Wilson Schaef, for example, lists the following as characteristics of codependency: dishonesty, not dealing with feelings in a healthy way, control, confusion, thinking disorders, perfectionism, external referencing, dependency issues, fear, rigidity, judgmentalism, inferiority/grandiosity, depression, self-centredness, loss of personal morality, stasis, and negativism. Who hasn't experienced these feelings? John and Linda Friel, in their book *Adult Children: The Secrets of Dysfunctional Families* (1988) argue: 'Is it not true that almost everyone has some form of dysfunction in their childhood that could lead to co-dependent symptoms? And if everyone has "it," does it not lose its conceptual and diagnostic meaning ... The [psychiatric diagnostic manual *DSM-III-R*] always describes symptoms, but asks us to look at length and severity of symptoms ... before we make a definite diagnosis.' Since apparently only the 'experts' can label codependents and since all of us potentially suffer from 'it,' we all are forced to seek their 'expert' advice, treatment, and workshops in order to 'get well'.

Codependency as a concept emerged during the late 1970s from the therapy community. Melody Beattie suggests in *Codependent No More* (1987) that the word emerged simultaneously from several treatment centres in Minnesota. With the concept of codependency, the therapeutic community attempts to co-opt both the feminist movement and the Twelve-Step movement represented by Alcoholics Anonymous.

Alcoholics Anonymous, one of the most successful grassroots movements of our time, was founded in 1935 by two upper-middle-class white males, Bill Wilson and Dr Robert Smith. It has literally saved the lives of thousands of men and women who otherwise would have died because of their drinking. Much is quite admirable about Alcoholics Anonymous, its offshoot organizations, and the Twelve Steps themselves. However, feminists and lesbians need to examine the roots of AA, et al. We must also make distinctions between those groups that are under the AA umbrella (such as Al-Anon and Alateen) and are therefore governed by AA's Twelve Traditions and those that are not (such as Codependents Anonymous). Alcoholics Anonymous attempts to combine the medical knowledge of alcoholism with the pragmatism of William James ('Keep coming back! It works!') and a form of Christian fundamentalism that is peculiarly American ('Let Go. Let God.'). Underlying the Twelve-Step approach to the treatment of alcoholism is a conversion experience, being 'born again', after one hits rock bottom. This process can involve either a religious experience, as traditionally understood (belief in a patriarchal God), or can mean an immersion in a community (the community of those recovering). Critical to this conversion is not only an understanding of the Twelve Steps but also its grounding in the Twelve Traditions of Alcoholics Anonymous.

The Twelve Traditions are the governing principles of AA, which are designed to keep AA a grassroots, member-focused organization. Not only do the Traditions distance the organization from experts and from treatment approaches, but they also address the forms of self-aggrandizement and endorsement that are seen at the core of alcoholic behaviour. They fully explain the 'Anonymous' part of the AA name. Twelve-Step groups not under the AA umbrella are not bound by the Traditions. And it is precisely these Traditions, to my mind the most positive features of AA, that are getting lost in the recovery industry.

It does not take a particularly astute observer of American life to realize how big the recovery industry is, judging from its numerous publications, workshops, treatment centres, best-selling books, etc. Its big names are major media stars; their words and ideas come at us from all directions. We are literally bombarded with their messages. And what they have done to the Twelve-Step movement is most interesting indeed.

Recently a friend and I visited one of the largest treatment centres for women in southern Minnesota. It was slick: the brochures were impeccable, the grounds were immaculate, and, of course, the facility was spacious and inviting. Critical to the centre's treatment program is its inpatient Twelve-Step groups. When I questioned the head psychiatrist about requiring patients to attend Twelve-Step meetings, since required attendance is antithetical to AA practice, she replied, 'Yes, that is a problem,' and changed the subject. Questions about how the therapists (many of whom were not recovering substance abusers) could participate in recovery groups were met with the same gracious stonewall of polite avoidance. The presence of therapists as experts, qualified only by training, not by experience, in such meetings, and the compulsory attendance contradict the Traditions and practices of AA. Further, the meetings take place, not in a grassroots setting accessible to all who need help, but in an expensive facility. One of the therapists frankly admitted that she had never even heard of the Twelve Traditions. She stated that the only reason the hospital had started the women's unit was because they knew it would make money. And lots of money it makes.

Codependency and its treatment lie at the heart of how the recovery industry seeks to manipulate and control women. Ostensibly the concept arises out of the Al-Anon movement, the group started by Lois Wilson and Anne Smith that was initially composed of wives of the men in AA. Al-Anon was founded on the concept that those who lived with alcoholics were affected by alcohol in some of the same ways as the alcoholic. At no time during its founding or since, however, was it held that alcohol affected the spouse physically as it affected the alcoholic. The behaviours of the significant other were seen not as a disease or an addiction, but as a stumbling block to the alcoholic's recovery. The current concept of codependency varies from this original belief quite significantly.

First, and perhaps most important, codependency is seen as a disease, a progressive, definable disease, with an inevitable outcome, which, if not treated, will result in death. Schaef even argues that, left untreated, the codependent will likely die before the addict. There is an implication that codependency may actually be a more serious condition than addiction to a substance. Codependency is characterized as an addiction that produces significant physical symptoms, which some experts believe occur before the codependent becomes involved with the substance abuser. As the Friels argue, '(W)e are stating clearly that we do not believe that people become co-dependent because they have been living with an addict. Rather we are stating that they are in relationship with an addict *because* they are co-dependent.' People in Al-Anon, on the other hand, are encouraged to create a healthy distance between themselves and the behaviours of the alcoholic, but they are not viewed as being ill prior to the relationship.

Second, almost all the behaviours ascribed to codependents are traditionally seen as feminine behaviours in this society. How the experts handle this issue, I believe, underlies much of how the codependent movement seeks to depoliticize feminism. Melody Beattie, for example, in *Codependent No More*, describes the characteristics of codependent behaviour as low self-worth, repression, obsession, controlling, denial, dependency, poor communication, weak boundaries, lack of trust, anger, and sex problems. These behaviours form feminine identity in American culture. If we resist these messages, we are penalized for our anger and lack of trust.

Because 'codependency' so accurately describes what many of us experience in our lives, we blame ourselves for the behaviour. In one of my introductory women's studies class, a student talked a great deal about how much she had learned from the book *Women Who Love Too Much* and how it had helped her understand her feelings about her ex-husband, who had battered her. I made an offhand comment that perhaps the best book would be not on women who love too much but on men who hit too much. In her journal, she wrote about how my comment 'blew her away'; she never thought that she could hold him responsible for his own behaviour. Codependency, thus, teaches us that femininity is a pathology, and we blame ourselves for self-destructive, feminine behaviours, letting men evade any responsibility for their violent and abusive behaviour. The Friels state, 'If someone tried to make love to me when I said I didn't want to, this would be an individual boundary invasion.' I would call that rape. (They consider incest the result of 'weak intergenerational boundaries.') Redefining rape as weak boundaries on the part of both victim and perpetrator blames the victim.

Critical to codependent analysis is the view that you cannot control the behaviour of the addicted person. Although obviously it is true that no one can control anyone else's behaviour, the extension of the argument is that a codependent cannot even criticize the behaviour of the addicted person. Anne Wilson Schaef states, in *When Society Becomes an Addict* (1987), that responsibility should no longer be considered to imply any kind of obligation, but rather should only be seen as the ability to respond, to explain your own behaviour. She writes, 'responsibility is the *ability to respond*. In the Addictive System responsibility involves *accountability and blame.*' In this view, women's responsibility is to look at their own behaviour; they can neither blame nor hold men accountable for violent and abusive behaviour. Sexism and, by extension, any system of oppression become only the problem of the victim; the perpetrator can no longer be held responsible.

Third, the therapy community depoliticizes feminism by insisting that the root cause of codependent behaviour is being raised in a dysfunctional family. The concept of dysfunctional family is based on the idea that it is possible to have a warm, loving, close nuclear family within the context of racist, capitalist, heteropatriarchy. It betrays the fundamental feminist insight that the patriarchal family itself is the primary institution in the oppression of women. Not only does this concept ignore the sexism and heterosexism involved in the reality of family life, but it also makes invisible the racism and classism inevitably underlying the 'warm, loving family' as conceived of by family therapists and psychologists. The fantasy of the 'functional' family imagines a well-employed father and perhaps, now, an equally well-employed mother, and children, able-bodied and well-adapted to society's definition of their race, class, and gender. Families like the single-parent African-American family or gay and lesbian families are seen as dysfunctional by definition and are therefore dismissed without any understanding of how those families may function far better for their members than the white, middle-class, 'ideal' family. As Donna Langston has pointed out to me, many of the characteristics of codependent behaviour, when seen in a working-class context, are actually critical aspects of survival skills. To learn to depend on others is what enables poor people to survive.

To work only on healing the pain from having been raised in a 'dysfunctional' family holds out the hope that it is possible to achieve a fundamentally healthy family in this society without challenging the basic institutions of capitalism, heterosexism, sexism, racism, and classism that produced the patriarchal family in the first place. When we, as feminists, work on our issues of childhood abuse and neglect, part of the purpose is healing our own pain, but we also must seek to understand the political context that makes such abuse widespread, accepted, and an everyday occurrence, and fight collectively to stop it. The lack of any racial or class analysis in any of the literature on codependency underlines the white, middle-class nature of its roots in the therapy community and reinforces my belief that it represents an attempt to depoliticize feminism. Codependency adherents argue that we can get 'well' without fundamentally altering the very institutions that created the situations in the first place. Beattie goes so far as to argue, for example, that a preoccupation with injustice is a further proof of addiction.

Why then is the concept of codependency so attractive to so many feminists and lesbians? A primary reason, in my view, is that codependency theory so accurately describes the reality of many of our lives. We feel powerless and unhappy. We live in a woman-hating culture where we pay a high price for resisting internalizing messages of feminine weakness and unworthiness. Codependency treatment offers hope that we can achieve our own private health. It allows those of us privileged by race, class, or sexual identity, among others, to avoid looking at our privileged statuses. Codependency theory feeds on our complacency; we are no more responsible for behaviour oppressive to others than any man is for his behaviour to women. It teaches us that only we are responsible for our fate, that social activism and discontent are merely further symptoms of our 'disease'. When white women are confronted by women of colour about their racism, they can now claim that racism is a 'disease', that they are not responsible for oppressive behaviour, and that their major task to 'get well.'

Codependency offers a relatively safe haven for those who can afford treatment. Its theory addresses many of the same concerns that we as feminists address, but without the high personal price of challenge and criticism. How many times have we felt judged wrongly or trashed in feminist groups without having been given adequate space to explain? Codependency treatment offers a context of unquestioning support that is all too often missing in our communities.

Codependency provides another way to resist the messages of femininity without fundamentally questioning the values of the racist, capitalist, heteropatriarchy we live with. We can get well, are encouraged to resist on a personal level, without ever really having to examine what made us 'ill' in the first place. Therefore, as we get 'better,' millions of other women will continue to be born into a culture that is misogynist to the core. Codependency theory offers a way to achieve a personal peace without examining the cost of that peace to others.

This article appeared in *Sojourner: The Women's Forum*, Vol. 15 (5), Jan. 1990. Reprinted with permission of the author.

NOTE

Thanks to Elliot, Donna Langston, Janet Lee, Mara, and especially Rosemary Curb for careful suggestions and comment, although the opinions expressed here are mine.

REFERENCES

Beattie, Melody (1987) *Codependent No More*, Harper/Hazelden.
Friel, John, and Linda Friel (1988) *Adult Children: The Secrets of Dysfunctional Families*. Pompano Beach, FL: Health Communications.
Schaef, Anne Wilson (1986) *Co-Dependence: Misunderstood – Mistreated*. Minneapolis: Winston Press.
– (1987) *When Society Becomes an Addict*. New York: Harper & Row.

DAVID SCHREIBER, MA

Hysterectomies, Mastectomies, and Codependencies

Nowadays it is nearly impossible for therapists to be unaware of feminist issues. Since therapists of both sexes work with clients of both sexes they must understand the unique concerns of same- and opposite-sex clients. The aware therapist develops a sense of what is generally good for and bad for clients who struggle with sex-role-related difficulties. The development of this therapeutic common sense is essential for effective therapy to occur within the context of modern society.

Feminists remind us of how the helping professions have over the years not always been helpful to women. For instance, in medicine, radical hysterectomies and mastectomies were very popular (with male surgeons) for many years. Recently, because of medical advances, a somewhat more egalitarian approach to patients, and the outcries of women, these radical physical insults are used with decreasing frequency. Psychiatry, too, has a tradition of oppressive mechanisms: overuse of hospitalization, chemotherapy, electro-shock therapy, and the diagnostic categories of depression and, especially, hysteria. These mechanisms are also falling into disuse, but they have done yeoman's duty over the years in preventing dialogue between the sexes. They have also been very effective in gagging those who wanted to speak up about incest and other forms of abuse.

Within the helping professions this oppression tends to change hands. Perhaps in a society that oppresses, the source is not as important as the continuation of oppression. Oppressors take notice. There is a new, one-size-fits-all disease category that seems particularly well designed for the oppression of women: codependency. Once again the chemical dependency industry has invented a disease so more people can be sick. Codependency as a diagnostic category is so flimsy that one would hope it never finds its way into the *DSM-III*. In spite of its vague and iatrogenic qualities, however, many chemical dependency practitioners seem enamoured with their new diagnosis.

Some would contend that codependency was invented to help the spouses of chemically dependent people; I disagree. Codependency was invented for three reasons: first, as a contemporary replacement for out-of-vogue, broad-brush diagnostic categories like hysteria; second, to increase the industry's pool of potential clients; and third, to engage spouses, usually women, in the gathering of ammunition for confrontation. An analysis of the codependent's role in intervention and family week reveals that she is usually not involved for her own therapeutic benefit, but rather has been coerced into an alliance with the counsellors aimed at crucifying ('with love and concern') the chemically dependent spouse.

What exactly is codependency? What kind of disease infects only those family members who attend family week? Does a name tag that says 'codependent' mean you are? Definitions of codependency, when they can be found, are invariably vague. Since codependency supposedly mimics chemical dependence in terms of symptoms and progression, the definition of codependency leans heavily on the definition of chemical dependency. Unfortunately, chemical dependency has never been adequately defined, and the hypothesis of alcoholic progression has not fared well in research findings. What does emerge from definitions of codependency is a description of what seasoned therapists would probably call lack of individuation. Lack of individuation is not a disease, nor is it even a constant state, since becoming more rather than less individuated is part of the human maturation process. To be not perfectly individuated is normal while striving for more individuation is noble. The noted therapist Dr Murray Bowen contends that perfect individuation is impossible. If he is right, we are all codependents; too bad for us but good financial luck for those counsellors who, with a true economy of thought and skill, specialize in treating codependency.

Codependency is designed to be a disease we all can experience, but it does seem more women than men receive this label. Children are frequently recipients of codependency but only in a secondary way, since they get it by virtue of their parents' dragging them to treatment. (It also seems that the disease is more often given to clients by female therapists than by male therapists. I have several ideas about why such an observation should be true, but space does not permit a discussion of them here.) What kind of counsellor makes people sick before helping them to get well? The modern version of Typhoid Mary? It is more likely someone who does not readily trust clients. Or someone who remembers not being trustworthy or treated as untrustworthy by counsellors prior to his or her own recovery and now projects that lack of trust onto clients. Or someone who believes that clients are delusional and must be convinced they are sick before they can get well. Or someone who is not comfortable working with normal people. Or someone who is not ready to be a therapist. Or maybe just a benevolent person who has never critically examined the entrapping iatrogenic nature of codependency.

If we abandon the codependency label, how can we help clients who stumble in the process of individuation? Not labelling them is the first way we can help them. But without a label how do we discuss their problems? Experienced therapists recognize that people who live with a chemical abuser's sometimes unpredictable and crazy behaviour will likely develop some unusual behaviours that are undesirable, but normal, responses to a troubled relationship. This process varies greatly from individual to individual, with some individuals actually gaining strength from this sort of experience. We can discuss clients' problems in terms that do not imply pathology and that are easily understood. Al-Anon and chemical dependency treatment provide examples of how to discuss these problems with individuation. From such sources come the terms *enabling* and *concerned person*. Each term describes behaviour, not internalized identity. Behaviours are easily identified, described, and discussed. Owing to the flexibility of behaviour, there is always room for change. Goals can be set and progress monitored. The client need never be treated as a sick person, and therapy will naturally terminate as goals are met. As the client returns to the normal condition of not being a client in therapy, both counsellor and client have succeeded.

How we employ language in therapy is crucial. When Al-Anon members and counsellors slip from behavioural descriptions like 'enabling' and 'concerned person' into labels like 'enabler' and 'codependent,' which encourage pathological identity, therapy has not only got off on the wrong foot, it hardly has a leg to stand on. Therapists are supposed to be expert in interpersonal communication. Maybe therapists need to pay less attention to how clients communicate and more attention to how therapists talk to clients. Honest, hopeful language is a key to therapeutic success.

My experience in clinical practice has resulted in some creative ways to work with individuation problems. Here is one specific example of how to help a client who suffers from lack of individuation and from being previously treated for codependency. First things first: the codependency label has to be convincingly removed. (This assumes the label is troublesome. Sometimes it is not. Some clients wear it in good health and this state should not be tampered with.) Trust is essential. Try trusting the client, treating him or her as your equal and as a normal person. Client's trust in the counsellor usually follows. Ask about previous counselling and express dismay at the imposition of the codependency label. Say that the label is not helpful and then substitute a behavioural description, such as 'you seem troubled by your reaction to your spouse's drinking.' Proceed, remembering that the ultimate goal is for you and your client successfully to terminate successful therapy.

This article appeared in *Viewpoints: The Quarterly Publication of the Minnesota Chemical Health Association* (Winter 1984), pp. 1–2. Reprinted with the permission of the author.

MARIANNE WALTERS, MSW

The Codependent Cinderella Who Loves Too Much ... Fights Back

According to the reams of self-help literature on bookstore shelves and in the women's mass circulation magazines, the American woman is fighting an uphill battle against lifelong dysfunction, addiction, and neurotic dependency. While sampling some of this outpouring, I discovered that not only are there 'Women Who Love Too Much,' but that these very same women are really 'Smart Women Who Make Foolish Choices'; that they 'Fear Success' and have a 'Cinderella Complex' that could be described as a rescue fantasy. Moreover, although some of them are now 'Beyond (Their) Codependency,' they have had mothers who 'Love Men Who Hate Women' and 'Toxic Parents' who suffered from an addiction to each other. This very same woman, trying to be 'The Perfect Woman' and reject the 'Doormat Syndrome' that had plagued her own mother, found that unfortunately she had become 'Too Smart for Her Own Good!' Perhaps she was one of those 'Daughters Who Love Their Mothers but Don't Love Themselves.' Or maybe, although she had worked through the 'My Mother/Myself' syndrome, and had been successful in 'Reclaiming Her Inner Child,' she was finding herself 'Falling Off the Fast Track.' Tired of trying to be a 'Super-Mom' and 'Have It All,' she was searching for a 'Mommy Track' where she could begin to cope with 'The Drama of the Gifted Child' and provide the empathy, space, and approving attention that her emotionally starved family needed. Yet, as a woman, she would need to remember that, for mothers and daughters, 'Loving and Letting Go' was what it was all about, and that, in the end, it was damn hard to have 'A Life of One's Own.'

Well, now, let's get serious.

There are several levels on which I think we need to take a critical look at the recovery/codependency movement. For, indeed, it has become a movement that has its roots deep in the social fabric of the last decade. The rapid development and popularity of the codependency/recovery movement and the concurrent proliferation of books and articles directed at women and their problematic relationships is no accident. The Reagan decade, with its glorification of the individual, of me, mine, the self, and the celebration of being good to oneself, encouraged a counter-reaction to the changes in families and intimate relationships that had been engendered by the women's movement. It was also a decade in which community had become less and less available to people; a decade marked by a sort of social alienation, when being involved in social causes seemed naïve. Taking care of your own needs became the hallmark of personal power and of the truly well-adjusted individual.

Consciousness-raising gave way to networking; potlucks were replaced by power lunches. And psychological buzzwords helped to define this culture of the self – separation, boundaries, individuation, hierarchy, self-esteem, space. Mental health was not measured in terms of interdependency, affiliation, connection, involvement, or taking care of others. Unsuccessful separation from one's family could lead to the most dire of behavioural disorders. There was no room for the concept of family as an ongoing process of negotiating and renegotiating affiliation – where the operative word is *affiliation* rather than separation. The pull, both economically and conceptually, was now the ideology of the self. And as money to alleviate poverty and to provide services to the disadvantaged disappeared, the haves found themselves without a cause – except themselves. At the same time, the expectations of women in the world were undergoing a dramatic transformation, and the traditional rules governing marriage, work, divorce, career, and family life, were in flux.

And it didn't hurt that the decade produced, for at least a sizeable portion of the population, a considerable amount of disposable income – income that could support psychology as yet another 'Me' commodity. So the decade of the 1980s was indeed ripe soil for the proliferation of any commodity that made people feel better, or that lay blame for any stress or distress on anything other than the body politic. The dysfunctional family had come of age and converged with the codependency movement and the literature of problematic women.

Of course, it is abundantly clear that many people have been greatly helped by their involvement in the deprofessionalized grassroots groups of the codependency movement. For some, this involvement has, quite literally, been a life-saving experience. Millions of people have found release there: recognition and validation of their pain; community with others who have had similar experiences; new freedom from anger, blame, mistrust; and safety – many for the first time in their lives. None the less, I have some reservations.

First, I believe that the codependency model blurs the power differential between the doer and the one who allows or enables the doing. Codependency in action reads 'co-culpability' or, equally liable. She who helps him who does is as responsible for the doing as the doer. This is not explicit in the model (although some proponents suggest that there is no addict, no abuser, without a codependent), but it is as much there, in inference, as those old axioms about the provocative girl who gets raped, or the overbearing wife who gets beaten up. Unfortunately, some systems thinking similarly blurs the distinction between the actor and the audience, an audience that, however indulgent of the performance, is, in fact, *not* doing the performing. Despite whatever reciprocal, complementary loops activate each, they are simply *not* the same order of business. What began as a way of helping people to understand how they get pulled into a set of behaviours and become part of a destructive system has been translated into a model in which the codependent is as instrumental in a set of dysfunctional interactions as the one with the behavioural problem.

For example, in a book about families with an alcoholic member, there is a description of the dysfunctional pattern of an 'alcoholic couple.' An *alcoholic couple* – the label itself is disconcerting, since in this instance only the husband drinks. Why do we call a whole family, or a couple, 'alcoholic' when only one member drinks? Doesn't it reflect a way of thinking, that everyone is metaphorically alcoholic, so that the distinction between the one who abuses and the ones who are engaged in the abuse is blurred? Now whatever goes on in that family becomes filtered through that label. No longer are they a family where someone plays tennis and others watch 'L.A. Law' together – or where one member gets angry about one thing and another gets jealous about something else – no, they are a family in which individual identity is submerged in the configuration of the addiction.

The writer of this book describes the couple's dysfunctional pattern as: drink, nag, drink, nag, drink. But, the author points out, the couple disagrees about the punctuation of that sequence: the wife punctuates the sequence *drink*, nag, *drink*, nag; whereas the husband's view is *nag*, drink, *nag*, drink. The author prescribes a therapy that validates both punctuations, intending to give an active role to both husband and wife. It follows that either way you cut it, the sequence is okay – the nagging may precipitate the drinking or the drinking may precipitate the nagging. The implication is that these are acts of equal significance, equal power in the relationship of the couple, equally productive of dysfunctional interaction.

Moreover, consider the message the author is conveying to this couple when you set them down in the real world of gender differences, when you attach a 'he' and 'she' to their roles with each other and in families. Codependents fit the archetypes usually drawn to describe a woman – overinvolved, depending upon others for approval, not taking care of herself, having poor boundaries, intoxicated with relationships, too willing to assume blame, putting the needs of others before herself. Publishers report that 85 per cent of the readership of codependent materials are women. So women are offered equal power in the creation of these dysfunctional patterns in families even as they are seeking power of another sort in the world. I'm not sure it's such a good bargain.

The self-help books for women are basically about the ways that women bring about their own destruction, usually leaving out any discussion of the way this self-destruction is socially sanctioned. How often do we encounter an 'ACOA' who is as angry or angrier with her mother who didn't protect her as she is with the person who abused her? And how often does the movement, and even our own therapy, encourage full expression of this anger, while encouraging forgiveness and re-bonding with the abuser?

I suggest that the codependent movement and the self-help literature, while clearly intended to empower, in fact pathologize behaviours and personal characteristics that are associated with the feminine. These characteristics presumably cause women to become addicted to men who hate them, to abusive relationships, to repeated affairs with irresponsible partners, or to overeating, compulsive shopping, premenstrual syndrome, or loving too much. And the literature offers us step-by-step solutions to healthier, more adult – autonomous, independent – behaviours, so we can establish appropriate boundaries, set our own agendas, take better care of ourselves, and attend to our own needs. Mature behaviours are conceptualized as taking care of oneself, putting one's needs first, loving oneself. Whatever happened to the poor reputation of narcissism?

While the model for the codependency self-help groups was the consciousness-raising groups of the women's movement, there is a marked difference between the ideology of these two movements. Both the codependent/ACOA/recovery movement and the women's movement offer community in a society where it has become a rare commodity. Both provide a safe place for people who feel lost, lonely, subordinate, damaged, or shamed, enabling them to come together and share their grief and find a path towards growth. But one movement encourages individuals to surrender to a spiritual higher power, while the other encourages people to join together to challenge and restructure power arrangements in the larger society. In one movement, community is used to empower the individual; in the other, community is used to empower the group as well. Their very names suggest the profound difference between these two movements – 'codependency' and 'adult child' on the one hand; 'consciousness raising' on the other. One is based on a deficit model of human personality; the other on a model of competency. One focuses on the personal roots of individuals' problems; the other on the social origins of problems that transcend the experience of the individual.

I am concerned about the codependency movement's promulgation of the disease model to explain a vast array of human behaviours; the use of what is essentially a medical term – *addiction* – to describe activities as disparate as substance abuse, loving, gambling, shopping, sex, incest, lateness, intimacy, affairs, relationships, eating, worry, work, and more. Codependency, which originally referred to some of the problematic behaviours of people married to alcoholics or drug addicts, now refers to an amorphous disease configuration that has become a national epidemic and that, apparently, can include almost any behaviour. In fact, the literature suggests that people in the helping professions are notorious codependents with an addiction to rescuing.

So pervasive is the 'illness' of codependency that if you are not in recovery, are not a survivor, then you must still be in the throes of the disease, or in denial. The term *adult children of alcoholics* originally referred to those whose adult lives were scarred by the substance abuse of one or both parents. But the typologies of ACOA began to appeal to a much wider audience and to include people who had grown up in any family that could be loosely described as dysfunctional – a vast cross-section of families whose characteristics could even include mothers who chose to work because they enjoy it!

One of the more disturbing aspects of the disease model is that it trivializes those truly addictive behaviours associated with substance abuse by likening them to so many ordinary human behaviours whose excesses are labelled addictive. And it comes dangerously close to equating the feelings of deprivation generated by having been insufficiently nurtured as a child to the utterly decompensating experience of having been sexually or physically abused by a family member.

It is very important for us to be able to distinguish an order of significance between things, if only to be able to set priorities, both socially and personally. In our professional work this task is even more compelling. The understanding of alcoholism and drug addiction as illness has been enormously useful for diagnosis and in the development of treatment modalities. And I know of no treatment for substance abuse that is as effective as the Twelve-Step model of AA and NA, a model that eschews blame and holds people responsible for their own recovery. But it is a disease model, holding that one is never cured, and that abstinence is necessary for the continued process of recovery. Imagine abstinence from loving, or worry, or shopping, or working! And the disease model conjures up the medical model, which gives rise to a culture of prescriptions, subordination to a higher authority, and conformity to treatment protocols. The movement books have contributed to the development of a readership that expects prescriptions – ten- or twelve- or fifteen-step programs for recovery; recipes, directions, typologies. Each disease must have its delineated program for recovery – most of which resemble each other.

Clearly the widespread appeal of the codependency movement has further elevated the authority of psychology as providing the ultimate explanation for all human behaviour. Increasingly the realm of psychological explanation has become a closed system, excluding other perspectives on human behaviour, narrowing our understanding of the complex cultural and social forces that shape or experience. Our preoccupation with the psychological leads us to enshrine simplistic formulas with the common wisdom, like the idea that achieving mental health merely is a matter of dispelling the demons of an unhappy childhood and 'being good' to ourselves. And there is no doubt that psychological knowledge has become a commodity in our ever-expanding marketplace – a fast growing and lucrative one at that. What is too often missing is the integration of the *social* construction of behaviour into our theories of causality, motivation, interpersonal dynamics, and individual problems.

Most popular books about problematic women briefly mention that the dysfunctional behaviours and patterns they describe are *learned*, that they have roots in the values, power structures, history, language, and institutional practices of a patriarchal, dominantly white, middle-class culture. Yet seldom is this idea reflected in their assumptions and formulations, or in their proposed solutions.

For instance, Dr Susan Forward, in *Men Who Hate Women, and the Women Who Love Them*, does have several paragraphs on the cultural support of men's aggression towards women and does refer to misogyny as learned behaviour. But here is how she describes the source of that learning (italics are mine): 'While both parents work together to raise their son, they also have separate jobs. Mother is the nurturer and the boy's primary source of comfort, while father helps him *to pull away* from mother so that he does not become *overly* dependent on her. However, in the family background of misogynists, just the opposite occurs ... so that the boy has *no other option* than to make mother the center of his universe. *Mother,* instead of meeting her son's needs for comfort and nurturing, is liable to try to get her son to meet her needs ... whether a *woman* does this through the extremes of overwhelming demands, severe rejection, or smothering control, the results are the same: the boy becomes too dependent on her.' Imagine how this information is experienced by a single mother of boys. 'Without realizing it, in adulthood he transfers this dependency, as well as the conflicts and fears that go with it, onto the woman in his life.' So much for the source of aggression and anger in men ... it's women!

In a book about 'adult children,' the author states, 'If someone tried to make love to me when I said I didn't want to, this would be an individual boundary invasion.' It still sounds like rape to me! These same writers consider incest the result of 'weak intergenerational boundaries,' and others go so far as to define it as an inappropriate expression of love. Whatever happened to the notion of the *abuse of power?*

Alice Miller, whose book *The Drama of the Gifted Child* inspired the 'inner child' movement, has twenty seven references under the indexed heading 'mother,' with a cross-reference to 'parent'; 'parent' has sixteen cross-references to 'mother.' There is *no* heading for 'father.' Yet the book is about the damage to the child of early dysfunctional *parenting*.

These are a few examples of closed-system thinking. To be informed by the many interesting realities and systems that shape our way of being in the world and to understand the social construction of behaviour can offer an antidote to the deficit constructions of most psychological theories. We badly need a broader landscape on which to locate our clients' problems and to help us see how their individual stories fit within the wider contours of our collective experience.

Recently, in a consultation group, a therapist presented the case of a working-class, first-generation Italian family he had been seeing for almost a year: mother, stepfather, and four children – two boys and two girls. The oldest daughter left home when she was seventeen because she couldn't get along with her stepfather and now lives with a maternal aunt. The second daughter, Gina, sixteen, became pregnant, an event that brought the family in for help. She was also dealing drugs. Both boys, twelve and eight, have school problems, while the youngest, the only child of this marriage, has muscular dystrophy. When Gina got pregnant, her stepfather became furious and threatened to disown her. She left home and is currently living with her boyfriend's parents. Now Gina wants to come home, but her stepfather refuses to allow it, although Gina is back at school, has had an abortion for which she had her parents' approval, and is no longer dealing. The therapist describes the stepfather as *extremely* rigid, the mother as the go-between in the family. When her husband is present, she takes his side, but when she is alone with her daughter, she takes the daughter's side. The situation has become intractable, with mother attempting to appease both sides in this warring family and stepfather and daughter barely able to be in the same room.

How do we begin to think about this family? At first, the consultation group focused on the triangulation of Gina between mother and stepfather, a pattern repeating itself in this family, as witness the angry, premature leaving home of the older daughter. The group considered issues related to marital conflict, family-of-origin, and stepfather's rigidity. But thinking about this family within a social context offered a different perspective, not structured around psychological 'deficits.' Here was a tough, working-class man, a first-generation American whose culture and ethnic traditions not only created expectations for his behaviour as head of household, but held him accountable for the protection of the women in his family. Living in the inner city, his fears for the safety of his stepdaughter, given her behaviours, were surely appropriate. How could the stepfather not feel he had failed, within his code of duty and ethics, in the light of the events in his family? And what was the mother to do? Her job was surely to be supportive and loving to her daughter as well as supportive and subordinate to her husband.

Using culture and social context as behaviour determinants, we viewed this family in terms of the stepfather's fear of failing his duty, not his rigidity; the mother's belief about what the family needed from her, not her triangulating behaviours. We approached our work with stepfather and Gina around ways that he could accomplish his paternal mission without continuing to jeopardize his connection with his step-daughter or compromising his view that people need to face the consequences of their behaviour in order to be safe in a risky world. Mother helped by contributing her expertise in creating alliances. And Gina, in understanding her stepfather's anger as concern for her safety, could begin to allow herself to experience his protection.

I recently saw a young black woman who is a chemistry major on scholarship at a local college. Although on graduating high school she had received a National Science Award and is an A student in college, she keeps dropping out of courses, defers credit by taking incompletes, forgets classwork, and makes endless changes in her course schedule, making it difficult to get into courses required for her major. She is frustrated and unhappy and considering dropping out. She's also concerned about two recent failed relationships with men. In previous therapy she had discussed some of the problems in her family: eleven children, never any space for herself, no privacy, little time with her working mother, and a father who, always tired from carrying two jobs, relates to his children only as disciplinarian. She had tried some behavioural prescriptions for coping with those behaviours she understood were self-destructive. She had explored her poor self-image, fear of success, and problems around them. In therapy she had located these issues in her conflictual relationship with parents, who never showed her approval or acknowledged her accomplishments, thus making more difficult her struggle to separate and be her own person.

Using a wider lens, my take was different. I saw a young woman caught between a rock and a hard place. Her family is struggling financially, seeking upward mobility, and she is the first to go to college. She becomes at once the hope of her family, the promise, the justification for the hard work of her parents – and at the same time her success, her fulfilment of that promise, will surely distance her from her family, from a world that feels familiar and safe. She will, in effect, be entering a new world, a world in which, sadly, her parents will be strangers. Her success will be costly; the price: distance from her family, alienation from her cultural roots. Further, as a black woman in a racist society, she probably fears that her relationships with black men will be compromised if she is successful in her own right; this makes her angry, and her anger, however justifiable, sometimes interferes in these relationships. Within this perspective, the goal would be to help her to find ways to remain affiliated to her culture and connected with her family while embracing success; to reduce the price she will have to pay for being young, black, beautiful ... and smart.

At our center this year we have been seeing a lesbian mother of three little girls. The mother, Leah, came in about her relationship with her eldest daughter, Betsy – a precocious, intrusive, mouthy kid, who interrupts her mother constantly, is intensely interested in her activities, offers advice on the parenting of the younger children, worries about her mother's welfare, and even tries to monitor her telephone conversations. Betsy also gets into difficulty at school and with peers because she is so argumentative. Leah feels this behaviour began about the time of her divorce – eighteen months ago – and when she set up household as a single parent with an open, committed relationship to another woman. The lack of boundaries, the permission to interrupt, mother's deference to her daughter's endless questions and comments, her willingness to be distracted, her patient listening to and exploring of her daughter's feelings, was such a compelling, even alarming scenario, that the therapist began early on to work with boundary formation, parental expectations, limits and Betsy's 'parentified' behaviours. It was hard going, with much resistance from both Betsy and her mother. Leah believed that children needed to express themselves and deserved such attention from their parents; she had received very little from her own family.

Consideration of the social determinants of behaviours in this family offers alternative interventions. First, a lesbian mother, feeling marginalized in a homophobic culture, would want, in every way, to legitimize her own daughter – validate her daughter's feelings and ideas and offer her the careful, respectful attention and emotional access that she herself feels denied. Since it would be difficult not to internalize the social disapproval attached to being a lesbian mother, she probably feels inadequate as a parent, guilty for denying her daughters a 'normal' family life, and fearful of the consequences of their being separated from their father. One way for Leah to compensate for these perceived deficits would be to give her daughter large doses of support, validation, and approval. In a society whose values are so oppressive to this mother, she must want most passionately not to oppress her daughter, not to impose her values, but to encourage her to be expressive, strong, and self-directed. And so she avoids setting limits, fearful of being authoritarian and oppressive.

This way of 'knowing' Leah moves us beyond our usual psychological concepts and language. It is informed by our understanding of, our sensibility to, and her experience of herself in the world, and offers both therapist and mother a frame of reference that legitimizes mother's behaviour even while reckoning with its excesses. The therapist can now use mother's competencies as a parent – her patience, her ability to listen, her connectedness – to modify those excesses caused by her self-doubts in a world that at best reinforces them, at worst *fundamentally creates* them.

When the newly elected president of Czechoslovakia, Vaclav Havel, appeared before a joint session of Congress, he said his experience of recent events in his country had given him one great certainty, that 'consciousness precedes being, and not the other way around.' The way we understand ourselves in relation to our world, the way we know who we are – our consciousness – will surely determine how we will be in that world. In our work as therapists we can't change the larger society, but we *can* help people to feel less oppressed in their lives by knowing that they are not just passively reacting to events, but are actors whose performance will be largely shaped by the way they *understand* the drama they are enacting.

This article appeared in *Family Therapy Networker*, July/Aug. 1990, pp. 53–7. Reprinted with permission.

CAROL TAVRIS, Ph D

Do Codependency Theories Explain Women's Unhappiness – or Exploit Their Insecurities?

Every few years there's a wave of best-selling books purporting to explain the origins of women's unhappiness. The symptoms these books attempt to treat are invariably the same: low self-esteem, passivity, depression, an 'exaggerated' sense of responsibility to other people, and an inability to break out of bad relationships. In nearly all of these books, the author begins by describing how she herself suffered from the disorder in question and, through persistence and effort, found The Cure.

In the 1970s a woman's problem was her 'fear of success.' No, said Colette Dowling in 1981, women have a 'Cinderella Complex' – a hidden fear of independence. No, said Robin Norwood in 1985, women's problem is that they 'love too much.' Not really, said Melody Beattie in 1987; women love too much because they are 'codependent' – 'addicted' to addicts and bad relationships.

'Codependency' is today's hot diagnosis. Beattie's 1987 book, *Codependent No More*, occupied top spots on the *New York Times* paperback best-seller list. (Following the formula, Beattie explains that she knows whereof she speaks, having first conquered her alcoholism and then her addiction to addicts.) More recent books on codependency include Lynne Namka's *The Doormat Syndrome*, Pia Mellody's *Facing Co-dependence*, and Anne Wilson Schaef's *Escape from Intimacy*.

Codependency is a national phenomenon – and big business. Thousands, perhaps millions of women are buying these books, joining recovery groups, and identifying themselves at social gatherings as codependents 'in recovery from their addiction.' What message do codependency theories convey?

Codependency was originally a term referring to the specific set of common problems faced by the spouses of alcoholics. The term caught on and quickly absorbed the 'disease' language that is now being applied to addicts of all kinds. Today it seems the codependency bug has struck virtually everybody: adult children of alcoholics; anyone living with any sort of 'holic' (alcoholic, foodaholic, workaholic, or sexaholic); people in relationships with partners who are mentally disturbed, chronically ill, or, adds Beattie, generally 'irresponsible'; parents of rebellious teenagers or children with behaviour problems; professionals in helping occupations, and so on.

Oddly enough for a 'disease' that has struck so many individuals, no one really agrees on what codependency is or defines its symptoms the same way. 'There are almost as many definitions of codependency as there are experiences that represent it,' says Beattie. Her own definition would exclude only a few saints and hermits: a codependent person is 'one who has let another person's behavior affect him or her, and who is obsessed with controlling that person's behavior.' Namka's definition of codependency is 'an addiction to dysfunctional love relationships, a preoccupation of meeting the needs of other persons to the point of feeling responsible for them at the expense of yourself.' Schaef thinks that codependency is a 'progressive disease' that covers up other 'addictions' to sex and love. 'Some therapists,' Beattie notes, 'have proclaimed: "Codependency is anything, and everyone is codependent."'

This is a curious kind of disease. What physician would write a book on diabetes, for example, that says, 'Diabetes is anything, and everyone is diabetic'? But codependency writers are not fazed by such questions, which they regard as defensive quibbling. A woman's skepticism is evidence of her codependence. 'Your judgementalism,' writes Schaef, 'is a characteristic of the disease.'

'The vagueness of these definitions makes it easier for everyone to have at least one of the symptoms,' says Leonore Tiefer, PhD, a psychologist at New York City's Montefiore Medical Center. 'This is the formula for bestsellerdom: if everybody has the problem, everybody needs to read about the cure or join the right group. The reformist spirit is on a new roll these days – more and more groups are ripe for conversion.'

Just as they share the 'disease' view of addiction, codependency books propose a common solution: the Alcoholics Anonymous Twelve-Step method, based on a 'spiritual awakening' in which the sufferer hands over her addiction to a 'Higher Power' to cure. Codependency books are full of warm admonitions to 'celebrate your perfection,' give yourself 'permission to be precious' (the title, as it happens, of Pia Mellody's six-cassette lecture series), and 'forgive ourselves.' Reading these books, therefore, feels somewhat like listening to friendly sermons that emphasize the healing power of love. They make perfect sense at the time, and the advice is undeniably good; but an hour later the reader is hungry for substance, and she may be forgiven for wondering the next day how to implement these wise ideas. 'Following the Ten Commandments is a good idea, too,' says Tiefer, 'but history shows the regrettably human gap between knowing what you should do and being able to do it.'

Tiefer observes that the codependency phenomenon draws much of its appeal from having a 'cure' that combines self-help with group support. 'In this way, it resolves the growing tension between the self-help movement and professional psychotherapy,' says Tiefer. 'There is an increasing conflict in our society between people's desire for guidance and their skepticism of authority. Skepticism is healthy, but it also makes people vulnerable to books and programs that are supposedly new and different. Whatever happened to "your erroneous zones"? To assertiveness training? To "when I say no, I feel guilty"? When such programs don't work over the long haul, participants blame themselves – and look for new solutions. They often end up going from one hit-and-run therapy to another. But the basic problem continues, because women's low *self*-esteem is a result of their low *social* esteem in this country.'

Codependency programs do alert people to one key cause of their troubles: the network of family relationships that enmeshes them. In this sense, the codependency framework is similar to family systems therapy. Both approaches regard each individual in a family as part of a larger pattern of reciprocal influences. Both approaches believe that when one family member begins to play the role of 'person with problem' (e.g., the alcoholic), the spouse often falls into the corresponding role of rescuer, martyr, problem solver. Both approaches share an emphasis on the importance, especially to women, of setting limits on what one is willing to do for others. But there the similarity ends.

Harriet Lerner, Ph D, a family systems therapist at the Menninger Clinic in Topeka, Kansas, and author of *The Dance of Intimacy*, has mixed feelings about the codependency phenomenon. 'I am sympathetic to its ultimate message to women,' she says, 'which is: set limits on the behavior from others that you will not tolerate; if necessary, leave harmful and abusive relationships; become able to live and think independently. But I question the means by which it wants women to achieve these admirable goals. I don't think it is useful or accurate for women to see themselves as sick and diseased instead of taking a larger view of the situation and seeing their symptoms as part of a complex system in which they are embedded.'

The family systems approach, adds Lerner, does not regard family conflicts, or even destructive patterns, as a result of individual sickness or pathology. 'It's normal to want to help a family member or friend in trouble,' she says. 'The problem arises only when a woman becomes overinvolved with that trouble and becomes underfocused on herself – a pattern that is encouraged in our culture. Family-systems therapy helps people observe and change the imbalances in families, but *having* a problem is not the same as *being* the problem, which is what the disease implies.'

Lerner also objects to what she considers the misplaced attribution of responsibility that codependency theories promulgate. 'Codependents may learn that they are as much to blame for their spouses' problems as their spouses are,' she says, 'because they are the "enablers," whose overconcern with their troubled partners allows the addiction to continue. The partners themselves, however, are usually not considered responsible for their abusive, rotten, or violent behavior, since, as Schaef writes, they have a "progressive disease" and "can't help themselves." Family-systems therapy does not apportion blame this way. Both partners are responsible for the pattern they develop, and both are responsible for changing their own part in it.'

Other psychologists worry that the codependency framework obscures the real-life concerns that keep women entangled in bad relationships. 'The language of codependency,' says Jacqueline Goodchilds, PhD, of UCLA, 'is just a modern way of explaining problems that women have had for decades, especially low self-worth and the role requirement to care for, and take care of, others. Women have been raised all their lives to put men first, to take care of everyone else in their lives, to marry the Right Person and happily take on the role of Assistant Person. Then they are surprised to discover that all this subordination of their personalities, abilities, and needs carries a psychological price.'

Goodchilds believes that codependency's emphasis on inner feelings and Higher Powers underestimates the importance of two outside forces that research psychologists know influence self-esteem: children and finances. 'A therapist will spend hours and hours with a woman trying to raise her low self-esteem with pep talks and persuasion,' she says, 'while both of them totally ignore the importance of kids and money. In many families, the kids are "hers" and the money is "his" – that's a virtual recipe for low self-esteem. Money in our society is enabling; it confers power to get your way. Children in our society are disenabling for women – because it's women who often must choose between financial success and family, and because children are largely their responsibility.'

In fact, there is mounting evidence that women remain stuck in destructive or abusive relationships more for 'rational' reasons than for pathological ones. Michael Strube, Ph D, of Washington University, recently published a review of years of research investigating why women leave abusive relationships – and why they stay (up to 50 per cent do). 'Overall,' Strube found, 'these studies paint a picture of women who lack the economic means to leave an abusive relationship, are willing to tolerate abuse so long as it does not become too severe or involve the children, and who appear to be very committed to making their relationships last,' that is, who have been in their relationships for a long time or oppose divorce for religious reasons. Such women also have friends and family who pressure them to stay in the marriage and disapprove of their efforts to leave.

'All of this boils down to the same old stuff,' says Lerner, 'that society is more comfortable with women who feel inadequate, self-doubting, guilty, sick, and "diseased" than with women who are angry and confronting. Women are, too, which is why they eat up many of these books like popcorn. Women are *so* comfortable saying, "I am a recovering addict; the problem is in me." They are so uncomfortable saying the F-word: "I am a feminist; the problem is also in society." Women get much more sympathy and support when they define their problems in medical rather than political terms.'

But that very comfort with self-blame, says Lerner, is the heart of the problem for women, and it is the reason that the concept of codependency poses such a paradox. 'On the one hand, the goal of these codependency books is to help women become stronger, in charge of their lives,' she says. 'On the other hand, their underlying message is subordination: first to your disease, then to a Higher Power.'

It is safer, certainly, to feel guilty rather than angry. 'As long as popular explanations keep saying that the reason for women's unhappiness is in them,' says Goodchilds, 'women won't deal with their real difficulties. Codependency is an effort to solve the problem without changing the situation.' When women begin to look outward, instead of always inward to their own faults and failings, their self-esteem is bound to rise. And perhaps books that blame women's unhappiness on women themselves will no longer have the tremendous appeal they have today.

This article appeared in *Vogue*, Mind Health column, Dec. 1989, pp. 220, 224–6. Courtesy Vogue. Copyright © 1989 by The Conde Nast Publications.

KAY HAGAN

Codependency and the Myth of Recovery: A Feminist Scrutiny

As a feminist and an adult child of alcoholics, I have taken great interest in the rise of popularity of codependency as a way to describe unhealthy intimacy patterns. My journey as an ACA over the past five years affected me almost as profoundly as my personal awakening to feminism in 1974. But until two years ago, my journey as an ACA was on one track, my journey as a feminist on another. They were parallel – I did not see any overlap between the two until the term *codependency* arrived on the scene. The relationship among addiction, intimacy patterns, and how popular culture has interpreted them for women is the subject of this essay.

Scrutinizing the avalanche of information about codependency from a feminist perspective, I want to address the following questions:
1. What exactly is codependency?
2. Why is it particularly dangerous for women?
3. Can we recover from codependency?
4. Is there intimacy after codependency?

What is codependency? By linguistic standards codependency is quite a new term, recognized and named less than fifteen years ago. It commonly refers to a set of intimate behaviours and patterns often associated with the substance addiction of a partner or family member. The specific naming of the syndrome is important because, as with the term *battering*, which emerged in the mid-1970s, when we can name a set of behaviours, we can often recognize the pattern in our own lives. Naming, as the mythmakers knew when they gave Adam the privilege, is empowering magic. When codependency was named into visibility, many women recognized the syndrome in our lives and noticed that we were not alone.

Codependency as a term appeared for the most part simultaneously in the fields of addiction therapy and mental health. In the addiction field, codependency emerged when therapists noticed that alcoholics who had successfully gone through treatment often started drinking again after returning home. Soon therapists began to bring in the families for counselling on how to behave with the recovering addict. Within the Alcoholics Anonymous organization, the Al-Anon groups represent this awareness that the behaviour of non-addicted family members is affected strongly by the addiction. If patterns of family members do not change as the addict's habits change, therapists noted, the family setting often seems to work against the recovery process.

At the same time in the field of mental health, therapists noted the dynamic of the family system, which adapts itself to problems and restructures to ensure efficient functioning. For instance, if a child becomes epileptic, the system quickly shifts into a stance designed to accommodate the unpredictable nature of the disease. In most cases, the problem (whether epilepsy, alcoholism, or an absent parent) becomes the focus of the system. Family systems therapists treated the entire family, not just the 'problem' member. An interesting term from this field is *fortress family*, describing the tendency for family members to maintain a tight protective secrecy around problems, particularly incest, making it nearly impossible for outsiders to learn the reality.

In both fields, codependency emerged gradually as a subtle but distinctive syndrome, a quiet and previously unnoticed context supporting a variety of more obviously destructive behaviours. Soon, therapists responded by offering a separate treatment for it, and now there are entire clinics for treating codependency. The naming of this pattern acknowledges the presence of a condition that is deeply embedded in our culture and that cuts across sex, race, class, ability, and other differences.

SOME DEFINITIONS OF CODEPENDENCY

The challenge of defining codependency is to describe accurately a behavioural phenomenon that is subtle, pervasive, and practised with uncanny precision, inventiveness, and unconscious, virtually automatic obedience. The variety of the following definitions drawn from both addiction and family systems therapies reflects recent attempts to define the term. When I applied a feminist perspective to these efforts, I noticed some interesting implications.

• A specific condition that is characterized by preoccupation and extreme dependence on a person, or object. Eventually, this becomes a pathological condition that affects the person in all other relationships. (Sharon Wegscheider-Cruse)

• Codependency is caused by those self-defeating, learned behaviours that diminish our capacity to initiate or participate in loving relationships. (Earnie Larson)

• A codependent person is one who has let another's behaviour affect him or her, and who is obsessed with controlling that person's behaviour. (Melodie Beattie)

• An emotional, psychological, and behavioural condition that develops as a result of *an individual's prolonged exposure to and practice of a set of oppressive rules,* rules which prevent the open expression of feeling as well as the direct discussion of personal and interpersonal problems. (Robert Subby; emphasis mine)

The last definition caught my feminist attention. While codependency may be difficult to describe accurately, oppression is certainly something I recognize. Relating the two is the crux of this essay.

Subby is a family systems therapist, and as such he identifies the 'set of oppressive rules' mentioned above as being characteristic of what he calls a 'dysfunctional' family. According to his definition, codependency does not result specifically or solely from relating to an addict, but rather from being reared in a dysfunctional family, which practises by rules such as

Don't talk about your feelings.
Communication is best if it is indirect and triangulated.
Be strong, be right, be good, be perfect (unrealistic expectations).
Don't be selfish.
Do as I say, not as I do.
Don't rock the boat.

Using the typical characteristics listed above, most American families qualify as dysfunctional in that they practise under similar oppressive rules whether or not a chemical addiction is present. Sharon Wegsheider-Cruse estimates that as many as 96 per cent of families are dysfunctional. When I heard this statistic, the parallel tracks of my journeys as a feminist and an ACA suddenly crossed. An alarm sounded inside me; for I suspected I was hearing a reversal.

As a feminist, I have learned that reversal is a common patriarchal communications trick. Something described one way in reality is the opposite. For example, the 'strategic defense initiative' is really the aggressive militarization of space. The 'natural look' describes a style of make-up. I want to suggest that when 96 per cent of American families display similar characteristics, what therapists describe as a 'dysfunctional' family is clearly the norm. Perhaps what we have been told is dysfunctional is actually, for our culture, normal. But what, then, is the family's function? What is the family supposed to be doing or producing? One obvious product, according to Subby, is codependency. Perhaps developing codependency is the main function of the nuclear family, since it does so with such extraordinary efficiency. With cooperation from 96 per cent of American families (plus or minus 4 per cent!), one might suspect this design is also deliberate.

While Subby describes the 'dysfunctional' family as operating by a 'set of oppressive rules,' prolonged exposure to which results in behaviour he describes as 'codependent,' feminist theorist and poet Adrienne Rich has described how the individual family unit under patriarchy is used as a training ground for dominance and subordination. From differing perspectives, both suggest that our earliest family models prepare us for relationships of unequal power. I now believe that *codependency* is a euphemism for the practice of dominance and subordination, and that its characteristics portray internalized oppression in intimate relationships.

Internalized oppression occurs when the subordinate takes in the beliefs of the dominator. The dominant group defines meaning, morality, and value, permeating society with images, institutions, structures, laws, and customs that reinforce these definitions. A white supremist society defines people of colour as inferior; a male supremist society defines women as inferior. Eventually, the subordinate group accepts the dominators' view as inevitable, as reality. This acceptance is a convenience for the dominators; for it is at this point in the process that the members of the subordinate group begin to oppress themselves, vastly simplifying the mechanics and perpetuation of oppression.

The oppressive rules of the patriarchal family system systematically train us to accept and expect the paradigm of dominance and subordination. Even the most benign of patriarchal families operates in a manner that cultivates the characteristics of *codependency*, a term that is much more acceptable than *internalized oppression*, which might encourage us to question authority or even 'rock the boat.'

So what are some of those characteristics? Perusing the current crop of self-help books on the subject, I find many checklists we can use to find out not just whether or not we are codependent, but exactly how codependent we are, since the 'disease' of codependency appears to be rampant. I have collapsed these features into several pivotal qualities:

External referencing. Always checking outside myself before making choices. I'm constantly monitoring my partner's behaviour in order to 'fix' or avoid conflict. This habit separates me from my own feelings, needs, and wants – my self.

Martyrhood. Taking care of others while sacrificing my own needs, keeping score, suffering silently, feeling unappreciated and resentful, or denying my feelings completely.

Poor self-esteem. Feeling less than, unworthy, undeserving, incapable, unlovable.

Controlling behaviour. Obsessing over my partner's behaviour, passive-aggression, manipulation by playing a victim, exposing vulnerability, or rescuing.

Demoralization. Feeling hopeless, despairing, helpless, futile, victimized, powerless.

Deriving a sense of self-worth from being needed. If I have defined and valued myself through taking care of my partner, I lose my sense of self when my partner goes into recovery, begins to get healthy, and doesn't need me. I may sabotage her/his recovery in order to maintain my self-worth.

When I look at these characteristics that examine the power dynamic at play, I notice that they describe a woman perfectly socialized into a male-supremist society, or a person of colour socialized into a white-supremist society, or any oppressed person in a system of dominance. Again, *codependency* is a precise description of the way we are trained to support a dominant/subordinate caste system.

As a woman in this culture, when I do not defer my needs to the needs of 'the man,' be he husband, father, brother, teacher, or boss, I am punished. Punishment may take the form of harsh words, a sullen look, withdrawal of affection, invalidation, a physical blow, rape, or death. I learn this lesson early in life. I learn it so well that I forget that I learned it. Deferring my needs for him and for others becomes my automatic choice. I become very creative at fulfilling the needs of others. I forget that I have needs. Life is easier when I don't have needs. In fact, when I am aware of my own needs, life under oppression becomes impossible. Finally, my needs *become* his needs.

Codependency is no accident, nor is it a disease, nor an individual character disorder afflicting us in a random manner, as popular self-help books and current therapeutic treatment would have us believe. A society of dominance trains the oppressed to be subordinate so that dominance may continue. For women this conditioning begins when we are born and extends throughout our lives via our family models, the images we see in the media, and interactions with institutions (church, school, government, military, corporation) where male dominance is infused. When we do not recognize the relation codependence has to the dominant culture, we risk falling prey to another aspect of our training in which we accept personal, individual responsibility and blame for having somehow developed 'unhealthy intimacy patterns.' In a culture of dominance, the oppressed are always at fault.

Upon occasion, the question is raised, 'what about men? Aren't they codependent, too?' By viewing codependency as the practice of dominance and subordination, I see that in patriarchy, men are trained to presume dominance, and society supports their dominance with institutionalized male privilege. So while men may indeed be 'codependent,' the neutrality of the term masks the unequal power dynamic between men and women in a sexist society. How men and women act out their codependent roles is necessarily different and should be regarded and treated differently.

CAN WE RECOVER FROM CODEPENDENCY?

Recovery is a term used to describe the phase in which an addict chooses to begin discarding addictive behaviour in favour of previous non-addictive behaviour; for example, 'I'm a recovering alcoholic,' or 'I'm in recovery from cocaine addiction.' Now we find recovery being applied to codependency: 'I'm in recovery from codependency.' Codependency is regarded by many as an addiction, in the same category as substance addiction, and the process by which we move into and out of it is seen in the same way. Once again, my feminist self squirmed in discomfort. I felt recovery was somehow inappropriate when applied to codependency.

I resisted this discomfort. I enjoyed claiming the power of recovery, the word felt active, exciting, vital, moving out of the numbness of codependency's robotitude. In terms of physical addiction to a substance, recovery is accurate: the addict decides to go back to a time when she or he was not addicted to the substance to reclaim that healthier way of being. But applied to codependency, the message is mixed. To say that recovery from codependency is possible implies that we can return to a previous time in our lives when we were healthier, when we related to our loved ones differently. It implies that there was a moment when something happened – we changed, we fell in with a bad crowd, or we took up bad ways – but now we are recovering what we lost. I suggest this is impossible.

Recovery from codependency is a myth. We cannot recover what we have never had. When we identify codependency as the practice of dominance and subordination, we see that as women we are conditioned to accept our subordinate position from the moment we are born. As Subby has determined, the typical family system thoroughly trains us in this behaviour. Born into patriarchy, we are groomed into codependency from the beginning of our lives. There was never a time that I was not codependent. To say I am 'in recovery' is inaccurate, can lead to self-blame, and distracts me from noticing the influence of the dominant culture. Herein lies the danger to women of unscrutinized acceptance of the popular approach to codependency.

If I believe that challenging codependency is solely a matter of recovery, then I ignore the political context of oppression in which I live. I accept full responsibility, viewing codependency as an individual character disorder, something wrong with me personally. As such, appropriate treatment would be therapy, Twelve-Step programs, or at the very least a slew of self-help books. I will fix myself, 'recover' my 'sobriety,' and then I will be capable of healthy intimacy. But when I try to 'recover' from codependency, there is nowhere to go. Every road out leads back to codependency because my focus is limited to my personal inadequacy and does not include the culture that designs, maintains, rewards, and benefits from codependent behaviour. With all due respect to the Twelve-Step programs of AA, these groups do nothing to develop a critical consciousness of the society that nurtures substance addiction and other forms of oppression. If I attempt to 'recover' from codependency without this analysis, the oppressor remains invisible, my oppression a misnamed affliction, and I in a cul-de-sac of self-blame. Whom does this benefit?

The subtle manipulation of our attention is one of patriarchy's greatest feats, keeping us distracted from focusing on the truths that would inspire us to action, revolt, resistance, and rage, much less vision, desire, felicity and joy. Take the best-selling pop psychology book, *Women Who Love Too Much*. The title is a classic reversal: women are at fault again, this time for loving – what we've been reared to do – 'too much.' My question is, where is the book for *Men Who Love Too Little*? Isn't this the real core of the 'problem'?

Anne Wilson Schaef's metaphor of the society as an addict is particularly mindtwisting. Leaving behind the 'white male system' of her first book *Women's Reality*, she has made addiction itself the focus, the pivotal demon, the monster at the core. But encouraging addiction and addictive behaviour is only one of the many tools the dominant caste uses to oppress. Violence, economic exploitation, homophobia, and sexism are some others. Schaef's insistence on focusing on addiction as the main problem successfully renders invisible the context, a dominant-subordinate culture that creates many interlocking systems to perpetuate the imbalance of power. I must take responsibility for my own decisions, yes, but I must also take into consideration that I live under oppression, that this is the *context* of my decision-making. I am not solely to blame for my codependence.

Imagine what might happen if, instead of saying 'I'm codependent,' thousands of women were saying 'I'm oppressed.' Imagine thousands of meetings in every city and town, where women gathered once, twice, or three times a week to discuss their oppression, what caused it, what it felt like, how they collude with it, what they might do about it. I venture to say this one slight shift in focus could galvanize women into radical, united action. Consciousness-raising groups were a pivotal part of the excitement and power of the women's liberation movement in the late 1960s and early 1970s. Might this be a reason for the propagandizing of codependency as a self-blaming double bind? In many ways, this perspective keeps us isolated from each other and prohibits us from seeing the political implications of our conditioning, the potential for personal empowerment, political action, or magic. I believe that by addressing our conditioning of dependence with a combination of self-examination *and* social consciousness, we can discover effective ways to challenge both our internalized oppression and the culture of dominance that surrounds us.

AFTERWORD

But if we cannot recover from codependency, what can we do? Is there intimacy beyond codependency? Leaving the familiar prison of dominance and subordination, we enter the wilderness of intimacy and begin a process of *discovery*. To move beyond my internalized oppression, I must be willing to examine my own behaviour and attitudes, find the roots of them in my past, and become aware of how my unique conditioning fits into and colludes with the overall design of the culture of dominance. I must be prepared also to explore entirely unfamiliar terrain: loving relationships among equals.

Without illusion, lying, indirect communication, passive-aggression, manipulation, self-sacrifice, projection, the need to control, rescue, persecution, codependence, dominance and subordination, what *is* intimacy, anyway? What does it feel like, look like, act like? How do we begin to connect with one another at the level of our essential selves? What are the guidelines for intimacy between and among self-loving, self-aware beings? We have no models, no guidelines, no environment of support. We must create them. Becoming partners in the wilderness, we must dare to rock the boat.

Selections from pages 27–39 from *Fugitive Information: Essays from a Feminist Hothead* by Kay Leigh Hagan. © 1993 by Kay Leigh Hagan. Reprinted by permission of HarperCollins Publishers, Inc.

KAREN M. LODL, MSc

A Feminist Critique of Codependency

INTRODUCTION

In a well-known National Film Board film, *Some American Feminists*, Ti-Grace Atkinson described an early experience of women in consciousness-raising groups when they discussed their problems with men. She observed that by talking together and sharing their stories, these women moved from a position of 'what is my problem because I can't find a non-abusive man' to a realization that men were a problem. In this process feminists came to understand that the personal is political, that the pain we experience in our lives has roots in the distribution of power within the society, not only in relationships or families.

Today a group of women meeting together to discuss their abusive relationships would be in a Twelve-Step program or other therapy group identifying themselves as having not only a problem but a disease: codependency. Codependency has emerged from the literature on addictions aided by the adult children of alcoholics self-help movement. It evolved from a concept to describe the experience of family members living with an alcoholic spouse or parent to a disease afflicting 96 per cent of the population (Schaef 1986).

Feminist therapists and observers (Brown 1990; Butler 1989; Faludi 1991; Haaken 1993; Hagan 1989; Kaminer 1992; Kasl 1992; Krestan and Bepko 1991; Lerner 1990; Petrie, Giordano, and Roberts 1992; Schrager 1993; Simonds 1992; Tallen 1992; Tavris 1992) have been concerned about the reverberations of victim blaming that are heard in women who use the terminology of addiction and the inspiration of popular self-help literature to describe the reality of their lives.

Women's bookstores devote more and more shelf space to 'recovery' and less and less to consciousness raising, political struggle, and analysis. In mainstream bookstores 'women's issues' are often shelved under psychology, health, and recovery.

CODEPENDENCY AS A DISEASE

There are many definitions of codependency or codependence (e.g., Mellody 1989; Schaef 1986, 1987; Wegscheider-Cruse 1985, 1990; Weinhold and Weinhold 1989). In general, codependency 'describes people who lack a defined inner self, feel defective, and, as a result, look outside themselves for self-esteem and self-definition' (Kasl 1992, 9). The literature on codependency tends to be gender neutral, but in reality we see that it describes women who adhere to a traditional set of roles learned in their family and reinforced by a sexist, heterosexist, classist, and racist society. The blueprint for survival provided to women and men by this culture is clear: women are socialized to be self-sacrificing and the emotional caretakers of men and children; men are trained to compete for mastery in the work force and to assume dominance in their families. Women who resist this arrangement were traditionally considered to be pathologically unwomanly and male identified and were urged to 'adjust.' Today, the price of this adjustment is again to be labelled with a disease: codependency.

This 'disease' is often considered progressive and incurable, akin to a physiological addiction, with symptoms that must be managed through 'working' a Twelve-Step program and associating with other persons in recovery. Diagnosis is made either through identification of symptoms or through acknowledging a 'dysfunctional' family of origin. A woman does not have to be symptomatic to have this disease. For example, adult children of alcoholics who do not recognize their codependency are considered to be in denial. Sharon Wegscheider-Cruse has been quoted as saying that '83% of nurses are firstborn children of alcoholics and, therefore, co-dependents by definition' (Schaef 1987, 30).

CODEPENDENCY AS A CULTURAL CONSTRUCT

One of the consequences of being a woman in this society is the experience of a devalued female self-concept; the codependency disease label reinforces this by encouraging women to see themselves as defective and to blame for problems within their current families. For example, the concept of codependency devalues women's reputed connectiveness and capacity for nurturing by pathologizing their commitment to a relationship. 'I am codependent because I stayed with my depressed lover for two years.' 'I am addicted to relationships because I stayed married for fifteen years.'

These self-diagnoses, aided and abetted by the self-help literature, deny the complexity and difficulty of making a decision about working through hard times with a loved one, ignore the cultural mandate for a woman to 'stand by' her mate, and minimize the consequences of economic dependence. The emphasis on addictive and self-defeating behaviours pathologizes women's survival skills and promises further self-blame for not surviving 'better.' It promotes self-labelling based on pathology and deviance (for example, 'women who love too much'), and again encourages women to take the blame for abusive relationships. 'What's wrong with my marriage is that I am codependent.'

Is it individual pathology that makes it difficult for women to know when to leave a non-satisfying relationship, is it gender socialization, or is it a combination of socialization, sexist domination, and the natural ambiguity of negotiating a painful love affair? The diagnosis of codependency allows for little insight into the subtleties of human relationship and struggle. When not blaming the victim, codependency blames the family of origin. In particular, blaming mothers as the source of pathology erases the impact of sexist, racist, and heterosexist power structures on even so-called normal families.

The language of codependency not only pathologizes all women's struggles within misogyny, but is particularly dangerous for abused women. Survivors of childhood sexual abuse receive intensive training in how to be acceptable women in contexts where acceptability is either impossible or intolerable to them. They have grown up under conditions that strongly reinforce and exploit the cultural mandate for women to devalue and ignore their own internal realities and to identify with externally generated self-concepts, whether from parents, lovers, abusers, self-help books, or well-meaning therapists. The concept of enabling behaviours coupled with the injunction to give up control advocated by proponents of relationship-addiction models implies that women not only control but are responsible for the abusive behaviours of the men in their lives. In fact, they share a disease with their abusers, whether it be labelled 'co-addiction' or 'codependency' (Utain and Oliver 1989).

CODEPENDENCY AS BEST SELLER

There are many possible explanations for the popularity of the 'codependent' or related 'adult child' label among consumers and therapists. The strength of the codependency movement is that it acknowledges the pain of growing up with substance-addicted and emotionally neglectful and/or abusive parents. Like other humanistic movements of the 1960s and 1970s, the codependency movement provides a common language to describe individual experiences and offers an opportunity for change through community. The structure and traditions of the Twelve-Step program, for example, 'Take what you can use and leave the rest,' provides the comfort of a blueprint for change and the freedom to find a common identity while minimizing conflict. The self-help aspect of the movement, with its meetings open to everyone any day in any city, allows easy and affordable access to this community.

The self-help movement against codependent and other so-called addictive behaviours speaks to a need for community and connection in a post-industrial world afflicted with a deep sense of alienation and disappointment. The language of race, class, and sex oppression has been appropriated by a new group of white, middle-class persons who also experience a deeply felt sense of marginality. In the 1960s the American New Left attempted to articulate this alienation by initiating a limited critique of class and race privilege. The women's movement followed with an analysis of sexism and heterosexism. Personal experience was transformed into the basis for a search for political solutions. As we continue to be confronted by social and political issues of overwhelming magnitude – pollution, poverty, nuclear war – there has re-emerged a longing to seek refuge in personal solutions. The 'reality of oppression' has been replaced by the 'metaphor of addiction' (Tallen 1992). We can both identify with and distance ourselves from individual pathology more easily than from systemic oppression. It is safer to identify a Marc Lepine as an adult child of alcoholics than to face the deeply rooted misogyny his crime represents. The search for a new self through recovery allows us to feel some sense of personal efficacy without challenging class, race, or gender privilege.

For therapists, the marketing of codependency treatment has become big business, characterized by a proliferation of books, conferences, and treatment centres. The application of a medical model of diagnosis and treatment to what in a previous era might have been considered existential problems of living reflects a shift in modern times from using philosophy, theology, and political analysis to medicine and science as sources of authority. The ability to diagnose and label, while implying self-empowerment for consumers, also endows the therapist with the status and credibility usually attributed to medical doctors in our society.

CODEPENDENCY AS A POLITICAL CONSTRUCT

Codependency as a critique of female dependency must be placed within the context of feminist thinking about the consequences of male-constructed gender for women. Although the male paradigm of adult development in western culture emphasizes separation and individuation, recent feminist thinking in North America describes a female concept of self that develops within relationships and through connection with others (Gilligan 1982; Jordan et al. 1991). We are societally rewarded and interpersonally nourished by our capacity to value contexts that encourage relationship and continuity of connection. We are socialized to be exquisitely aware of the emotional and material needs of others in our environment and to make meeting those needs a priority. Within patriarchy, however, this skill is politically acceptable only when used in the direct service of men and sometimes children. (Mothers continually risk compromise in order to balance the responsibility to be nurturing without becoming 'smothering' and 'overprotective.) Women who offer this advanced level of caring to ourselves, other women, and sometimes children risk being considered 'selfish,' 'unnatural,' and 'sick.' Women who refuse to offer this level of caring to men and sometimes children are definitely labelled selfish, unnatural, and sick.

Kate Millett (1970) described the socio-political impact of misogyny on the construction of female and male identities within patriarchy. Judith Bardwick and Elizabeth Douvan (1972) went on to document the psychological consequences to women of the traditional female role in terms of conflict and ambivalence. Jean Baker Miller (1976) explored the impact of the devaluation of women's 'positive' qualities and the stigmatization of our 'negative' qualities in terms of internalized subordination. Feminist therapists continued to identify the consequences of powerlessness and devaluation in the issues that women brought to therapy: limited behavioural and emotional options resulting in repressed anger, fear, anxiety, and depression, diffused sense of self leading to an unease with setting personal boundaries and lack of confidence in self-direction, confusion between internal and external causes resulting in self-blame and hypervigilance, and inability to articulate needs and to self-nurture (Collier 1982). Traditional analysis of female gender traits emphasized a positive and negative valuation based on patriarchal assumptions. Liberal feminist solutions to this socialization recommended that women revise their gender role by becoming more androgynous, often characterized as exchanging so-called negative female traits for a mix of more positive male and female traits. Radical feminist analysis went beyond simple socialization to explain the development of feminine character within the context of a misogynous culture and to advocate for a woman-centred culture. Early feminist thinking, therefore, attributed the wounding of the female psyche not to socialization to be nurturant per se but to the consequences of living this socialization within a misogynist culture. The next step has been to empower women to revalue and reclaim nurturance and connection as qualities vital not only to women's survival but to the welfare of the planet.

Feminist psychoanalytic thinking, rejecting Freudian drive theory in favour of object relations and attempting to explain the transmission of inequality on a deeper level than socialization, has emphasized the negative (Dinnerstein 1976) and positive (Chodorow 1978; Surrey 1984) impact of women's nurturance and affiliation expressed through the mothering relationship. There has only recently emerged a discussion of the impact of the father on this relationship (Kaschak 1992). The outcome of this work has been to reify women's capacity for empathy and relationship separate from the understanding that this nurturance takes place within a misogynist context, essentially depoliticizing feminist analysis of gender in favour of psychology. It is interesting, therefore, that as feminists have moved away from criticizing the female role and moved towards promoting these qualities to human society as a whole, a new movement dedicated to re-pathologizing these concerns has emerged.

Like object relations theory, the concept of codependency depoliticizes the original feminist critique of gender socialization, but with very different results. Self-in-relation theory, for example, honours women's capacity for connection while paying only passing reference to political context. Codependency thinking devalues women's capacity for connection while ignoring political context. Although mirroring early liberal feminist criticism of female dependency in terms of its debilitating impact on the female psyche, codependency depoliticizes this critique by labelling female carriers of this conditioning as individually diseased. Despite Anne Wilson Schaef's (1987) attempt to neutralize her own political analysis by moving from 'Women's Reality' to the 'Addictive System,' codependency theory reminds us that despite our attempts to reclaim female affiliation and nurturance, we cannot ignore the willingness of a woman-hating society to reduce these qualities to pathology and victim-blaming. The final context is always political.

For feminists, codependency and related Twelve-Step programs have been seductive. Women activists and therapists experience our share of the statistics on rape, incest, battering, and emotional abuse. We have sought and found safety and community in feminist groups. Our experiences in our political groups, however, have sometimes been emotionally bruising and physically exhausting, sometimes leaving us feeling as silenced and unsafe in our organizations as in our homes and workplaces. Urgent personal and political pain combine to create a pattern of intense commitment and activism, followed by disappointment, exhaustion, isolation, and burn-out. We have sought healing through therapy and a new direction by moving into graduate schools and the professions, or by retreating to lovers, home, and children, or, sadly, into silent bitterness. For many women, the rhetoric of codependency mirrors the reality of our private and public struggles.

Sandra Butler (1989) has described the depletion of political energies as activist women burn out and go into recovery programs. It is more socially acceptable for a woman to engage in a self-help process or therapy to overcome her behavioural and emotional deficits, for instance too much caring, than to join a feminist political action group. In fact, joining such a group to fight against injustice becomes another symptom of codependency. As Butler has commented, 'In trying to create a safe place for ourselves where we won't be in danger, we've succeeded only in guaranteeing that we won't be dangerous.'

MAKING THE SHIFT TO A CONSCIOUSNESS MODEL

The answer is not to replace codependency with yet another diagnostic label for women – such as Kasl's (1992) 'internalized oppression syndrome.' We have enough of those already. We need to replace the language of disease with the language of healing, and we need to find the connections between psychological and political healing and to use a language that tells true stories for both. Women have been told false stories, and our true stories have been silenced (Christ 1980). In therapy we must encourage our women clients to find their own language to tell their own stories. What we need is not another diagnostic category, but a whole model of how to work on the interface between psychological and political wounding and healing. Nancy Cole (1991) describes this connection when she observes that the dissociation common to women survivors of childhood sexual abuse allows us not to know what happened to us, but also, perhaps more importantly, not to know what we want to do about it. Sandra Butler (1989) offers this transition to what is needed:

What do we do then in order to reintegrate the need to mend our very real wounds, to heal in community, to live in both the inner and outer world? We use the concept of the celebration of scar tissue. To see as a survival mechanism everything that got a woman to the point of beginning her healing work. Whatever that was. Addiction does not necessarily begin as a self-indulgent search for pleasure without responsibility, nor does codependency stem from a deeply felt need to deny oneself, rather we see it as a failed attempt at a legitimate goal. Many of these behaviours come from a sense of incompleteness and a belief that the need to find something outside of ourselves is the journey we need to make in order to make ourselves complete.

What is important is that the search is for wholeness. Can we not find a way to celebrate the scar tissue of the search itself. And begin with an honouring of that fact. That we might rethink the need for a disease model and shift to a consciousness model. The choice between recovery or denial does not cover the complexity of a world in painful need of personal and political transformation.

In a consciousness model, grief, anger, and pain become not disease symptoms but signposts on the road to social and political change. Just as it has been said that all therapy is about grief, social transformation is also grief work. Peace activists know the importance of despair work as a catalyst to political activism. Feminists are remembering that we know this as well.

Feminist therapy must make the connection between psychological and political healing. To connect the abuse of a woman's body with the same consciousness that sends armies across borders and tortures political prisoners is dangerous and necessary. To the extent that misogyny drives women 'crazy,' we need safe places to rest and heal.

To the extent that patriarchy subjugates women, we must leave our safe places and embrace political consciousness. Feminist therapy and consciousness-raising groups must be stations along an underground railroad that not only transports survivors to freedom but also finds ways to prepare them for the struggle to create freedom.

The power of working together as women comes from honouring and respecting the creativity, strength, and courage we have brought to survival. When this survival is removed from the context of individual pathology, and resituated within that of a misogynist culture, women who never liked women, who are frightened of women, and who have never liked the female in themselves can learn to honour and value other women and themselves. Therapy as the testimony of survival and resistance, therefore, becomes a revolutionary act.

We can meet together as a community of witnesses to give testimony and to create new ways of surviving that honour rather than devalue, that empower rather than merely protect, and that translate into choices for action and transformation beyond survival. The legacy of Audre Lorde (1984) teaches us that with language and action, women move beyond survival, recovery, and healing, and into freedom and being a freedom fighter.

CONCLUSION

The concept of codependency exploits a set of attitudes consistent with our culture. As a model of addiction it encourages a purely personal and individualistic approach to working on feelings and behaviours that are in fact massively supported by external societal factors, such as media exploitation of sex-role stereotypes, limited economic opportunities, and socially reinforced power dynamics in the home, workplace, and street. It fits a negative self-concept that has been encouraged by a woman-hating culture. Having a disease explains to a woman why her trained behaviour is not working – she is defective – without having to challenge the source of that training. Its emphasis on intrapersonal and intrapsychic factors ignores the similarity of codependency behaviours with the same behaviours of any oppressed group trying to survive in any system (Flood 1990). It encourages women to emphasize personal solutions, providing a false sense of empowerment while taking energy away from political solutions to political problems.

Therapeutic modalities for codependency that rely on confrontation and the breaking of denial and that are premised on adherence to a vocabulary and program of prescribed 'recovery' to prevent 'relapse' actually recreate the original family and society experience of individual blame for systemic problems. Goodness is again externally defined, and the struggle is one to overcome illness rather than to organize for change. The achievement of survival in adverse circumstances is diagnosed rather than honoured.

Ideas like codependency and relationship addiction, although having the appealing credibility of a grassroots self-help movement, undermine our resolve to challenge and confront larger systems to work for political change. As feminist therapists and activists we must continue to seek ways to combine psychological and political consciousness to generate both healing solace and political energy. The task of healing both our inner and our outer worlds requires work towards individual empowerment and cultural transformation.

NOTE

This paper is the result of many conversations with Sandra Butler. Thanks also to Lynn Sloane and Elaine Silverman for their helpful comments.

REFERENCES

Bardwick, J.M., and E. Douvan (1972) Ambivalence: the socialization of women. In J.M. Bardwick (ed.), *Readings on the Psychology of Women*. New York: Harper & Row.

Brown, L. (1990) What's addiction got to do with it: a feminist critique of codependence. *Psychology of Women Newsletter* of Division 35, American Psychological Association, *Winter*, 4.

Butler, S. (1989) Some negative thoughts about positive thinking: a critique of addiction theory. Paper presented at Beyond Survival: Conference on Women, Addiction and Identity, April, Toronto, Ont.

Chodorow, N. (1978) *The Reproduction of Mothering*. Berkeley: University of California Press.

Christ, C. (1980) *Diving Deep and Surfacing* (2nd ed.) Boston: Beacon Press.

Cole. N. (1991) *The Politics of Dissociation: A Feminist Perspective on Multiple Personality Disorder*. Conversation hour at the Eighth International Conference on Multiple Personality / Dissociative States, Nov., Chicago, Il.

Collier, H.V. (1982) *Counseling Women*. New York: Free Press.

Dinnerstein, D. (1976) *The Mermaid and the Minotaur: Sexual Arrangements and Human Malaise*. New York: Harper & Row.

Faludi, S. (1991) *Backlash: The Undeclared War against American Women*. New York: Crown Publishers.

Flood, B. (1990) *The Politics of Co-Dependency or, Do We Live in the Problem or Does the Problem Live in Us*. Poster presentation at Association for Women in Psychology 1990 National Conference, March, Tempe, Arizona.

Gilligan, C. (1982) *In a Different Voice: Psychological Theory and Women's Development*. Cambridge, MA: Harvard University Press.

Haaken, J. (1993) From Al-Anon to ACOA: codependence and the reconstruction of caregiving. *Signs: Journal of Women in Culture and Society, 18*, 321–45.

Hagan, Kay (1989) Codependency and the myth of recovery. *Fugitive Information, 1*, 1–13.

Jordan, J.V., A.G. Kaplan, J.B Miller, I.P Stiver, and J.L. Surrey (1991) *Women's Growth in Connection*. New York: Guilford Press.

Kaminer, W. (1992) *I'm Dysfunctional, You're Dysfunctional*. New York: Addison-Wesley.

Kashak, E. (1992) *Engendered Lives*. New York: HarperCollins.

Kasl, C.D. (1992) *Many Roads One Journey: Moving beyond the 12 Steps*. New York: HarperCollins.

Krestan, J., and C. Bepko (1991) Codependency: the social reconstruction of female experience. In C. Bepko (ed.), *Feminism and Addiction*. New York: Haworth Press.

Lerner, H.G. (1990). Problems for profit? *Women's Review of Books, 7*, 15–16.

Lorde, A. (1984) *Sister Outsider*. New York: Crossing Press.

Mellody, P. (1989) *Facing Codependence*. San Francisco: Harper & Row.

Miller, J.B. (1976) *Toward a New Psychology of Women*. Boston: Beacon Press.

Millett, K. (1970) *Sexual Politics*. Garden City, NJ: Doubleday.

Petrie, J., J.A. Giordano, and C.S. Roberts (1992) Characteristics of women who love too much. *Affilia, 7*, 7–20.

Schaef, A. (1986) *Co-Dependence: Misunderstood – Mistreated*. Minneapolis: Winston Press.

– (1987). *When Society Becomes an Addict*. New York: Harper & Row.

Schrager, C.D. (1993) Questioning the promise of self-help: a reading of *Women Who Love Too Much*. *Feminist Studies, 19*, 177–92.

Simonds, W. (1992) *Women and Self-Help Culture: Reading between the Lines*. New Brunswick, NJ: Rutgers University Press.

Surrey, J. (1984) The 'self-in-relation': a theory of women's development. *Work In Progress*, No. 13. Wellesley: Stone Center Working Paper Series.

Tallen, B. (1992) Codependency: the de-politicization of feminism. Paper presented at Association of Women in Psychology 1992 National Feminist Psychology Conference, Feb., Long Beach, CA.

Tavris, C. (1992). *The Mismeasure of Woman*. New York: Simon & Schuster.

Utain, M., and B. Oliver (1989) *Scream Louder*. Deerfield Beach, FL: Health Communications.

Wegscheider-Cruse, S. (1985) *Choice-Making*. Deerfield Beach, FL: Health Communications.

Wegscheider-Cruse, S., and J. Cruse (1990) *Understanding Co-dependency*. Deerfield Beach, FL: Health Communications.

Weinhold, B. and Weinhold, J. (1989) *Breaking Free of the Co-dependency Trap*. Walpole, NH: Stillpoint Publishing.

CHRISTINE MCKAY, MSW

Codependency: The Pathologizing of Female Oppression

During the last two decades feminist research in psychiatry and psychology has demonstrated the ways in which concepts of mental health are male defined and how psychiatric and psychological theories reflect and reinforce the existing power relations that oppress women by equating female socialization with 'pathology' or 'maladjustment' (Chesler 1972: Smith and David 1975; Penfold and Walker 1983). Psychiatric and psychological theories support gender, as well as race and class, domination by obscuring cultural and economic factors and by 'labelling as "social," problems which are in fact political and economic' (Morgan 1981, 20). Patricia Morgan (1981) addresses the ways that psychiatry and psychology function to conceal and contain the tensions inherent in contemporary capitalist, as well as sexist and racist, society: 'Social problem management through the capitalist state serves to depoliticize political questions: to incorporate demands through quasi-medical models, to individualize and personalize structural problems, and to obscure any class interests inherent in them' (21).

Women, like other oppressed groups, are vulnerable to this growing trend of medicalizing political and economic problems, a process that transforms broader political issues into individual pathologies (Conrad 1980). Codependency is the most recent quasi-medical model to reinforce the existing power relations by equating female socialization with pathology.

The term *codependency* started to be used in the North American alcoholism treatment field in the early 1970s and originally referred exclusively to the behaviour of partners, primarily female, of alcoholics (Weisner and Room 1984). By the 1980s, however, the concept had expanded to include any suffering that results from focusing on the needs of others (Whitfield 1989). This redefinition of codependency increased the market of potential codependents and created a demand for therapists specializing in codependency as well as for intensive, in-patient treatment programs. By 1990 a survey conducted by the American Psychological Association's Division 35 (on Women) found that codependency was the second most frequently addressed issue in therapy (Brown 1990).

Despite this trend, many feminists have challenged the notion of codependency (Fabunmi, Frederick, and Jarvis Bicknese 1985; Asher and Brissett 1988; Hagan 1989; van Wormer 1989; Babcock 1990; Haaken 1990; Krestan and Bepko 1990; Tallen 1990; Walters 1990; Sloven 1991; Irvine 1991; McKay 1992). Within the addictions and mental health fields these feminist critiques of codependency have been marginalized.

In this critique, codependency is viewed as a social construct that is shaped by economic, historical, and social forces, not as a diagnostic category that has emerged from an objective or a neutral science. The evolution of codependency is situated in an economic, historical, and social context through a discussion of three of the issues raised by feminist critiques: one, a discussion of who profits from the creation and promotion of codependency; two, how the 'symptoms' ascribed to codependency are related to historical and current views of female mental health as well as women's subordinate status in North American society; and three, the impact of male violence on women. Finally, feminist models of healing for women in relationships with alcohol abusers are forwarded.

A central premise of this paper is that the proponents of codependency ignore feminist research, theory, and practice. Female behaviour that is seen by the codependency 'experts' as a personal failing or pathology is viewed instead by feminists as an appropriate response to the 'socially produced conflicts and contradictions shared by many women' (Weedon 1987, 33). Women for whom such conflicts are magnified, for example, women in relationships with alcohol abusers and women who are or who have been abused, are at greater risk of being labelled codependent (Frank and Golden 1992).

Feminist critics of codependency are concerned with the personal and political implications of codependency theory and practice. What feminists identify as a political issue – namely, the devaluation of self that results from institutionalized oppression – is reframed as a personal pathology by the proponents of codependency. This medicalizing of female experience is an example of social-problem management

(Morgan 1981), a form of social control that serves to manage and channel political struggles into individualized and personalized ones. This pathologizing of women's oppressed status undermines the feminist struggle to transform the 'politics of domination' (hooks 1988) and diverts women's attention, anger, and energy from the real sources of their oppression: the inequitable economic, social, and political structures that discriminate against women to differing degrees depending on race, class, sexual orientation, and age, globally. This analysis asserts that codependency theory and practice both reinforce male, as well as race and class, privilege and serve to maintain oppressive power relations. Codependency is viewed as part of a growing 'backlash' against feminism that has emerged in the regressive 1980s (Faludi 1991).

DEFINITION AND MODELS OF CODEPENDENCY

While many definitions of codependency exist, the definition adopted at the First National Conference on Codependency held in 1989 states that codependency is: 'a pattern of painful dependency on compulsive behavior and approval seeking in order to gain safety, identity and self-worth' (Lawton 1990, 1).

This definition was agreed upon by 'a committee of more than 20 eminent therapists and theorists' (ibid.) thereby legitimizing the concept of codependency as a diagnostic category. However, many theoretical differences among these theorists persist. For example, there is little agreement among the 'experts' on whether codependency is a primary disease (Schaef 1986; Whitfield 1989) or a dysfunctional behaviour (Subby 1984; Beattie 1987; Potter-Efron and Potter-Efron 1989; Spann and Fischer 1990). Other proponents of codependency (Cermak 1986; Cocores 1987; Whitfield 1989; Wegsheider-Cruse and Cruse 1990) have suggested that codependency be considered a personality disorder and included in the current edition of the *Diagnostic and Statistical Manual of Mental Disorders (DSM-IV 1994)*, the psychiatric profession's diagnostic code book. A personality disorder is defined in the *DSM-III-R* (1987) as a 'constellation of enduring, inflexible and dysfunctional traits that cause either significant functional impairment or subjective distress' (335).

The disease and personality disorder frameworks of codependency lodge the construct within a medical model of treatment. These frameworks extend the disease model of alcoholism, dominant in North

America, to include family members and promote individual and/or group therapy in out-patient or in-patient settings as well as participation in Al-Anon.

The construction of codependency as a disease legitimizes a medical model of treatment. Katherine van Wormer (1989) notes that the 'medicalization of alcoholism has reaped enormous benefits in terms of revenue for diagnosis, research, and treatment' and that 'there is a parallel trend to medicalize codependency' (60). Jo-Ann Krestan and Claudia Bepko (1991) agree, and they contend that profit making is in part responsible for the shift 'from describing a problem to ascribing pathology'; for if 'one is dealing with a disease, there is justification for establishing high-cost programs to treat it' (218).

The proponents of the dysfunctional behaviour model of codependency utilize a behavioural/social learning approach with an emphasis on family-systems theory (Larson 1987; Bradshaw 1990). Systems theorists tend to lodge the source of all problems within the family unit and distribute responsibility and blame for any problem equally among family members. Many systems theorists contend that 'Symptoms in any member of the family, whether social (e.g., child abuse, delinquency), physical (e.g., depression, schizophrenia) or conflictual (e.g., marital conflict) are viewed as evidence of dysfunction in the family relationship process' (Helm 1970, 342).

Critics of family systems theory (Carniol 1987; Haaken 1990; Hare-Mustin and Marecek 1990) claim that systems theorists ignore the power differentials between women and men. Ben Carniol, in his book *Case Critical: The Dilemma of Social Work in Canada* (1987), argues that the main emphasis of systems theory is on individual or family adjustment within existing social relations, conditions that are shaped by capitalism, sexism, and racism.

While the disease/personality disorder and dysfunctional behaviour frameworks of codependency differ, both models promote similar kinds of treatment: individual and group therapy in either an in-patient or out-patient setting as well as participation in Al-Anon, the self-help group for partners of alcoholics. The membership of Al-Anon is 80 per cent female (van Wormer 1989).

Al-Anon is patterned on the Twelve-Step model put forward by Alcoholics Anonymous (AA). While the Twelve-Step model has positive features, such as being widely available to the public at no cost, critics of the model argue that it is rooted in Christian doctrine (Bufe 1988) and therefore does not address cultural and religious differences (Herman 1988).

Other criticisms of the Twelve-Step model include: the disease model of alcoholism is not substantiated by empirical research (Fingarette 1988); the disease model is apolitical in orientation (Herman 1988); the 'disease' label robs the individual of autonomy (Fingarette 1988) and responsibility (Peele 1989).

In addition to these issues concerning theory and practice, the literature on codependency is vague (Babcock 1991). According to Ramona Asher and Dennis Brissett (1988), the definitional and conceptual ambiguity that characterizes the popular and psychotherapeutic literature on codependency has a twofold effect: one, that almost all women can be diagnosed as having 'codependency' and two, resistance to such an all-encompassing label is difficult.

Women, particularly white, middle-class women (Tallen 1990), are the main targets of the codependency message. Statistics suggest that most women stay with their alcohol-abusing partner, while the majority of men in the same circumstances leave (Kokin and Walker 1989). Women who stay in these situations, whether out of fear for their own safety, financial dependence, or in compliance with traditional female socialization, are now considered to be suffering from codependency.

Given the similarity between the 'symptoms' of codependency and behaviour that is associated with traditional female social conditioning, any woman who wishes to be involved in her partner's addictions treatment is likely to be labelled 'codependent.' Should a woman disagree with the diagnosis of codependency, her scepticism is used as evidence of her 'codependence' (Tavris 1980; Harper and Capdevila 1990) and 'further proof that this is a "sick woman"' (Fabunmi, Frederick, and Jarvis Bicknese 1985, 2).

Codependency is presented by the 'experts' as gender neutral and is based on the implicit assumption that codependency affects both genders equally. The proponents of codependency ignore gender as well as the variables of race, class, poverty, and sexual orientation. Consequently, the construct of codependency is gender, race, and class blind (McKay 1992).

Within the addictions literature on codependency only Schaef (1986, 1987) puts forward an analysis of gender relations and an admission that many of the 'symptoms' of codependency are reinforced differentially according to gender. Despite an acknowledgment that women are oppressed, Schaef (1986) claims that codependency is a 'basic, generic disease' (40). Like other proponents of codependency, she extends the disease model of alcoholism to include family members.

While Schaef (1987) co-opts some of the language of feminism and suggests that the 'White Male System' supports the development of codependency, she ignores feminist research regarding gender and power relations. Behaviours that feminists have identified as resulting from oppression (Miller 1976) are labelled a disease by Schaef (1986). This pathologizing of female oppression transforms what feminists define as political and social issues into a personal disease (Kaplan 1990).

Few proponents of codependency discuss the factors of race, class, or sexual orientation in relation to codependency, and those theorists who do (Coggins 1990; hooks 1993; Finnegan and McNally 1989) fail to critique its link to the medicalization and individualization of political problems.

Coggins (1990) combines the Recovery Medicine Wheel, a Native American healing tool, with the disease model of addictions and Schaef's notion of codependency. bell hooks, in her book *Sisters of the Yam: Black Women and Self-Recovery* (1993), also appears to endorse Schaef's concept of codependency. While hooks acknowledges that 'black women are socialized to assume the role of omnipotent caregiver' (75) she links the passive acceptance of this female socialization to codependency. Finnegan and McNally (1989) discuss how homophobia contributes to the development of codependency. They, too, cite Schaef (1986) as well as Cermak (1986).

Coggins (1990), hooks (1993), and Finnegan and McNally (1989) discuss the psychological impact of oppressive power relations in relation to race, gender, and sexual orientation. However, these authors appear to agree with the conceptualizations of codependency and fail to examine critically the construct of codependency or its economic, historical, and social underpinnings.

THE BUSINESS OF CODEPENDENCY

In the United States, the addictions treatment industry is big business (Fingarette, 1988). The cost of a typical twenty-eight-day in-patient treatment program for alcohol or drug abuse ranges from $7,500 to $35,000 (Peele 1989) and is usually paid for by insurers. Similar programs have been promoted by the addictions treatment industry for so-called 'codependents' (Long and Wolin 1989). In the 1980s the movement to provide treatment for the spouses and children of alcohol abusers, estimated to be upwards of 80 million Americans, became the largest growth area of all in the alcoholism treatment field (Peele 1989).

Stanton Peele (1989) notes that during the 1980s 'the shift from government funding of public facilities to the support of third-party financing of alcoholism treatment created a tremendous expansion of private inpatient treatment' (49). As a result of this change in policy: 'Between 1978 and 1984 the number of for-profit residential treatment centers increased by 350% and their caseloads by 400%' (ibid.).

These for-profit institutions, which are largely owned by conglomerates (Peele 1989), benefit from the medicalization of codependency. When many of these institutions have a surplus of empty beds, the creation of this new pathology provides a vast new market for those for-profit treatment facilities to exploit (Long and Wolin 1989). The November 1987 issue of *Addiction Program Management*, for example, addressed the issue of 'how to fill hospital beds with co-dependency patients' (Long and Wolin 1989, 42). Krestan and Bepko (1991) argue that codependency has been 'created by a set of diagnostic labels that reflect primarily the self-serving and self-reinforcing standards of the treating profession itself' (219).

Other commercial and corporate interests have also benefited from the creation of codependency. Wendy Kaminer (1990) states: 'This amorphous disease is a business, generating millions of book sales.'(1).

Major publishing houses, such as Harper & Row, Prentice Hall, and Thomas Nelson, all have their own lines of recovery books. Smaller publishing concerns also are benefiting. Health Communications Inc., for example, publishes only books on recovery. It publishes about 102 recovery titles, including Janet Woititz's *Adult Children of Alcoholics*, Charles Whitfield's *Healing the Child Within*, and John Bradshaw's *Bradshaw on: The Family*. Collectively, these books have sold close to 2 million copies and have made at least a few of the authors wealthy. Bradshaw, for example, commands $6,500 per day for speaking engagements, in addition to having all his expenses paid and first-class airfare (Katz and Liu 1991).

The phenomenon of codependency has also been accompanied by mass media saturation. These books and their authors are promoted in articles in *Time* and *Newsweek*, in talk show interviews, and even in television therapy with John Bradshaw. This media blitz has popularized the notion of codependency for mass consumption and has effectively created a demand for mass treatment (van Wormer 1989).

HYSTERIA, MASOCHISM, AND CODEPENDENCY

Historically, women have been viewed as inferior and subordinate to men and the mental health establishment has legitimized this claim. Freudian theory, for example, has characterized adult women as being narcissistic, masochistic, and dependent (Mowbray, Lanir, and Hulce 1984). Feminist researchers argue that the historical formulations of female psychological development have obscured power relations and, consequently, have constructed 'a fundamental alliance between "women" and "madness"' (Showalter 1985, 3).

Feminist critics position the emergence of codependency within this historical context (van Wormer 1989; Babcock 1990; Irvine 1992; McKay 1992). One of the trends that feminist researchers have identified in examining the history of psychiatry and psychology is that of labelling 'femininity a disease' (Chesler 1972; Ehrenreich and English 1978; Penfold and Walker 1983; Showalter 1985; Ussher 1991). The construct of codependency, like the notions of 'hysteria' and 'masochism,' perpetuates this trend.

Leslie Irvine (1992) draws parallels between the emergence of codependency and that of neurasthenia (the most extreme form of hysteria), a predominantly female malady that reached epidemic proportions within the middle and upper classes at the turn of the century. She contends that both conceptualizations are culturally 'acceptable' channels for expressing female discontent (Irvine 1992), at least for white, middle-class women.

The constructs of both 'hysteria' and 'codependency' emerged after periods of increased feminist activity, eras when women threatened male privilege by challenging the restrictions of their enforced social roles as women, wives, and mothers (ibid.). The epidemic of 'hysteria' at the turn of the century, for example, followed a time when middle-class women were beginning to organize for political rights and entrance into higher education and the professions (Showalter 1985); and the 'women's liberation movement' of the 1970s preceded the emergence of 'codependency' during the 1980s.

In both cases, women's discontent is rendered a pathology, and consequently, a medical means of social control is legitimized. Both examples demonstrate how the medical profession, as part of the dominant political apparatus, channels women's discontent into socially acceptable forms, forms that ultimately support male privilege and co-opt the feminist movement.

Feminist critics of codependency view the construct as part of the growing 'backlash' (Faludi 1991) against feminism (Irvine 1992; McKay 1992). A backlash against feminism is defined by Bordo (1989) as being a reassertion of 'existing gender configurations against any attempts to shift or transform power-relations' (14). It is predictable that a psychological construct that suggests that vast numbers of women are 'sick' or 'dysfunctional' would emerge in the 1980s following the gains made by the women's movement during the 1970s.

Nor was codependency the only psychological construct with sexist underpinnings to emerge in the 1980s. In tandem with the mass marketing of codependency within the addictions field, there was a concerted push by a group of male psychoanalysts within the American Psychiatric Association (Faludi 1991; Herman 1992), the overseeing body of the mental health field, to have the 'masochistic personality disorder' included as a diagnostic category in the *DSM-III-R* (APA 1987).

Feminist critics within the mental health field, such as Paula Caplan (1985), linked this proposed diagnostic category with the pathologizing of traditional female social conditioning and argued that the myth of female masochism has been perpetuated and legitimized because it 'helps justify the continuing subjugation of women' (29–30).

Despite much resistance from male professionals within the American Psychiatric Association, feminists within the mental health field succeeded in getting the 'masochistic personality disorder' dropped from inclusion in the *DSM-III-R* (APA 1987) only to have essentially the same sexist construct, in the new guise of the 'self-defeating personality disorder,' included in the appendix (for an illuminating discussion of the politics surrounding this process, see Caplan 1991). Neither alleged personality disorder is included in *DSM-IV* (APA 1994).

The 'self-defeating personality disorder' describes a 'disorder in which a person persists in behavior that does not allow him or her to reach his or her goals' (van Wormer 1989, 54). According to Paula Caplan (1988), much of the behaviour included in the criteria for the 'self-defeating personality disorder' diagnosis is a 'combination of adaptation to the misogyny in our society and an obedient execution of the traditional female role' (198). Feminist critics of this proposed diagnostic category argue that it is as sexist and victim blaming as the masochistic personality disorder diagnosis (Franklin 1987).

The feminist critiques of codependency are similar to those arguments put forward against the 'masochistic' or 'self-defeating' personality disorder. They are also just as compelling. For example, both proposed diagnostic categories emerged almost simultaneously in the 1980s; both ignore the social devaluation of women; both imply that women actively collude in destructive situations; both obscure the incidence and effects of violence against women; both profit the addictions or mental health industry; and finally, both serve as mechanisms of social control that undermine feminism.

CODEPENDENCY AND ABUSED WOMEN

Many of the concerns raised by workers in the anti-violence movement are also relevant to a critical analysis of codependency. In *Women, Violence and Social Change* (1992), for example, R. Emerson Dobash and Russell P. Dobash argue that the more the anti-violence movement adopts 'an individual, psychological position on abused women the greater likelihood that it will dismiss or ignore the political, social and economic issues surrounding the problem of male violence against women' (234).

The proponents of codependency theory and practice ignore the political, social, and economic factors that keep women in relationships with alcohol abusers and fail to acknowledge the social and political problem of violence against women. In fact, violence against women is subsumed under the codependency framework. Melody Beattie (1987), for instance, states that codependents 'tend to have been victims of sexual, physical, or emotional abuse, neglect, abandonment, or alcoholism' (38). According to Beattie (1987), and other proponents of the codependency framework, women who stay in abusive relationships are, by definition, 'codependent.'

Research on codependency (Brewer, Zawadski and Lincoln 1990; Lyon and Greenberg 1991) also ignores the impact of violence on women, specifically male violence in intimate relationships, and fails to address whether or not so-called codependents have also experienced sexual, physical, or emotional abuse. This is a neglected confounding variable given the prevalence of male violence towards women in North American society.

Studies of domestic violence have indicated a relationship between alcohol abuse and wife battering (Walker 1979; Rainbolt and Greene 1990). The evidence suggests, however, that 'violent behaviour in the home is not a direct result of alcohol abuse' (Rainbolt and Greene 1990, 4) and that even if these men stop drinking they will often continue their abusive behaviour. Within the addictions field, however, 'treatment programs often write off physical abuse as symptomatic and secondary to the substance abuse in lieu of laying the responsibility directly with the physical abuser' (Fabunmi, Frederick, and Jarvis Bicknese 1985, 3). The impact of violence against women, as a personal and political issue, must be considered, because many of the women who are being labelled 'codependent' by the addiction and mental health fields are being abused or have been abused in childhood.

Incest

Although estimates of incest vary, Kathleen Whipp (1991) cites two surveys that report incest as occurring in 19 per cent and 21 per cent of women. In another study of 900 women chosen by random sampling techniques, Russell (1984) found that one woman in three had been sexually abused in childhood. Recent studies reveal that 44 per cent to 70 per cent of the women using psychiatric services are incest survivors (Whipp 1991). The perpetrators of incest are men in 98.8 per cent of cases (OACWI 1990). These estimates suggest that many of the women who are labelled codependent are incest survivors.

The most common behavioural manifestations of incest are serious depression, self-injury, anxiety, somatization, panic attacks and phobias, compulsive risk taking, angry outbursts, prostitution, substance abuse, eating disorders, and imbalances in interpersonal relationships (Whipp 1991). These behaviours, which are decontextualized by the psychiatric profession, are attempts to cope with trauma. Many of the 'symptoms' of codependency, such as weak boundaries, lack of trust, and anger (Beattie 1987), are similar to the behaviours that incest survivors develop.

Incest survivors typically identify chronic depression, rather than incest, as the presenting problem in therapy (Gelinas 1981). In addition to the 'disguised' presentation of incest-related trauma, difficulties exist surrounding disclosure, including the repression of memory. Most mental health as well as addiction workers have not been trained in identifying or helping incest survivors.

Incest survivors have been given other psychiatric diagnoses such as 'borderline personality disorder,' 'alcohol dependence,' 'eating disorders,' and 'multiple personality disorders' (Whipp 1991). For example, Bryer et al. (1987) found that 86 per cent of women with the psychiatric diagnosis of 'borderline personality disorder' were incest survivors;

while Putman et al. (1986) discovered that 97 per cent of the women with 'multiple personality disorders' had been sexually abused, often brutally, by male family members in childhood.

The psychiatric profession revictimizes incest survivors by decontextualizing their coping behaviour and pathologizing the trauma associated with incest (Whipp 1991). The proponents of codependency also ignore the trauma associated with incest and decontextualize the coping behaviour of incest survivors by erroneously labelling some of this behaviour 'codependency.'

Battered Women

Many of the women who are labelled 'codependent' are in violent and abusive relationships. Conservative estimates suggest that one in ten Canadian women are victims of male violence in the home (MATCH International 1990). Research on battered women has demonstrated that any woman – regardless of personality characteristics, family history, race, age, or class – can find herself with an abuser (Frank and Golden 1992). Battering also occurs in lesbian relationships where, owing to the internalization of oppressive power relations, one partner uses violence in order to control and dominate.

Women stay in abusive relationships for multiple and complex reasons: the availability of community support, the legal and criminal justice systems' response to wife battery, her employability, and whether she has children (Frank and Golden 1992); in addition to female socialization, fear, depression, emotional paralysis, and financial dependence (Penfold and Walker 1983). Women of colour and lesbians experience the additional problems of prejudice and discrimination. Financial dependence is the most common reason women give for staying in abusive relationships (Penfold and Walker 1983). Many of the same factors keep women in relationships with alcohol abusers.

A potential hazard of the codependency framework is that behaviour that is adaptive and necessary for survival within the context of an abusive relationship will be labelled 'codependent' by addictions workers. According to Fabunmi, Frederick, and Jarvis Bicknese (1985): 'a preoccupation with the spouse is a learned survival skill which enables the abused women to anticipate and sometimes avoid situations where she (or her children) will be physically hurt' (3).

Many psychological theories of wife battery, such as those incorporating the diagnosis of the masochistic personality disorder, promote the myth that battered women 'somehow asked for it' and focus blame on the victim (Penfold and Walker 1983). Proponents of codependency also imply that women in alcoholism-complicated relationships, such as battered women, provoked or 'somehow asked for it' and are complicit in their own suffering. An example is the accepted notion within the addictions field that 'enablers help to kill alcoholics' and that 'the most common cause of alcoholism is the non-alcoholic' (Miller and Gold 1989, 7).

The codependency model, according to Harriet Lerner (1989), does not hold substance abusers accountable for 'their abusive, rotten, or violent behavior, since, as Schaef writes, they have a "progressive disease" and "can't help themselves"' (cited in Tavris 1989, 226). Krestan and Bepko (1990) agree and argue that codependency is 'simply another tool in the oppression of women, fostering denial of male accountability' (219). These feminist critics contend that the codependency framework, like the psychological theories that explain wife battery (Dobash and Dobash, 1992), absolves men of responsibility for their behaviour (Krestan and Bepko 1990; Tallen 1990; Walters 1990).

A number of the concerns raised by researchers and clinicians exploring the psychological impact of male violence on women, such as the potential for decontextualizing behaviour that serves survival, are also relevant to codependency. These concerns are ignored by the proponents of codependency.

FEMINIST APPROACHES TO HEALING

Conceptual definitions and models influence therapeutic practices. Jane Sloven (1991) highlights the importance of choosing a model from which to view problems in living. She states: 'The choice of a lens in treatment influences not only our clients' perceptions of their problems and of themselves, it also determines treatment choices and treatment outcomes' (Sloven 1991, 195). The proponents of codependency label the female partners of alcohol abusers 'sick' and promote a corresponding medical model of treatment.

The problems of women in relationships with alcohol abusers, especially chronic and heavy drinkers, are a legitimate concern. Women stay in these relationships for numerous reasons, including financial dependence, love, and the traditional female role imperative to nurture others, especially family members, often at the expense of self. Women in relationships with alcohol abusers, like women in relationships with partners who have cancer, suffer from stress, not individual pathology. Women who are in stressful relationships, whether alcoholism related or not, can be helped by a feminist approach to therapy that considers the impact of institutionalized and internalized sexism.

A feminist approach to therapy grew out of the contemporary women's movement and is rooted in the broader framework of the psychology of women, which includes the disciplines of social work (Levin 1983; Burstow 1992), psychiatry (Miller 1976), and counselling (Ballou and Gabalac 1983; Butler 1985; Greenspan 1983; Jiminez and Rice 1990; Herman 1992). Other feminists (Dominelli 1988; Fulani 1988; hooks 1993) have challenged the gender, race, and class biases within traditional psychology.

Feminists argue that traditional therapy supports gender, race, and class domination by obscuring cultural and economic factors. They argue that traditional therapy functions 'as a mechanism of social control, preserving the status quo and protecting the patriarchal (as well as race and class) structure of society by perpetuating sex-role stereotypes in both its theoretical stance and practical application' (Sturdivant 1980, 66).

While a number of therapists have articulated visions of feminist therapy (Greenspan 1983; Levine 1983; Ballou and Gabalac 1985; Burstow 1992), at present there is no unified approach (Ballou and Gabalac 1985; Butler 1985). Areas of disagreement and consensus regarding philosophical assumptions, principles, and guidelines are identified by Ballou and Gabalac (1985). While divergent positions exist, all feminist therapy shares the assumption that women have less social, political, and economic power than men. As well, all feminist therapy shares a commitment to transform this oppression by empowering women.

Ballou and Gabalac (1985) identify the three key principles that inform all feminist therapies: one, that women are oppressed; two, that what is labelled female pathology is caused by external, not internal, sources; and three, that women must attain economic and psychological independence in order to combat the first two problems (23–4). These principles are expanded upon by Butler (1985) in her guidelines for feminist therapy. According to Butler, the process of examining sex roles and power differentials in feminist therapy as well as learning to differentiate between internal and external sources of distress helps women to identify the harmful effects of all kinds of exploitation. Women's strengths, which have been systematically devalued in patriarchal culture, are also validated.

A feminist approach to therapy situates the problems women experience within an individual as well as a social, economic, and political context. The exploration of sex-role stereotypes and internalized oppression in feminist therapy helps women to engage in a process of cognitive and emotional restructuring that transforms the devaluation of self that occurs as a result of patriarchal, as well as racist and classist, power relations. The personal, cultural, and economic factors that keep women in unsatisfying relationships are validated and examined as coping skills that arise in 'response to an untenable psychopolitical situation' (Greenspan 1983, 264). This process is well described by Ballou and Gabalac (1985) and can be expanded to fit the needs of women in relationships with alcohol abusers.

For women in relationships with chronic and heavy drinkers a feminist approach to therapy can be combined with post-traumatic stress therapy, a model that is increasingly used to describe the trauma experienced by survivors of incest (Whipp 1991) and abuse (Herman 1992). The same model has been utilized by other theorists to describe the psychological and physiological impact of oppression on Native peoples (Rowell and Kusterer 1991).

Feminist critics of codependency, such as Frank and Golden (1992), contend that the 'post-traumatic stress disorder,' or 'PTSD,' is a more accurate diagnostic framework than the codependency model for many women in alcoholism-complicated relationships. While the PTSD label is an improvement over the codependency framework, the model also has limitations.

One of the advantages of the PTSD diagnosis is that 'while other psychiatric "disorders" supposedly develop out of a person's *individual psychological and biological make-up*, "PTSD" may arise out of a past traumatic experience that would be "markedly distressing" to anyone' (Whipp 1991, 39). According to Whipp, PTSD is the only *DSM* diagnostic category that does not revictimize the incest survivor when incest is detected.

In her book *Trauma and Recovery* (1992), Judith Herman combines a medical approach with a feminist approach and puts forward the need for a new psychiatric diagnosis that acknowledges the effects and manifestations of prolonged, repeated trauma and the 'profound deformations of personality that occur' (119). She suggests using the label 'complex post-traumatic stress disorder' (119).

The complex post-traumatic stress model describes the psychological and physiological impact of prolonged and severe stress and includes 'those subjected to totalitarian systems in sexual and domestic life, including survivors of domestic battering, childhood physical and sexual abuse' (ibid., 121). While this model may not apply to all women in alcoholism-complicated relationships, it certainly applies to those women in relationships with chronic and heavy drinkers. These women live in a state of chronic unpredictability and stress. Many of the indicators for PTSD apply to women in these relationships: a sense of helplessness; shame, guilt, and self-blame; a preoccupation with the relationship with the perpetrator; acceptance of the belief system or rationalizations of the perpetrator; isolation and withdrawal; and a sense of hopelessness and despair (ibid.). Herman outlines a therapeutic approach for working with women who have been abused, a model of practice that validates the coping skills that these women have developed in response to trauma. This model could be adapted for use with women in relationships with chronic and severe alcohol abusers.

A disadvantage of the PTSD framework is that it is lodged within the psychiatric framework of the *DSM* and that consequently a medical model of treatment is promoted. This leads to many of the same problems that were discussed in relation to including codependency as a personality disorder in the *DSM*. Feminists, such as Frank and Golden (1992) and Herman (1992), are attempting to make the *DSM* more responsive to the trauma experienced by women in abusive relationships.

Audre Lorde (1984), however, argues that 'the master's tool will never dismantle the master's house' (112). A potential danger in applying the PTSD and complex PTSD models to groups oppressed by gender, race, or class is that social problems become individualized and viewed as medical, rather than social and political, issues.

CONCLUSION

In this article, the feminist critiques of codependency theory and practice were reviewed. As well, the economic, historical, and social underpinnings of codependency were exposed. Feminist critics of codependency argue that the construct is sexist and needs to be re-examined. These feminist critiques of codependency are marginalized within both the addictions and the mental health fields.

Feminist researchers in psychology and psychiatry have documented a pervasive historical trend, associated with peaks of feminist activity, of labelling 'femininity a disease' and have argued that definitions of mental health reflect a male bias. Despite sustained feminist critiques of male bias within the mental health field, the prevailing conceptualizations of codependency are gender, as well as race and class, blind and are informed by a male-defined standard of mental health.

Codependency is viewed by some feminist critics as part of a broader trend within advanced capitalism: the increasing tendency to medicalize, and individualize, problems that are social and economic in origin. This medicalization of social problems intensifies when the interests of the dominant class are threatened and functions as a method of social control by depoliticizing discontent. As women are the primary recipients of the codependent label, feminist critics claim, with justification, that codependency is an ideological assault on feminism. Codependency theory can be seen as an attempt to replace women's developing political analysis of female oppression with a personalized and pathologized alternative.

The medicalization of social problems also profits the addictions treatment industry. The emergence of codependency has benefited the proponents of codependency and the addictions treatment industry, largely owned by conglomerates in the United States. While the 'experts' get rich promoting their books through extensive speaking engagements, the addictions treatment industry exploits a huge market and flogs expensive in-patient residential treatment in order to fill empty treatment beds with codependents. This glut of treatment beds has resulted from empire building within the treatment industry, an overexpansion of for-profit treatment facilities during the early 1980s.

A central concern that is addressed throughout this paper is the potential for women to identify with the codependency construct because it describes and pathologizes many of the conflicts and contradictions women in North America experience, conflicts that are exacerbated for women in relationships with chronic and heavy drinkers.

Feminist critics contend that codependency theory and practice blames and harms women, especially women who have been abused or are in abusive relationships. Given the incidence of violence in women's lives, a fact that is ignored by the proponents of codependency, it is likely that the behaviour associated with a history of sexual, physical, and emotional abuse will be labelled 'codependent.' Research on codependency also fails to address the issue of male violence in intimate relationships.

Workers in the addictions and mental health fields who uncritically adopt and promote the codependency model perpetuate the oppression of women. These critiques of codependency challenge workers in these fields to question their assumptions regarding the construct of codependency and provide alternative models that empower women individually and collectively to resist patriarchal, as well as racist and classist, oppression: the root cause of codependency.

REFERENCES

American Psychiatric Association. *Diagnostic and Statistical Manual of Mental Disorders* (1987: *DSM-III-R*; 1994: *DSM-IV*). Washington, DC: American Psychiatric Association.

Asher, R., and D. Brissett (1988) Codependency: a view from women married to alcoholics. *International Journal of the Addictions, 23,* 331–50.

Babcock, M. (1990). Caught in the culture: women and addictions services. Unpublished manuscript.

– (1991) Who are the real co-dependents? *Focus* (Aug./Sept.), 28, 44–5.

Ballou, M., and N. Gabalac (1985) *A Feminist Position on Mental Health.* Springfield, IL: Charles C. Thomas.

Beattie, M. (1987) *Codependent No More.* New York: Harper & Row/Hazelden Foundation.

Bordo, S. (1989) The body and the reproduction of femininity: a feminist appropriation of Foucault. In A. Jaggar and S. Bordo (eds), *Gender, Body, Knowledge: Feminist Reconstructions of Being and Knowing.* New Brunswick, NJ: Rutgers University Press.

Bradshaw, J. (1990) *Homecoming: Reclaiming and Championing Your Inner Child.* New York: Bantam Books.

Brewer, L., M. Zawadski and R. Lincoln (1990) Characteristics of alcoholics and codependents who did and did not complete treatment. *International Journal of the Addictions, 25,* 653–63.

Brown, L. (1990) What's addiction got to do with it: a feminist critique of codependence. *Psychology of Women Newsletter* of Division 35 American Psychological Association (Winter), 4.

Bryer, J.B., B.A. Nelson, J.B. Miller, and P.A. Krol (1987) Childhood sexual and physical abuse as factors in adult psychiatric illness. *American Journal of Psychiatry, 144,* 1426–30.

Bufe, C. (1988) Guilt and god for the gullible. *Utne Reader* (Nov./Dec.), 54–5.

Burstow, B. (1992) *Radical Feminist Therapy: Working in the Context of Violence.* Newbury Park, CA: SAGE.

Butler, M. (1985) Guidelines for feminist therapy. In L. Rosewater and L. Walker (eds), *Handbook of Feminist Therapy: Women's Issues in Psychotherapy.* New York: Springer.

Caplan, P. (1985) *The Myth of Women's Masochism*. New York: E.P. Dutton.
- (1988) The name game: psychiatry, misogyny and taxonomy. In M. Braude (ed.), *Women, Power, and Therapy: Issues for Women*. New York: Haworth Press.
- (1991). How *do* they decide who is normal? The true, but bizarre tale of the *DSM* process. *Canadian Psychology, 32*, 162–70.
Carniol, Ben (1987) *Case Critical: The Dilemma of Social Work in Canada*. Toronto: Between the Lines.
Cermak, T. (1986) *Diagnosing and Treating Co-Dependence*. Minnesota: Johnson Institute.
Chesler, P. (1972) *Women and Madness*. New York: Avon Books.
Cocores, J. (1987) Co-addiction: a silent epidemic. *Psychiatry Letter. 5*, 5–8.
Coggins, K. (1990) *Alternative Pathways to Healing: The Recovery Medicine Wheel*. Deerfield Beach, FL: Health Communications.
Conrad, P. (1980) On the medicalization of deviance and social control. In D. Ingleby (ed.), *Critical Psychiatry: The Politics of Mental Health*. Harmondsworth: Penguin Books.
Dobash, R.E. and R. Dobash, (1992) *Women, Violence and Social Change*. London: Routledge.
Dominelli, L. (1988) *Anti-Racist Social Work*. London: MacMillan Education.
Ehrenreich, B., and D. English (1979) *For Her Own Good: 150 Years of Experts' Advice to Women*. London: Pluto Press.
Fabunmi, C., L. Frederick, and M. Jarvis Bicknese (1985) The codependency trap. Available from the Southern Minnesota Regional Legal Services, P.O. Box 1266, Winona, MN 55987. Unpublished.
Faludi, S. (1991) *Backlash: The Undeclared War against American Women*. New York: Crown Publishers.
Fingarette, H. (1988) Alcoholism: the mythical disease. *Utne Reader, 30* (Nov./Dec.), 64–8.
Finnegan, D., and E. McNally (1989) The lonely journey: lesbians and gay men who are co-dependent. *Alcoholism Treatment Quarterly, 6*, 121–35.
Frank, P., and G. Golden (1992) Blaming by naming: battered women and the epidemic of codependence. *Social Work, 37*, 5–6.
Franklin, D. (1987). The politics of masochism. *Psychology Today* (Jan.), 52–6.
Fulani, L. (1988) 'All power to the people!' But how? In L. Fulani (ed.), *The Psychopathology of Everyday Racism and Sexism*. New York: Harrington Park Press.
Gelinas, D. (1981) Identification and treatment of incest victims. In E. Howell and M. Bayes (eds), *Women and Mental Health*. New York: Basic Books.
Greenspan, M. (1983) *A New Approach to Women & Therapy*. Blue Ridge Summit, PA: TAB Books.

Haaken, J. (1990) A critical analysis of the codependence construct. *Psychiatry*, 53, 396–406.

Hagan, K. (1989) Codependency and the myth of recovery. *Fugitive Information*, 1, 1–13. Available at Escapadia Press, P.O. Box 5298, Atlanta, GA 30307.

Hare-Mustin, R., and J. Marecek (1990) Beyond difference. In R. Hare-Mustin and J. Maracek (eds), *Making A Difference: Psychology and the Construction of Gender*. New Haven, CT: Yale University Press.

Harper, J., and C. Capdevila (1990) Codependency: a critique. *Journal of Psychoactive Drugs*, 22, 285–92.

Helm, P. (1970) Family therapy. In G. Stuart and S. Sundeen (eds), *Principles and Practice of Psychiatric Nursing*. St Louis, MO: C.V. Mosby.

Herman, E. (1988) The Twelve-Step program: cure or cover? *Utne Reader*, 30 (Nov./Dec.), 52–3.

Herman, J. (1992) *Trauma and Recovery*. New York: Basic Books.

hooks, b. (1988) *Talking Back: Thinking Feminist – Thinking Black*. Toronto: Between the Lines.

– (1993) *Sisters of the Yam: Black Women and Self-Recovery*. Toronto: Between the Lines.

Irvine, L. (1992) The pathologizing of love: a sociological analysis of codependency. Masters thesis. Boca Raton, FL: Florida Atlantic University.

Jiminez, M., and S. Rice (1990) Popular advice to women: a feminist perspective. *Affilia*, 5, 8–26.

Kaminer, W. (1990) Chances are you're codependent too. *New York Times Book Review*, 11 Feb., 26–7.

Kaplan, J. (1990) The trouble with codependency. *Self*, 12(July), 112–13, 148.

Katz, S., and A. Liu (1991) *The Codependency Conspiracy*. New York: Warner Books.

Kokin, M., and I. Walker (1989) *Women Married to Alcoholics*. Toronto: Macmillan.

Krestan, J., and C. Bepko (1990) Codependency: the social reconstruction of female experience. *Smith College Studies in Social Work*, 60, 216–232.

Larson, E. (1987). *Stage II Relationships: Love Beyond Addiction*. New York: Harper & Row.

Lawton, M.J. (1990) Co-dependency: the search for definition. *Addiction Letter*, 6(Aug.), 1–2.

Levine, H. (1983) Feminist counselling: approach or technique? In J. Turner and L. Emery (eds), *Perspectives on Women in the 1980s*. Winnipeg: University of Manitoba.

Long, T.R., and S. Wolin (1989) Co-dependents: is in-patient treatment necessary? *Alcoholism & Addiction* (Oct.), 41–2.

Lorde, A. (1984) *Sister Outsider*. Trumansburg, NY: Crossing Press.

Lyon, D., and J. Greenberg (1991) Evidence of codependency in women with an alcoholic parent: helping out Mr Wrong. *Journal of Personality and Social Psychology*, *61*, 435–9.

MATCH International Centre (1990) *Linking Women's Global Struggles to End Violence*. Ottawa: Match International Centre.

McKay, C. (1992) *The 'Co-dependency' Myth – A Feminist Critique*. Independent Enquiry Project. Ottawa: Carleton University.

Miller, J.B. (1976) *Toward a New Psychology of Women*. Boston: Beacon Press.

Miller, N., and M. Gold (1989) Enablers help to kill alcoholics. *US Journal of Drug and Alcohol Dependence*, *13*, 7.

Morgan, P. (1981) From battered wife to program client: the state's shaping of social problems. *Kapitalistate*, *9*, 17–39.

Mowbray, C., S. Lanir and M. Hulce (1984) Women and mental health: new directions for change. *Women and Therapy*, *3*, 1–16.

OACWI (Ontario Advisory Council on Women's Issues) (1990) *Women and Mental Health in Ontario: A Background Paper*.

Peele, S. (1989) *Diseasing of America: Addiction Treatment Out of Control*. Lexington, MA: D.C. Heath.

Penfold, S., and Walker, G. (1983) *Women and the Psychiatric Paradox*. Montreal: Eden Press.

Potter-Efron, R., and P. Potter-Efron (1989) Assessment of co-dependency with individuals from alcoholic and chemically dependent families. *Alcoholism Treatment Quarterly*, *6*, 37–59.

Putnam, F.W., J.J. Guroff, E. Silberman, L. Barban, and R. Post (1986) The clinical phenomenon of multiple personality disorder: 100 recent cases. *Journal of Clinical Psychiatry*, *47*, 285–93.

Rainbolt, B., and M. Greene (1990) *Behind the Veil of Silence: Family Violence and Alcohol Abuse*. Center City, MN: Hazelden.

Rowell, R., and H. Kusterer (1991) Care of HIV infected Native American substance abusers. *Journal of Chemical Dependency Treatment*, *4*, 91–104.

Schaef, A. (1986) *Co-Dependence: Misunderstood – Mistreated*. San Francisco: Harper & Row.

– (1987) *When Society Becomes an Addict*. San Francisco: Harper & Row.

Showalter, E. (1985) *The Female Malady: Women, Madness & English Culture 1830–1980*. New York: Pantheon Books.

Sloven, J. (1991) Codependent or empathically responsive? Two views of Betty. In C. Bepko (ed.), *Feminism and Addiction*. New York: Haworth Press.

Smith, D., and S. David (1975) *Women Look at Psychiatry*. Vancouver: Press Gang Publishers.

Spann, L. and J. Fischer (1990) Identifying co-dependency. *The Counselor, 8,* 27.

Sturdivant, S. (1980) *Therapy with Women: A Feminist Philosophy of Treatment.* New York: Springer.

Subby, R. (1984) Inside the chemically dependent marriage: denial and manipulation. *Co-Dependency: An Emerging Issue.* Pompano Beach, FL: Health Communications.

Tallen, B.S. (1990) Co-dependency: a feminist critique. *Sojourner: The Women's Forum,* 15(Jan.), 20–1.

Tavris, C. (1990) The politics of codependency. *Family Therapy Networker,* 14(Jan.-Feb.), 43.

Ussher, J. (1992) *Women's Madness: Misogyny or Mental Illness?* Amherst, MA: University of Massachusetts Press.

van Wormer, K. (1989) Co-dependency: implications for women and therapy. *Women and Therapy, 8,* 51–63.

Walker, L. (1979) *The Battered Woman.* New York: Harper & Row.

Walters, M. (1990) The codependent Cinderella who loves too much ... fights back. *Family Therapy Networker, 14,* (July/Aug.), 53–7.

Weedon, C. (1987) *Feminist Practice and Poststructuralist Theory.* Oxford: Basil Blackwell.

Wegscheider-Cruse, S., and J. Cruse (1990) *Understanding Co-Dependency.* Deerfield Beach, FL: Health Communications.

Weisner, C., and R. Room (1984) Financing and ideology in alcohol treatment. *Social Problems, 32,* 167–88.

Whipp, K. (1991) Lost in the diagnosis: incest survivors in psychiatry. Masters thesis. Ottawa: Carleton University.

Whitfield, C. (1989) Co-dependence: our most common addiction – some physical, mental, emotional and spiritual perspectives. *Alcoholism Treatment Quarterly, 6,* 19–36.

'We believe that there are a significant number of professionals in the addictions and mental health fields, as well as consumers, who are ready to "deconstruct" many of the popularly enforced notions in addictions work, but who have been isolated from each other, owing to the silencing of their ideas in much of the public arena. This anthology lessens that isolation by bringing together some of the feminist critiques that challenge the simplistic and sexist norms embodied in the construct "codependency."'

From the introduction

UNIVERSITY OF TORONTO PRESS

ISBN 0-8020-7230-5

9 780802 072306